EMMANUEL LEVINAS

Emmanuel Levinas:

The Problem of Ethical Metaphysics

EDITH WYSCHOGROD

Fordham University Press
New York
2000

Perspectives in Continental Philosophy, No. 8
ISSN 1089–3938

Library of Congress Cataloging-in-Publication Data

Wyschogrod, Edith.
    Emmanuel Lévinas : the problem of ethical metaphysics / Edith Wyschogrod. — 2nd ed.
        p. 1.   cm. — (Perspectives in continental philosophy ; no. 8)
    Includes bibliographical references and index.
    ISSBN 0-8232-1949-6 (hardcover). — ISBN 0-8232-1950-X (pbk.)
    1. Lévinas, Emmanuel.   I. Title.   II. Series.
194—dc21   99-40971
                                                                                  CIP

Printed in the United States of America
04 03 02 01 00 5 4 3 2 1
Second Edition

CONTENTS

ACKNOWLEDGMENTS

I am deeply grateful to the many interpreters of Levinas who have, over the years, enriched my understanding of his work and, in conformity with his own principles of interpretation as a process of expansion, have extended his thought to open new conceptual vistas. I cannot refrain from singling out Adriaan Peperzak from among them both for his meticulous readings of Levinas and for bringing Levinas's work to the attention of a wider philosophical public.

Without the help of John D. Caputo the present project could not have gone forward. The ways in which I have benefited from conversations with him both face-to-face and via e-mail are too numerous to mention. I am especially grateful for the coordinated efforts of three graduate students—Martin Kavka, Stephen Hood, and Eric Boynton—for their tireless tracking and evaluation of current translations of Levinas's texts and for their preparation of the index.

PREFACE TO THE SECOND EDITION

Interest in the work of Emmanuel Levinas has grown exponentially since the first edition of the present work appeared in 1974. It goes without saying that Levinas's thought has influenced discussion in ethics and the philosophy of religion. His vision of alterity, of responsibility for the Other, has also spilled over into literary and cultural analysis, political philosophy, and social thought. Ethical discourse in Levinas's sense, what he calls the language of criticism, opens the way for a novel articulation of concrete problems in these fields. To risk a cliché, Levinas would seem to be a philosopher for the next century.

In these introductory remarks, I shall frequently turn to works that had not yet been written or published when the first edition of this book appeared. I shall attend closely to these later works but not as supplements to those discussed in the earlier edition, in compliance with Derrida's astute warning that supplements constitute not innocuous additions to texts but rather their reorientation. Nor do I do so in the spirit of affirming a *Kehre*, a turning in Levinas's later work. In a conversation with Levinas in which he reflected upon such allegations, he remarked with *un clin d'oeil* (a wink), "*Je ne suis pas Heidegger.*" At the same time, his later writings cannot be viewed as issuing seamlessly from the earlier ones as though deducible from them.

To read Levinas, to really read him, is to allow oneself to be claimed by a text whose predicative statements may be concealed imperatives. What is more, in Levinas's view, exegesis necessitates the reader's intervention, the eliciting of meanings that are not predetermined, and presupposes that texts contain more than they contain. The exegesis of his own writings is not exempt from this textual expansiveness. Perhaps interpreting Levinas's ethical metaphysics today is to read him proleptically, even messianically in Derrida's sense of the term as heralding a future that will never arrive but whose advent is the object of an intense desire. Such a desire is not a conatus for the realization of some specifiable value—Levinas does not fail to make room for justice as the sphere where wrongs can be redressed and values concretely actualized—but an inherently unfulfillable yearning for the Good beyond being.

In this preface I shall examine some of Levinas's responses to the argument that if transcendence outstrips cognitive or affective grasp, there is an unbreachable gulf between the beyond of being and actual experience. What boots it to insist upon a transcendence divorced from mundane life that can offer no guidelines for determining right and wrong in one's day-to-day existence? Levinas must devise new strategies for bringing to light the imbrication of transcendence as a call to responsibility for the Other in the world of history, politics, economy, and culture, a world that manifests itself alternatively as totality, ontology, and the said, to cite some of his metaphors. Far from endorsing an Hegelian dialectical solution to this problem, one in which ethics would be a negation that allowed for a higher synthesis and the creation of a new totalization, Levinas envisions a phenomenology of difference, of an unbreachable gap between totality and exteriority.

Levinas also addresses the question of transcendence in terms of incommensurable languages. A specific language, Hebrew, serves as a trope for designating the Hebrew Bible and its rabbinic interpretation viewed as a system of semiotic expansion. Although it is the language in which transcendence is inscribed, Hebrew requires but resists translation into Greek, a synecdoche for Western thought that bears the legacy of classical philosophy. In the comments that follow, I interpret such conceptual transposition as a portable strategy, one that is carried over into Levinas's account of the Saying, the signification-of-one-to-another prior to words, and the said, the language of speech and writing as ordinarily understood and through which the Saying must manifest itself.

In the ensuing remarks, I examine several strands of Levinas's thought that constitute its provocation as it has been termed: his account of God and philosophy, of the problem of incommensurable languages, and finally of corporeal figurations of the psyche as vulnerability. Levinas's writings are seen as a summons to engage in a new philosophy, one that is neither an ontology nor a proclamation of faith. Although I make merely passing mention of the thought of Maurice Blanchot, Jacques Derrida, and Jean-Luc Marion, I bear in mind not only the ways in which Levinasian notions have affected their thinking but, conversely, the significance of their perspectives as constituting the mise-en-scène against which Levinas may be understood today. My discussion takes shape as argument and counterargument and is largely guided not by the question of whence but of whither Levinas.

Reading Levinas is never a solitary act but always already includes an Other who is not an authorial presence but an intruder who penetrates the interiority of the subject as proscribing violence and mandating radical altruism. I consider the face of a Levinasian text akin to a human face, a countenance that prohibits harming another and decrees benevolence toward her or him.

TRANSCENDENCE AND ALTERITY

In bypassing "the pure ether of thought"[1] that characterizes rational accounts of God, Levinas argues for a God beyond being, a God who eludes both the positive assertions of kataphatic theologies and the apophatic language of negation to which mystical theologies resort. For Levinas, the rationality of Western theological thinking is inextricably bound up with the thinking of being that captures transcendence in the net of ontology. In his ongoing critique of Heidegger's effort to reclaim the meaning of being that had been progressively obscured in Western philosophy, Levinas argues that being remains for Heidegger the ultimate referent to the detriment of the Good. What has been lost is the exteriority of the Good, what lies outside of being as being's Other.[2]

By contrast, Levinas argues that meaning can exhibit itself as the strangeness of the Other's face. It inheres in the human countenance not as a form apprehended in perception but as an ethical datum exuded, as it were, from the exposure and defenselessness of the Other. The demand of the Other issues "from an unknown God who loves the stranger." Never couched in the language of apodictic predication, God talk in Levinas can be thought of as prefaced by an unstated "perhaps" in the Derridean sense, a perhaps that points to an irresolvable uncertainty.

It would be a radical misunderstanding of the transcendence of the face to construe it as a visible instantiation of the sacred. Such an interpretation confers upon the face the status of an idol so that the gaze of the Other becomes not simply a vacant stare (as would be the case if transcendence were altogether denied) but a dangerous and alluring invitation to idolatry. Jean-Luc Marion comments, "The idol consigns the divine to the measure of the human gaze."[3] In a compelling passage, Levinas writes: "The epiphany of a face is a *visitation*. Whereas a phenomenon is already, in whatever respect, an image, a captive manifestation of its plastic and mute form, the epiphany of a face is alive" (HAH 51/BPW 53). To live does not, for Levinas, indicate a *conatus essendi*, the desire to persevere in existence, but rather an undoing of form.

Nor is the face to be interpreted as a vessel, a receptacle for the sacred sparks of light that have broken off from a divine plenum and are now entrapped in matter to be released through fervent prayer, as suggested in Martin Buber's appreciative reading of Hasidism's interpretation of Kabbalah, the doctrine of the Jewish mystical tradition. For Levinas a sacrality that abrades even if it does not fully undermine the exteriority of the Other may enhance the intensity of religious experience but loses sight of the primordiality of the ethical meaning of the *tout autre*.

Could it not be claimed that if the face of the Other is evidence for a hidden God that Levinas has, in fact, forged a natural theology of the face? In rebuttal, it can be said that the face as a source of meaning is not part of the orderly design of a world pointing to a divine plan but is rather a disruption of the order of the world. Far from manifesting transcendence as present, the face signifies as being in the trace or track of the One that has always already passed by. Ever wary of the potential for the transgressive violence that may lurk in the ecstasy, the possession or seizure by a sacrality that is rooted in presence, Levinas sees the trace as belonging to an archaic past that can never be brought into plenary presence.

It could also be charged that if transcendence is featureless as

Levinas claims, it is pure nothingness and Levinas is, willy-nilly, in the camp of the death-of-God theologians. But the Good by which one is claimed, he contends, survives the critique of contemporary death-of-God theologies that "perhaps signif[y] only the possibility to reduce every value arousing an impulse to an impulse arousing a value" (AE 158/OBBE 123). For Levinas, the Good lays hold of me rather than I of it, whereas, for death-of-God theologians, transcendence is absorbed by the world.

A more troubling allegation is that if absolute transcendence is, of necessity, featureless and, at the same time, God is not to be identified with the human Other (a point explicitly stated), must Levinas not, *faute de mieux*, equate God with pure being, being without objects? This is an especially vexing problem because pure being, what Levinas calls the *il y a*, is described as the threatening nocturnal obverse of environments, of the elemental, earth, sea, sky, and the like, in which we are immersed and is the source of a mythical or pagan religiosity.[4] Unlike the world of objects that emerge from a horizon, such a milieu seems to come from nowhere, a nonplace from which God is absent. But, as Blanchot points out in a 1980 text in honor of Levinas, the reverse of transcendence is already in a relation with transcendence so that the latter is always "ready to veer off to the point of possible confusion" with the absolute indeterminacy of the *il y a*[5] whose ominous murmur oscillates in so many of Blanchot's own fictions. Might one then infer that the *il y a* mimes the transcendence it occludes? Could it not be asserted that in the absence of criteria for distinguishing the "nowhere" of the *il y a* from transcendence and thus in conformity with a certain Kierkegaardian ambiguity with respect to the word of God and its other, demonic temptation, that an ambiguity criticized by Levinas has insinuated itself into Levinas's ethics?

Levinas might respond that resolving the issue requires a fresh look at the problem of human freedom and its limitations. The either/or of a theology of risk is framed within the confines of a philosophy that posits freedom as the unencumbered spontaneity that engenders moral acts. But, for Levinas, there is a responsibility without limit prior to freedom, an obligatoriness that (in his words) is as inextinguishable as the flames of the burning bush that would not be consumed as described in the Biblical narrative.

In a number of later works, Levinas depicts this responsibility as accusation in the absence of any specifiable infraction, as an indictment of the ego as ego. In this state, one does not actively choose but is rather expelled into a passivity extrinsic to being and its moves. Thus, Levinas writes: "In a responsibility for the other of life and death, the adjectives unconditional, indeclinable, absolute take on a meaning . . . wear[ing] away the substrate, from which the free act arises. . . . This finite freedom is not primary . . . but it lies in an infinite responsibility where the other . . . can accuse me to the point of persecution. . . . That is why finite freedom is not simply infinite freedom operating in a finite field. The will which it animates wills in a passivity it does not assume" (AE 159–60/OBBE 124).

THE UNCONTAINABLE INFINITE

Levinas's adumbration of epiphanies often relies upon tropes of excess, a strategy commonly deployed in Nietzschean fashion by recent French thinkers, among them Bataille, Deleuze, and Kristeva, to describe the exercise of power and will. For Levinas, it is the Other who is felt as unassimilable surplus, the Other who invades one's own psychic space as an excess that resists enclosure. The face that manifests itself in phenomenality yet departs from the form that encloses it is given as "a more" that signifies an irrecusable command. It should not be forgotten, however, that this excessiveness must break into the world and that, for Levinas, it is both impossible and undesirable to build a *cordon sanitaire* around a transcendence that deposits its traces in reason and language.

But if thought is to be penetrated by transcendence, Levinas must find an object that cannot be thought, an object whose excessiveness shatters the thought that tries to think it. The idea of the Infinite as analyzed in Descartes's Third Meditation meets this requirement. The Infinite is conceived not as different from the finite, as its negation, but rather as nonindifferent to the finite (DVI 109/BPW 138). The Infinite is "monstrous" in the sense of being extravagant and immoderate, a monstrousness that may also be viewed etymologically as monstration or showing forth.

The unfulfillable desire ignited by the excessiveness of its object attests the ethical dimension of an Infinite that might otherwise be perceived as merely unimaginable magnitude. Such desire for the Other is without eros. Thus, Levinas: "[T]his endless desire that is beyond being is dis-inter*estedness,* transcendence—desire for the Good." Far from having wandered away from the Infinite, Levinas sees it in terms of what it mandates: thought thinking more than it thinks as the unthinkable responsibility for the Other (DVI 111/BPW 139, emphasis in original).

For Levinas, the Infinite is not, as it is for Buber, what lies beyond the human capacity for thought as a supplement to thought's deficiency. In Buber's view, to know anything whatever is to become cognizant of knowledge's limitation, to become aware of the Infinite as that which the finite thinks by default. Thus, for Buber, the sheer fact that there is human knowledge becomes a proof for the existence of the Infinite. By contrast, Levinas sees the idea of the Infinite as implanted within oneself. "The Idea of God is God in me," Levinas says (DVI 105/BPW 136), in me not as contained by a *cogito* as guarantor of what it thinks but rather "[as] the *cogitatum* of a *cogitatio* which, to begin with, contains that *cogitatio,* signifies the non-contained par excellence. . . . The objective reality of the *cogitatum* breaks up the formal reality of the *cogitatio.*" Beyond the unity of the *cogito* and more primordial than it is "the psyche in the subject, the-one-for-the-other . . . signifyingness itself. . . . This is the gravity of the body extirpated from its *conatus essendi*" (AE 181/OBBE 142).

Levinas detects a danger in positing psychic submissiveness, one that traditional theologies have named pride in one's humility, a pride that exists as a residue of activity within the passivity of the psyche. At the same time and (ambiguously) the Infinite does not cease to infinitize, as it were, the obligation to the Other. To avert the reversion to activity, passivity must expose itself and do so wordlessly and without image, redouble itself so that no act could arise from it. One does not, in this context, deploy signs, but rather one makes oneself into a sign, a process that Levinas designates as sincerity (AE 182/OBBE 143). Incapable of dissimulation, sincerity scandalizes in its assumption of limitless responsibility. Although sincerity is not a modification of intentional consciousness in the standard phenomenological sense, it has a referent that precludes its folding back upon itself. This referent does not itself appear or become the subject of a theme: it is "the glory of the Infinite."

Just as Levinas has given new and positive meaning to the term metaphysics and reversed the bad odor into which the word "sincerity" had fallen through Sartre's derogation of it as impossible, in still another surprising move, Levinas infuses new meaning into a traditional theological term. Glory describes not the luminosity of divine presence but rather the suspension of the conatus to know or do, the pure receptivity or passivity of a subject who places her- or himself at the disposal of the Other and is open to the point of total defenselessness. "Glory is but the other face of the passivity of the subject," he insists (AE 184/OBBE 144). Through persecution and martyrdom as an intrapsychic process, one becomes a hagiographic sign without narrative.[6] Thus, far from embodying an intellectual vision in the Thomistic sense, the subject is "a seed of folly, already a psychosis" (AE 180/OBBE 142). Here Levinas, in a remarkable transvaluation of values, preempts by conceding what Freudians might perceive as masochism. Submissiveness is reinstated as self-donation.

A number of traditional philosophies of religion have depicted the divine-human relation as necessitating the transfiguration of corporeality so that divine glory is the agent and the glorified body the result of this transformation. On Aquinas's reading, divine presence is known by intellect "on the sight of and through corporeal things" as a result both of "the perspicacity of intellect" and from "the divine glory" that will affect the body after its final renewal.[7] For Levinas, as we have seen, glory disrupts the cognitive subject, transcends its intraworldly imbrication in facts and states of affairs, and opens subjectivity to an excess of Goodness that exceeds intellectual comprehension. Subjectivity must give itself as a Saying or discourse prior to actual speech, prior to predicative language, the precondition that makes possible the subsequent thematization that language accomplishes in what is termed "the said." I shall consider this bifurcation in detail in due course. In the present context, I want only to note that Saying points to the glory of the Infinite, a glory that resists entrapment in immanence and, at the same time, leaves the subject no place to hide. On the one hand, the glory of the Infinite traumatizes egoity, expels the subject from itself as self-presence and, on the other, glory is the outcome of that trauma, the willingness of the subject to substitute the self for another. "The an-archic identity of the subject," says Levinas, is "flushed out without being able to slip away" (AE 184/OBBE 144). The one who, in self-giving, says to the Other, "Here I am," placing the self at another's disposal, bears witness to the Infinite. By intertwining transcendence and immanence, Levinas is able to assert: "The Infinite does not appear to him that bears witness to it. On the contrary, the witness belongs to the glory of the Infinite." Yet, paradoxically, "it is by the voice of the witness that the glory of the Infinite is glorified" (AE 186/OBBE 146).

In a move that appears to be one of reversal in which outside becomes inside, Levinas claims that the exteriority of the Infinite is interiorized. Thus, he appears to endorse the inwardization he roundly condemns elsewhere as mystification. But Levinas sees no contradiction: the Infinite as an outside maintains its exteriority even when inwardized because glory persists in this internality, disrupts thematization and "gives sign" to the Other. In a visual metaphor rare in Levinas's accounts of transcendence, glory is described as dazzling and as arousing adoration.[8]

One might ask whether the glory of the Infinite is not a mere pleonasm, for how can glory add anything to the Infinite to which nothing *can* be added. But if glory can be interpreted as Saying, substituting oneself for another, taking responsibility for the Other, proclaiming peace or proscribing violence, and if infinition *is* this process as Levinas seems to think, then glory is the very dynamism of the Infinite.

Some Problems of Translation

The idea of the Infinite provides an entering wedge for considering the incommensurability of the language of ethics and that of ontology. For Descartes, the Infinite contracts itself, "the more in the less" so as to inhabit the finite while still remaining outside it. One of Levinas's favorite rabbinic aphorisms, "The Torah speaks the language of men," presupposes that the Torah is the Word of God as the rabbis believe and that it too can contract itself so as to be rendered comprehensible to human beings without exhausting its extramundane meaning through a process of labyrinthine discusssion.[9] Traditional rabbinic interpretation may begin with the plain or obvious sense of a verse but elicits the verse's implied meanings through a process of augmentation that relies upon conceptual and philological affinities. Texts that are "mischievous, laconic . . . in love with the possible" are orchestrated by "hypercritical minds, thinking quickly and addressing themselves to their peers" (QLT 15/NTR 5).

It is one thing to gloss traditional verses in an intratextual process of expansion but another to render these texts pervious to philosophical transposition. A favorite conundrum of analytic philosophers, the possibility of translating an absolutely unknown language, highlights the necessity for a preexisting repository of known meanings in the language to be translated, for without this backdrop of existing meaning, the task may be impossible. Walter Benjamin in his well-known essay on the subject writes: "While a work of literary translation does not find itself in the center of the language forest but on the outside facing the wooded ridge, it calls into it without entering, aiming at this single spot where the echo is able to give, in its own language the reverbation of the work in the alien one."[10]

How much more complex is translating the conceptual repertoire of the Hebrew Scriptures together with their rabbinic commentaries, the Talmud, into the philosophical language of the West or, as Levinas prefers, into Greek. For here the challenge is not to find verbal equivalents for hitherto unknown expressions but rather to "translate" biblical themes into the language of philosophy, one that has itself already been affected by biblicism. Among the numerous possibilities of misprision in this context is that of appearing to generate a synonymy that had already been created in Hellenistic and medieval syntheses but whose preexistence had, by now, become invisible.

Levinas could reply by invoking the context in which conceptual transposition functions. He does not deny the instrumental value of ordinary language or that of a philosophical language fine-tuned to express complex concepts. He does claim that language condensed in the synecdoche "Hebrew" is a coordination with the Other to be read as always already ethical in contrast to the ontological language of philosophy. What is more, this coordination with the Other may be described in terms of a relation to certain books, a relation that can be described as a movement-toward-God (*l'à-Dieu*). Levinas does not posit the counterintuitive claim that the book is itself an icon of transcendence but rather that, insofar as the book is "in language," it is "phenomenology, the 'staging' in which the abstract is made concrete." [11]

In discussing Levinas's philosophy of language, it has been argued that his account of the relation of Saying, the language anterior to speech that provides the warranty for its truth, to the said, language that is a discourse about beings, is a reworking of Heidegger's elaboration of the difference between Being and the assemblage of beings. [12] Or, perhaps more persuasively, Levinas's account of the saying and unsaying (*dédire*) of the Saying in the said may be seen in the context of the Heideggerian Dasein's corruption of its primordial modes of world habitation as analyzed in *Being and Time*. Because the Saying and the said reflect a distinction between a preoriginary and derivative mode of language, to read this difference, even if only formally, as replicating Heidegger's account of authentic and fallen modes of being would be to misread Levinas's effort to forge a language that unsays the language of ontology: "The otherwise than being is stated [*s'énonce*] in a Saying that must also be unsaid in order thus to abstract the otherwise than being from the said in which it comes to signify" (AE 8/OBBE 7). [13] Ethics must both enter and be extricated from the various ontological matrices in which it has historically been embedded.

Because God cannot be thought apart from ethics, God too must be freed from the ontological encumbrances of this history, one that Levinas believes helped spawn the violence endemic to actual history. A God who is *autrement qu'être* (otherwise than being) and *au-delà de l'essence* (beyond essence) resists cognitive apprehension. Thus, Levinas contends that "[p]hilosophical discourse should be able to include God—of whom the Bible speaks. . . . But as soon as he is conceived, this God is situated within 'being's move' . . . as the being (*étant*) par excellence. If the intellectual understanding of the biblical God, theology, does not reach to the level of philosophical thought [it is not because it fails to explicate the being of this being] but because in thematizing God it brings God into the course of being" (DVI 95/BPW 130). Unlike Heidegger's oft-cited claim that language is the house of being, for Levinas "speech delineates an original relation" that is the ethical precondition for other-world relations rather than their expression (EN 18/BPW 6). Neither predicative nor interrogative, the connection with the Other spoken in the vocative is the fundamental gesture of language: to name in the primordial sense is to invoke, solicit, or call (EN 20/BPW 8).

It could be argued that, like Kierkegaard's Single One, Levinas's account of the Other neglects to reckon with social existence. But it is precisely the fact that there is a multiplicity of persons, a socius that, for Levinas, opens the need for a language that can universalize and that, in Husserl's terms, requires a consciousness that thematizes. The recognition that there is not only the Other but other others imposes the need for comparison. Thus, Levinas: "The act of consciousness is motivated by the presence of a third party alongside of the neighbor approached. . . . There must be justice . . . a comparison among incomparables . . . thematization, thought, history and inscription" (AE 20/OBBE 16).

If the preceding argument holds, it cannot be said that Levinas repudiates the language of being as having fallen from a prelapsarian state, but rather that its sphere of applicability must be clearly delineated and reined in. Ontological language acquires its meaning from a sociality that is understood in terms of proximity, of the one who is near and whose approach does not diminish her or his alterity and that, in turn, arouses an awareness of the Saying in the said (AE 19/OBBE 16).

In *Otherwise than Being, or Beyond Essence,* not only does Levinas explore the connection between a preoriginary Saying and language as uttered and written—the said—but he also provides what must be recognized as a new and intricate post-Heideggerian description of being's relation to language. Levinas maintains not that language issues from being but, conversely, that "the birthplace of ontology is in the said" (AE 55/OBBE 42). Referring to what he calls the amphibology of being, its built-in binarism, Levinas claims that being can refer either to entities, real or ideal, on the one hand or it can express the manner of an entity's existing on the other. In the latter sense, being reflects the temporality of verbs, their openness to time, designated as essence and perhaps better expressed by the English gerund "essencing." While the atemporal connotations of "essence" in Aristotelian and Scholastic usage would appear to preclude its application to the temporality of language, it is precisely the doubleness of being, its expressing of temporal passage as well as its proclivity to timeless nominalization, that Levinas means to highlight.

Without essence there would be no manifestation, no apophansis through language, no truth. "Essence is not only conveyed, it is temporalized in a predicative statement," Levinas claims (AE 51/OBBE 39). Verbs can be nominalized and nouns set into motion as verbs, so that even apparent tautologies reflect this verbality. "A is A" means "A A's" as in "The red reddens." (Recall Heidegger's "*Die Sprache spricht.*") For Levinas, such propositions do not express an identity or even an activity but rather an essence, temporalization as such that already resounds in assertory language so that (surprisingly) actual verbs are secondary reflections of a diachrony already inherent in predication: "Essence is not only conveyed in the said, is not only expressed in it, but originally—though amphibologically—resounds in it qua essence" (AE 51/OBBE 39). When nominalized, the verb "to be" shows itself in various modes of ideality, as an entity or as a narrative expressing fixed time. Yet, Levinas declares, these modes of nominalization "are still in an amphibology" that continues to imply essence (AE 54/OBBE 42). It could be argued that the Saying is absorbed by the said, but, to the contrary, the resounding of temporalization that essencing exposes, awakens the Saying in the said (AE 55/OBBE 43).

In still another unexpected move, Levinas links being's essencing to art, arguing that, in art, there is a primordial resounding of essence. Reflecting both suspicion and admiration, Levinas's account of art treats the art work as a manifestation of the beautiful, which, as such, is supported by and supports Western conceptions of being. Art renews being, refurbishes exhausted verbal and visual languages, yet, in its exoticism, lures one into a dangerous mythical zone. In its self-manifestation, art is sheer phenomenality, a panoply of decontextualized images without world: art demands exegesis. Poetry, or language as *Dichtung* (in Heidegger's phrase), solicits the prose of interpretation. There is more than an echo of Maimonides's suspicion of images as promoting idolatry in Levinas's perspective. Even if Scripture deploys images in conveying theological truth, it does so in order to appeal to the masses who, Maimonides believes, cannot grasp rational arguments. Although Levinas would hardly endorse the latter premise, his distrust of images leads him to insist that the language of exegesis, prose, is not an arbitrary superimposition upon an art work but rather is itself a manifestation of essence.

The danger of idolatry for Levinas lies not in its dissimulation of a higher sacrality but rather, as Jean-Luc Marion has shown, in the idol as a distillate of genuine power. In the absence of prose that is in the trace of alterity, one may be drawn back into the faceless being of the *il y a*, the realm of a mythical sacred. But once there is language, the signifyingness of the Other wends its way through the said, cuts through being's canniness, its cunning, at every level (AE 61–62/OBBE 48). In sum, there is no escape from the call of Ethics, the responsibility of one-for-another in that the traces of alterity are inscribed in language.

WHITHER LEVINAS: TROPING VULNERABILITY

Neither an analysis of consciousness nor an account of being-in-the-world, Levinas's thought is nevertheless a phenomenology, a description of what is refractory to description, while at the same time it is a reorienting of thought's direction from that of truth and being to ethics as a relation of the address to an addressee. As phenomenological description, philosophy solicits metaphor, seeks a language that would bring beings into the light of truth, and is thus a mode of illumination. Levinas's phenomenological philosophy while remaining philosophy is, on occasion and of necessity, pictographic while at the same time resisting representation as a bringing into presence.

It is Levinas's strength to have forged a new philosophical language critical of luminosity, of the seduction of art's shimmering surfaces, without traducing all art or endorsing narrowly didactic art. Just as abstract art does not eschew the use of color in the interest of form but rather applies it deftly, attentive reading uncovers Levinas's own use of sophisticated literary devices. A text that is an address could become a scarcely disguised moral tale, homiletical, and self-gratulatory. That this does not occur can be attributed at least in part to the breadth of Levinas's literary cultivation. It can be argued that he is indebted both to the palette of nineteenth-century French literature and to modernist writers such as Kafka and Beckett for whom the overlapping of literary and philosophical concerns is manifested in the troping of transcendence as absence.

Although it lies beyond the scope of these remarks to discuss such affinities in detail, I cannot resist suggesting that Levinas's account of the insatiable desire for the Other that grows through what it feeds on may reflect a transposition of Proust's description of Swann's desire for Odette, of the narrator's passion for Albertine or that of M. de Charlus for Morel. Levinas's account of time's passing as aging conjures up Proust's incomparable description of what is virtually a *Todestanz,* a scene in which faces become palimpsests, age etched over irrecoverable youth. On the significance of Proust, Levinas remarks, "It is as if I were constantly accompanied by another self, in unparalleled friendship, but also in a cold strangeness that life attempts to overcome. The mystery in Proust is the mystery of the other."[14]

Although Levinas's account of a loving noneroctic concern for the Other is clearly indebted to rabbinic commentaries on the meaning of *rachamim* (mercy), it is difficult to imagine that Levinas, in the exhortation to give the bread from one's mouth to the Other, to substitute oneself for the Other, did not think also of Flaubert's hagiographic tale, "The Simple Life," in which the peasant woman Françoise elects to be held hostage to the children in her charge and to her beloved nephew. To be sure, for Levinas, artworks demand the exegesis of prose, but has Levinas not at the same time tried to invent a new and artful prose that exhibits neither the austere abstraction of modernism nor the oneiric palette of surrealism to depict the relation of transcendence to quotidian existence?

That a poetics of exegesis is not foreign to Levinas is attested in these remarks drawn from his essay for Paul Ricoeur:

> In the poetic imagination, the unheard can be heard, called out to and expressed; a text can be opened up to the hermeneutic process

more widely than the precise intentions which had determined it. . . . When it is marked by the exceptional character of the messenger, the imperative or teaching which comes from outside would be able to vouch for itself in the mind of the listener. . . . The transcendent would be able to seduce and open up the imagination rather than constraining the will. There would be a mediation here connecting freedom to a certain obedience, a dependence without heteronomy reconciling transcendence and interiority.[15]

Beyond textual exegesis whose language remains that of a historically constituted vocabulary are the corporeal manifestations of transcendence. It may be recalled that, for Merleau-Ponty and in the tradition of Husserl, corporeality is understood as a point of orientation through which things are perceived and persons understood. On this reading, the intentions of another's consciousness seem to inhabit one's own body while one's intentions penetrate the body of the Other.[16] In several striking phenomenological analyses of corporeality in his early work, Levinas depicts the body as the source of movement, of effort and its attendant retrograde *lapsus,* fatigue.[17] Later, Levinas depicts corporeality as ethical, the body as vulnerable uncovered, without dissimulation: "The one is exposed to the other as a skin is exposed to what wounds it" (AE 63/OBBE 49). In a series of respiratory and dermal metaphors, Levinas describes the passivity of this exposure as being "stripped to the core as in an inspiration of air" or as "the pain, this underside of skin . . . more naked than all destitution" (AE 64 /OBBE 49). To be thus denuded is to put out of play, to bracket, the lived body depicted in phenomenological philosophy in order to expose the body of ethics.

Levinas's troping of gender issues in terms of erotic and maternal love has given rise to considerable commentary that cannot be considered in detail here.[18] Erotic love is envisioned by him as a relation beween man and woman, a comportment toward the body as flesh that is itself refractory to grasp, a body whose form slips away and becomes erotic nudity. The feminine body of eros eludes the language of ontology and in that sense is infradiscursive, although the possibility of woman's self-revelation as the face is not precluded: "The femininity of woman can neither deform nor absorb her human essence." Erotic heterosexual love itself must be refigured and the sphere of love transcended through

what may issue from it, the birth of another, of a child. The intimacy and self-enclosure of the lovers who are not one-for-another
but reflections of one another may thus be overcome in a phenomenon Levinas calls fecundity (DL 57/DF 34).[19]

It is all too obvious that the troping of woman as seductive materiality and man as rational discursivity perpetuates lamentable
cultural stereotypes. A Levinasian reply might concede the point
without surrendering the claim that it is precisely the language of
ontology that is chastised by the passivity of a more primordial
Saying. Such chastisement, neither psychological manipulation
nor physical coercion, could be reinscribed as an expression of
empowerment. Along other lines, it could also be argued that
Levinas has failed to perceive the fecundity of the caress itself as
an invitation to the Other to become what she or he is not yet.
The ever-increasing avidity of erotic love might be viewed as a
reaching for that which has not yet come into existence.[20]

A crucial issue in Levinas's later work, the depiction of the psyche as fissured by an alterity that cannot be expelled, is troped as
the maternal body. Inscribed in a chain of images—vulnerability,
respiration, wounding, susceptibility—it is not the body of eros
but rather the body that is linked to fecundity that becomes signification itself, the gestation of otherness in the same. As a figure
of the psyche, the maternal body does not signal the expulsion of
the child into the world but rather is lived as the pain of child-
birth in the most interior regions of the body: "In maternity, what
signifies is reponsibility for others and suffering both from the
effect of the persecution and from the persecuting itself in which
the persecutor sinks. Maternity which is bearing par excellence,
bears even responsibility for the persecuting by the persecutor"
(AE 95/OBBE 75).

If erotic relations could themselves be fecund (a claim that Levinas roundly denies) and, if the time of fecundity is the time of
what is always yet to come but never arrives, then the erotic relation may be envisaged as a trope for messianic time in the Derridean sense: a future that is always solicited but cannot become
present. For Levinas, it is not the body of eros but rather the
maternal body that is transformed into a prophetic body, the
body of Sarah rather than that of Abraham (DL 57/DF 34). Yet,
it must be conceded that, for Levinas, the prophet as a prefig-

urement of the Messiah no longer depends upon the identity of woman as woman, an identity that slips away. Thus, Levinas avers (DL 62/DF 38): "The hand that caresses and rocks . . . is no longer feminine. Neither wife not sister nor mother guides it. It is Elijah, who did not experience death, the most severe of the prophets, precursor of the Messiah."

It might be assumed that Levinas's messianism identifies him as an eschatological thinker in a traditional sense.[21] Yet Levinas does not hesitate to reply that the *eschaton* as an unchanging state of perfection reduces the difference between individuals, a difference that safeguards the Other's transcendence. For Levinas, "the danger of eschatology is the temptation to consider the man-God relation as a . . . fixed and permanent state of affairs. I have described ethical responsibility as insomnia or wakefulness precisely because it is a perpetual duty of vigilance."[22] The God of ethics is not the *telos* of a historical process culminating in a static eternity or in a panorama that unfolds before the backwards glance of a rational Absolute but is rather the persecuted God of the prophets. Levinas concludes: "I can never have enough in my relation to God . . . for he remains forever incommensurate with my desire."[23]

A note on the new edition: The present work differs from its predecessor in that easy-to-locate standard English translations that have appeared since the earlier edition was published have been substituted for my own. My reservations (few in number) with regard to the rendering of key terms are noted, minor corrections made, and an index added. To substitute feminine for masculine pronouns used in the earlier edition would alter the meaning of many passages. Were I to recommence, I would unhesitatingly do otherwise now.

NOTES

1. The expression is used by Karl Jaspers of Spinoza. See *Spinoza,* volume 2 of *The Great Philosophers,* trans. Ralph Mannheim (New York: Harcourt Brace Jovanovich, 1964), 94.

2. Emmanuel Levinas, "De la signifiance du sens," in *Hors sujet* (Montpellier: Fata Morgana, 1987), 138–39; translated by Michael B.

Smith as "The Meaning of Meaning," in *Outside the Subject* (Stanford: Stanford University Press, 1993), 91.

3. Jean-Luc Marion, *God without Being: Hors-texte,* trans. Thomas A. Carlson (Chicago: University of Chicago Press, 1991), 14.

4. See chapter III for an elaboration of this theme.

5. Maurice Blanchot, "Our Clandestine Companion," in *Face to Face with Emmanuel Levinas,* ed. Richard Cohen (Albany: State University of New York Press, 1986), 49.

6. On the commanding character of hagiographic narrative, see my *Saints and Postmodernism: Revisioning Moral Philosophy* (Chicago: University of Chicago Press, 1990).

7. *Summa Theologica* in *Basic Writings of St. Thomas Aquinas,* ed. Anton Pegis (New York: Random House, 1945), I:12, 3 reply obj. 2, p. 96.

8. Levinas, "Transcendence and Intelligibility," BPW 157.

9. Levinas, *L'au-delà du verset: Lectures et discours talmudiques* (Paris: Minuit, 1982), 7. Translated by Gary D. Mole as *Beyond the Verse: Talmudic Readings and Lectures* (Bloomington: Indiana University Press, 1994), x.

10. Walter Benjamin, *Illuminations: Essays and Reflections,* trans. Harry Zohn (New York: Schocken, 1968), 76. Benjamin comments (82) that great texts already contain their potential for translation between the lines, and sacred texts more so than others.

11. Levinas, *L'au-delà du verset,* 9; *Beyond the Verse,* xii–xiii.

12. Although there are numerous accounts of Levinas-Heidegger parallels, a nuanced reading of the present problem can be found in Adriaan Peperzak, "From Intentionality to Responsibility: On Levinas's Philosophy of Language," in *The Question of the Other,* ed. Arleen B. Dallery and Charles E. Scott (Albany: State University of New York Press, 1989), 3–22. For a condensed but powerful critique of Heidegger's thought as "a deduction of ipseity out of being," see Levinas's "De la déficience sans souci au sens nouveau," DVI 77–89, translated by Bettina Bergo as "From the Carefree Deficiency to a New Meaning," in *Of God Who Comes to Mind* (Stanford: Stanford University Press, 1998), 43–51.

13. In an article rich in complex relays describing what must be unsaid (de-diction) in relation to language prior to speech (pre-diction), John Llewelyn puts the matter thus: "The thing that is undone here is the word. To undo words said is the saying word's most dramatic and drastic deed. It is this because it is the undoing of the sayer." See his "Levinas: Critical and Hypocritical Diction," in *Philosophy Today* 41 (supplement 1997): 36.

14. Levinas, "L'autre dans Proust," in *Noms propres* (Montpellier: Fata Morgana, 1976), 120; translated by Michael B. Smith as "The Other in Proust," in *Proper Names* (Stanford: Stanford University Press, 1996), 102.

15. Levinas, *L'au-delà du verset*, 107–8; *Beyond The Verse*, 86–87.

16. Merleau-Ponty, *The Phenomenology of Perception*, trans. Colin Smith (London: Routledge and Kegan Paul, 1962), 178–81.

17. Chapter I considers some of these essays. Human deficiency as inability to perform a task, a thwarting of effort, could be seen as resembling the backwards pull of lassitude in the early work, although Levinas does not make this connection. See DVI 77–79; *Of God Who Comes to Mind*, 43–44.

18. For analysis of the feminine in Levinas see Catherine Chalier, *Figures du féminin: Lecture d'Emmanuel Levinas* (Paris: La nuit surveillée, 1982). Also see the essays by Tina Chanter and Luce Irigaray in *Re-reading Levinas*, ed. Robert Bernasconi and Simon Critchley (Bloomington: Indiana University Press, 1991).

19. Chapter V discusses fecundity.

20. This is Luce Irigaray's claim in "The Fecundity of the Caress," trans. Carolyn Burke, in *Face to Face with Levinas*, 233.

21. This question is posed in a somewhat different fashion by Richard Kearney in his interview with Levinas ("Dialogue with Emmanuel Levinas") in *Face to Face with Levinas*, 30.

22. Ibid.

23. Ibid., 32.

PREFACE TO THE FIRST EDITION

Emmanuel Levinas recounts the main events of his life in a brief essay, "Signature," appended to a collection of essays on social, political and religious themes entitled *Difficult Freedom*. He was born in 1905 in Lithuania and in 1917, while living in the Ukraine, experienced the collapse of the old regime in Russia. In 1923 he came to the University of Strasbourg, where Charles Blondel, Halbwachs, Pradines, Carteron, and later Guéroult were teaching. He was deeply influenced by those of his teachers who had been adolescents during the time of the Dreyfus affair and for whom this issue assumed critical importance. Continuing his studies at Freiburg from 1928 to 1929, he served an apprenticeship in phenomenology with Jean Héring. Subsequent encounters with Léon Brunschwicg and regular conversations with Gabriel Marcel served to distinguish, to sharpen and bring into the foreground, his own unique point of view. He also attests a long friendship with Jean Wahl. Together with Henri Nerson he undertook a study of Talmudic sources under the guidance of a teacher who communicated the traditional Jewish mode of exegesis. It is no accident that Levinas begins his autobiographical account, which is indeed no more than a spare outline of events and formative influences, with the information that the Hebrew Bible directed his thinking from the time of his earliest childhood in Lithuania.

In addition to those friends and mentors whose influence is attested in "Signature," it is not difficult to discern other strains in Levinas's thought. He continues the tradition of Martin Buber and Franz Rosenzweig to whom he acknowledges indebtedness elsewhere. It is, however, from Husserlian phenomenology that Levinas derives the rigorous and systematic methodological tools of inquiry that distinguish his thought from that of other religious thinkers whose rich and novel insights often lack sound philo-

sophical foundations. Indeed, Levinas was one of the first to introduce Husserl's work into what by now can be called the French
phenomenological school. His interpretation of Husserl incorporates Heidegger's critique of pure phenomenology in its assumption that the importance of phenomenology lies in providing a
foundation for a genuine understanding of ontology. Yet Levinas's own work can be read as a profound critique of this very
recovery since Levinas separates ontology from what he terms
"metaphysics" and prescinds from ontology its privileged role. By
separating metaphysics from ontology he is able to predicate a
unique bond between metaphysics and ethics. The interpretation
of this relationship forms the substance of his work.

The thought of Emmanuel Levinas is no less than an attempt
to accomplish a radical reversal of traditional procedures by
grounding metaphysics in ethics rather than in constructing an
ethic upon preestablished metaphysical foundations. Levinas argues that traditional Western philosophy, including the work of
Husserl and Heidegger, sustains a distinction between the one
and the other. In empirical systems this distinction is retained as
real; in idealistic systems it is rejected as illusory. But, Levinas argues, whether real or illusory, the distinction is always made and
always rests upon the presupposition that it is constituted by a
consciousness that discriminates. The one and the other are apprehended as distinct only to an observer who provides a point of
view. But the very possibility of incorporating the one and the
other into a single point of view compromises the radical alterity,
the "exteriority" of the other. Alterity that can be conjoined with
or separated from the one by thought is not true alterity but part
of what Levinas calls "the same." Radical otherness derives from
a more primordial source. It can never be adequately thought,
for it lies beyond ontology. It is reflected in the world through
the advent of other persons.

It is not the purpose of this essay to trace the diverse strains
that find their way into Levinas's work except in those instances
in which Levinas deals explicitly with inherited concerns. Since
careful attention is given to the work of Husserl, I shall take into
account Levinas's interpretations of Husserl's method and his critique of Husserlian phenomenology as a proper foundation for
the discerning of values. I shall also try to indicate the reasons for

Levinas's rejection of Heidegger's analysis of Dasein since Levinas's own phenomenological analyses can be regarded as attempts to found alternative modes of access to man's being-in-the-world. These interpretations can be conceived as constituting an ongoing polemic against Heidegger's attempted reconstruction of ontology. I shall on occasion indicate, for the sake of making plain Levinas's own understanding of a problem, its analogous development in other thinkers. I would hope that the conspectus of *Totality and Infinity* will be seen not only as deriving from Levinas's immediate predecessors but also as expanding and reworking key motifs in the philosophies of Descartes, Kant, and Hegel. But the major thrust of this book will lie in revealing neither the Cartesian view of the infinite nor Kant's understanding of the relationship between the realm of moral law and human activity, nor Hegel's view of history as Levinas appropriates these themes. Rather, attention will be directed to apprehending what is unique and innovative in Levinas's own thought. It will be my purpose to evaluate the feasibility of the effort undertaken by a profound and original thinker to reconstruct metaphysics upon ethical foundations.

It only remains to be said that a deep debt of gratitude is owed to Professor Levinas, who was professor of philosophy at the University of Paris at Nanterre and head of the Israelite Oriental Normal School in Paris, for his replies to my inquiries. In no sense are any interpretations of his work (save in the case where critical sources are cited) to be attributed to anyone other than myself. I also wish to thank Professors Robert Denoon Cumming, John Macquarrie, and Daniel D. Williams for their help in preparing this book and Professors Joseph L. Blau and Horace L. Friess for their ongoing interest in my work over a period of many years.

All citations of Levinas's texts are to existing translations; a handful have been slightly altered. Quotations from Talmudic sources are derived from the Soncino translation of the Babylonian Talmud. References to Levinas's works adhere to the system of abbreviations located herein.

This study was initially completed before the publication of *Otherwise than Being, or Beyond Essence* and thus only considered the portion of that work that had been previously published as "Substitution." The preface to the second edition deals more fully with this work.

ABBREVIATIONS OF WORKS BY LEVINAS

AE   *Autrement qu'être ou au-delà de l'essence.* The Hague: Martinus Nijhoff, 1974.

BPW   *Emmanuel Levinas: Basic Philosophical Writings.* Edited by Adriaan T. Peperzak, Simon Critchley, and Robert Bernasconi. Translated by the editors et al. Bloomington: Indiana University Press, 1996.

CPP   *Collected Philosophical Papers.* Translated by Alphonso Lingis. The Hague: Martinus Nijhoff, 1974.

D   "Discussion of Existentialism by Nicolas Berdiaeff, Maurice de Gandillac, Georges Gurvitch, Alexandre Koyré, Emmanuel Levinas, Gabriel Marcel." In Jean Wahl, *A Short History of Existentialism,* 35–56. New York: Philosophical Library, 1949.

DE   *De l'évasion.* Introduction and notes by Jacques Rolland. Montpellier: Fata Morgana, 1982.

DEE   *De l'existence à l'existant.* Paris: Vrin, 1947.

DEH   *Discovering Existence with Husserl.* Translated and edited by Richard A. Cohen and Michael B. Smith. Evanston, Ill.: Northwestern University Press, 1998.

DEHH   *En découvrant l'existence avec Husserl et Heidegger.* 3d ed. Paris: Vrin, 1974.

DF   *Difficult Freedom.* Translated by Seán Hand. Baltimore: Johns Hopkins University Press, 1990.

DL   *Difficile liberté.* 3d ed. Paris: Albin Michel, 1984.

DVI   *De Dieu qui vient à l'idée.* Paris: Vrin, 1982.

EE   *Existence and Existents.* Translated by Alphonso Lingis. The Hague: Martinus Nijhoff, 1978.

EN   *Entre nous: Essais sur le penser-à-l'autre.* Paris: Grasset, 1991.

ENT   *Entre Nous: On Thinking-of-the-Other.* Translated by Michael B. Smith and Barbara Harshav. New York: Columbia University Press, 1998.

HAH *Humanisme de l'autre homme.* Montpellier: Fata Morgana, 1976.

MHO *"Martin Heidegger and Ontology."* Translated by the Committee of Public Safety. *Diacritics* 26, no. 1 (1996): 11–32.

NTR *Nine Talmudic Readings.* Translated by Annette Aronowicz. Bloomington: Indiana University Press, 1990.

OBBE *Otherwise than Being, or, Beyond Essence.* Translated by Alphonso Lingis. The Hague: Martinus Nijhoff, 1981.

QLT *Quatre lectures talmudiques.* Paris: Minuit, 1968.

RO "La réalité et son ombre." *Les Temps Modernes* 38 (1948): 771–89. Translated by Alphonso Lingis as "Reality and Its Shadow," CPP, 1–13.

S "La Substitution," *Revue Philosophique de Louvain* (1968): 487–508. Translated by Peter Atterton, Simon Critchley, and Graham Noctor as "Substitution," BPW, 80–95.

TA *Le temps et l'autre.* Montpellier: Fata Morgana, 1979.

TeI *Totalité et l'infini: Essai sur l'exteriorité.* The Hague: Martinus Nijhoff, 1961.

TI *Totality and Infinity: An Essay on Exteriority.* Translated by Alphonso Lingis. Pittsburgh: Duquesne University Press, 1969.

TIH *The Theory of Intuition in Husserl's Phenomenology.* Translated by André Orianne. Evanston, Ill.: Northwestern University Press, 1973.

TIPH *Théorie de l'intuition dans la phénomenologie de Husserl.* Paris: Alcan, 1930.

TO *Time and the Other.* Translated by Richard Cohen. Pittsburgh: Duquesne University Press, 1985.

TrO "The Trace of the Other." Translated by Alphonso Lingis. In *Deconstruction in Context,* edited by Mark C. Taylor, 345–59. Chicago: University of Chicago Press, 1986.

EMMANUEL LEVINAS

I

Early Themes

THE STRUGGLE to understand the significance of life has challenged existential philosophy from its inception. Overwhelmed by complexity, contemporary man turns from technology with its attendant institutions backed by formidable systems of information to seek the meaning of his existence. According to Emmanuel Levinas, these intricate structures are integrated into a totality that imposes its own purposes upon individual life. The totality in its turn is a vastly ramified extension of self. Man has sown his dragon's teeth. How can he break the circuit of the self, or to put the question in Levinas's terms, how can he find the meaning of the Other?

In Levinas's texts from 1951 onwards, the original project of the self as self is a reduction of the Other to the one. This is possible because the one and the Other are constituted as such by a consciousness that discriminates. According to Levinas, the Platonic theory of ideas already presupposes this, since not only is alterity incorporated by the thinker as an *idea* of otherness, but it turns out to be something that he already knows. All knowledge can be elicited from him since his original repertoire includes everything that can possibly be thought. It is clear that Levinas reads Plato in much the same way as Kierkegaard: we can never learn what we did not know, and therefore Socrates's insight into the nature of knowledge leads to a genuine impasse. But Levinas adds the significant corollary that we can never know the Other because all knowledge is self-knowledge. A rethinking of the problem of the Other is required.

While Platonic metaphysics has correctly understood the nature of this problem, it was unable to develop a set of tactics for bypassing or solving it. The reason for this is that Plato's idea of the one is dominated by ontology. The one is inseparable from being. Levinas insists that the problem can be raised to a new level of insight only if the entire tradition of Western metaphysics is set aside as having arisen in the context of a totalizing ontology that must be transcended if an otherness truly exterior to totality is to emerge.[1] Like the gods created by the eternal God of the *Timaeus,* "whose very excellence enables it to keep its own company without requiring anything else,"[2] the self of traditional metaphysics finds itself alone in the world. How can the solitary self escape the narcissism of its original project? Is there no exit from its hall of mirrors?

Despite the totalizing intention of Plato's idea of the one, the Socratic theory of knowledge suggests a possibility for the transcendence of ontology. Having situated the good beyond being, a supraontological source of value anterior to ontology can be glimpsed from the Socratic teaching. But for Socrates "the Good" and happiness are linked: the latter derives from the former. The failure to distinguish them is, from Levinas's point of view, the error of Socratic metaphysics. "It is better (happier) to be than not to be" is the maxim of the ontologizing self. Happiness characterizes the self before its discovery of the Other. Solitude is attached to the awakening of alterity in Levinas's mature thought as being is related to the Good in Socratic metaphysics. Just as being is illumined in the light of the good, the meaning of the self is brought to fulfillment in the presence of the Other. What is the perspective of ontology so that the good is seen only as arising beyond it? What is solitary human consciousness before confrontation with the Other who appears but cannot be accommodated by it? In this chapter, I shall try to show Levinas's answers to these questions in his early work, before they are incorporated into the more elaborate architecture of his major work *Totality and Infinity.*

BEING AND BEGINNING

Contemporary philosophical speculation is forced to contend with the distinction between what exists and the act of its existence. The verb "exist" appears before thought as devoid of content, a kind of dizzying emptiness. It becomes intelligible only when expressed as a participle, "existing." Being is that by which the existing exists. From this idea of being, thought moves naturally to the idea of a "cause of existence," to a "being in general." This being, which has traditionally been identified with God, is such that its essence is its existence (DEE 15/EE 17). Such a "being in general" has frequently been interpreted as occurrence or activity or event. When we say that something is, we use being as an attribute. But Levinas, adhering to the Kantian view that being is not a predicate, maintains that if it is an attribute it adds nothing to the subject. Nor does Levinas believe that being is a genus, following Aristotle in this respect (DEE 17/EE 18).[3] The meaning of being, for Levinas, becomes visible only when "being in general" becomes the being of the existent through the event that is the present (DEE 18/EE 19).

How does the difficulty of separating being from existence arise? It is a consequence of the everyday way in which we regard temporality, of the accustomed habit of atomizing time and situating the instant beyond every event as something static. Temporality is thus dissociated from activity. We view the instant as a discrete fragment. But for Levinas being is not something discrete and unrelated to existence; instead existence confers a dynamism on being. The relation of being to existence cannot be conceived as a content that is somehow given in the instant; the instant is the very event by which being posits itself. The instant is a kind of "polarization" of "being in general" (DEE 18/EE 18).

The act of beginning brings to light the nature of this event. To know beginning we need not discover a cause that created the being that begins, but we must ascertain what, in such being, receives existence. Not that beginning is a bestowal of something upon a substratum; there is no residuum bequeathed by a preexisting subject. I believe, however, that when Levinas maintains that *something* receives existence he cannot escape the charge that he is, in fact, implying a substratum of continuity. The shadow of the metaphysics of substance, of the notion of "matter" antecedent to creation, lurks behind such an idea. This is borne out by Levinas's writing: "Even creation *ex nihilo* which implies pure passivity on the part of the creature, imposes on it, in the instant of its upsurge, the instant of creation, an act over its Being, a subject's mastery over its attribute" (DEE 17–18/EE 18). For Levinas, beginning is already a possession and activity of being. In spatial terms, the instant is not a "block" but is somehow "articulated."

Levinas means that the instant is, in its upsurge, dramatic and novel and thereby distinguished from the eternal, which lies beyond the sphere of activity and event.

It is my view that Levinas's understanding of the instant can best be grasped in the context of Kierkegaard's reflections upon the difference between Socratic and Christian concepts of temporality.[4] Since, according to Kierkegaard, the Socratic questioner assumes that the one to whom inquiry is directed already has the truth, then "[t]he temporal point of departure is nothing; for as soon as I discover that I have known the truth from eternity without being aware of it, the same instant this moment of occasion is hidden in the Eternal, and so incorporated with it that I cannot even find it so to speak, even if I sought it; because in my eternal consciousness there is neither here nor there, but only an *ubique et nusquam.*"[5] But if the moment is to have decisive significance, the seeker cannot have known the truth up to the moment at which he learns it: "Now if things are to be otherwise the Moment in time must have decisive significance . . . because the Eternal which hitherto did not exist, came into existence in this moment."[6]

Levinas does not confer upon each instant the unique and unprecedented distinction that Kierkegaard attributes to the moment. Nevertheless, his view of the relationship between the instant and eternity can, I believe, be seen as restating the Kierkegaardian position: eternity is, for Levinas, simple and strange to the event. Levinas bestows upon the instant the quality of novelty that Kierkegaard reserves for the moment. His critique of quotidian temporality, of the instant as an atom of time no different from similar atoms in an endless series of homogeneous fragments, presents a parallel to the Socratic view of temporality as Kierkegaard understands it. The instant, like the moment in Kierkegaard's thought, is bereft of a heritage and therefore provides the condition for genuine beginning.

INDOLENCE AND FATIGUE

Levinas contends that human spirituality depends not upon our relation with things that go to make up our world, but upon a relation that, by reason of our very existence, we are compelled to maintain. It is a relation with the bare fact that there is being. A concern with this relation between the self and its existence becomes particularly acute in certain prereflective lived states in which existence is seen as a burden to be assumed. Evasion, indolence, fatigue, and insomnia are such states. They represent attempts to avoid the imperatives that existence imposes but cannot in any sense be said to represent judgments about existence. Only upon subsequent reflection are they constituted as contents of consciousness. Indeed, reflection falsifies their character as events.

Evasion and indolence are interpreted as attempts to escape from existence, to flee from one's own being. The escape from being, which is an underlying motif in all of Levinas's thought, is in his early work designated as ex-cendence (DE 73). The flight from being to which ex-cendence refers is an inauthentic manifestation of escape conceived within the framework of ontology. Excendence, the effort to flee one's own being by the refusal to assume it, is doomed to failure. It must be distinguished from the legitimate transcendence of ontology through the relation with other persons, the theme of Levinas's reflections in *Totality and Infinity* as well as in much of his later work.

In evasion, being is experienced as an imprisonment from which one must break free. It is the need to take leave of oneself, to elude the fact that one is oneself. Being takes on a gravity and seriousness that makes its interruption seem imperative:

> Temporal existence takes on the inexpressible savor of the absolute. The elementary truth that there is being—being which counts and which weighs—is revealed at a depth which measures its brutality and gravity. The pleasant game of life loses its character as game. Not that sufferings which threaten life make it unpleasant; but the depth of suffering is the result of the impossibility of interrupting it and of a fevered feeling of being riveted down (DE 70).

In both indolence and evasion there is steadfast refusal to begin. In indolence this refusal is not the result of deliberation, for no quandary has been put before consciousness. It does not derive from any inherent impossibility to perform a specified act since the crucial element in indolence is that it is always *possible* to overcome it. This is the bad conscience of indolence. Indolence is tied to beginning as the impossibility of beginning. Any given task may be sufficiently complex to require a number of individual acts for its proper execution. Indeed, it is the character of extended labor to be discontinuous, to show many starts and stops. Indolence belongs to the trajectory of the task as a refusal to undertake what each instant of its execution demands (DEE 33/EE 26).

The beginning of a task is distinguished from the beginning of a game. The game possesses nothing and bequeaths nothing; it leaves no trace of itself in reality. Its commencement does not represent a true instance of beginning (DEE 34/EE 27). In a genuine beginning we already possess something, namely, the instant itself. If we interrupt what we have begun, our enterprise may end in failure, but we have not expunged the beginning. Though we may be thwarted in our intentions, the beginning we have made is now inscribed in being. Unlike the case of play in which beginning lacks seriousness and weight, the beginning of a task is a cutting of one's moorings, a risk. To begin is to accept one's future; indolence is an abstention from the future (DEE 39/EE 29).

Even in Levinas's earliest work the notion of beginning is not a simplistic overcoming of inertia, the expenditure of effort against the resistance offered to it by being. In Levinas's thought, beginning is conceived within a framework of authentic human possibilities, of legitimate engagement in the tasks of existence. In one of his first essays, an essay distinctly Marxist in provenance,[7] the capitalist is depicted as the embodiment of effort, of initiative and discovery, the antithesis of the lazy man (DE 68). He is anxious about his future, about realities that threaten to intrude upon the pleasant equilibrium of his present state. It is clear that Levinas does not wish to identify the capitalist as the authentic counterpart within the sphere of social existence of the lazy man. I believe that the apparent inconsistency between the negative picture of capitalism and the description of the capitalist as one who is willing to assume the tasks of existence becomes understandable once the notion of beginning is understood within a sociohistorical context. For Levinas, beginning involves disturbance, getting up with all the attendant insecurity that such activity implies (DEE 33/EE 26). The hallmark of the "bourgeois mind" is for Levinas the quest for security. Thus, the "imperialism" of the capitalist represents not genuine beginning, but the attempt to retain self-sufficiency. The lazy man and the capitalist, despite an apparent difference in their modes of existence, seek imperturbability and a retention of the status quo.

Unlike the being of indolence, the being of fatigue appears to be tied to certain distinguishable body processes. Levinas points out, however, that a phenomenological account of fatigue seeks to understand it as event, to uncover its meaning by getting inside it as a lived condition of existence rather than to reduce fatigue to its physiological components. While lassitude, which is distinguished from fatigue, is drowsiness and already belongs to the sphere of sleep, fatigue is the lived alternation between effort and its relinquishment. It is a relaxing of one's grip while still hanging on. Unlike indolence, one cannot avoid fatigue since it is not merely the consequence, but the modus vivendi, of effort. Fatigue is the slackening of the vital impulse or élan that inheres in effort (DEE 44/EE 31). Because of fatigue the duration of effort is entirely composed of stops; it is a "stiffening, a numbness, a curling up" of effort (DEE 41/EE 30). Fatigue is a condemnation of freedom, for it is inevitable, a consequence of the phenomenon of effort. Because of fatigue, the phenomenon of effort is characterized by stops. Effort cuts in on time and assumes the instant, yet is always behind the instant. It comes to grips with the instant as an inevitable present; effort is the fulfillment of the instant. The coming to grips with existence that effort represents is the first manifestation of the constitution of the existent as someone who *is* (DEE 48–49/EE 34).

BEING-IN-GENERAL: THE *il y a*

We have seen that for Levinas certain basic prereflective states of existence obstruct the act of beginning. These states, however, assume beginning as a realized human possibility, that is, they are lived against the background of a preexistent possibility of beginning. Their upsurge demands the existence of the existent who suspends the act of beginning. A fundamental interrogation of being, however, cannot take for granted the act of beginning that serves as the backdrop for indolence, evasion, and fatigue.

Such an investigation must raise the question: Is there being before beginning? In order to begin there must be an existent who begins. Is there being without an existent, without a being who begins? "Let us imagine all things, beings and persons, returning to nothingness. What remains after this imaginary destruction of everything is not something, but the fact that *there is* [*il y a*]" (TA 25–26/TO 46).

This state of affairs is not a return to primordial chaos, to the pure *apeiron* or unlimited, for we are asked to suppose a world. Nor is it to be confused with the nothingness evoked by "being-toward-death," by the anguished concern of being-in-the-world. It is a fear of being rather than a fear of nothingness that characterizes the stance within the *il y a*. The being that persists in the face of the destruction of the world, the theme of apocalyptic literature, is the being of the end of the world. This being to which the disappearance of the world makes us attentive is the being of neither persons nor things nor of the totality of persons and things. The *il y a* is a presence in the absence of things; it is a field of forces, the sheer fact of being when there is nothing at all. The *il y a* is perfect anonymity. It lacks the solidity and contour of the *en-soi,* the being of things. It "is the very work of being, which cannot be expressed by a substantive but is verbal" (TA 26/TO 48). It is without aperture, a kind of pleroma characterized by eternity since there is no point of departure in it. Cratylus's gloss on Heraclitus best expresses the state of the *il y a*: it is the river where one cannot even bathe once (TA 28/TO 49).

The *il y a* is the being that is prior to the being of the existent, so that it is the being that precedes solitude. It is impervious to form, lacking both interiority and exteriority. The formlessness of the *il y a* precludes its appearing in clarity, removes it from the dimension of light. It is as the absolutely unillumined. Night is our experience of the *il y a*. It envelops us in a presence while obliterating the forms of things. For Levinas night cannot be conceptualized; it is simply there. Even the self loses its identity in night. The disappearance of things and of self is a retrograde movement into what cannot disappear. This can be termed "nocturnal space"; it is filled with obscurity as though obscurity itself constituted its content (DEE 94–95/EE 58).

The mode in which one encounters the *il y a* is that of horror.[8]

The only way in which one can wrench oneself free of the *il y a* is by mastering it. The mastery of being comes about through the upsurge of consciousness.[9] Horror robs consciousness of its subjectivity by precipitating a plunge into participation, into the absolute impersonality of the sacred. The *il y a* is not a precursor to the God of revelation who will emerge from it in the course of an evolutionary process, but the absence of God (DEE 99/EE 61). The horror that one experiences before it is a breakdown of the boundaries of subjectivity rather than anguish before death. The *il y a* is the very impossibility of death, an existence that continues without interruption until the point of annihilation. Thus, for Levinas, unlike Heidegger, it is the continuity of being without interruption rather than a fear of its cessation that is fundamental to our experience of being.

I think it is important to note Levinas's attempt to communicate an ineffable experience, horror, and an essentially contentless existence, the *il y a*. The appropriate mode of mastering that which has content is knowledge. This principle is fundamental to Platonic thought: we have knowledge of form, but that which lacks form can only be apprehended as ignorance. That which is merely unintelligible presence, in which all distinction is absent, remains impervious to the grasp of intelligence. The conceptual scheme of Platonic metaphysics has been recast by Levinas in his early work into a contemporary phenomenological framework. Platonic ignorance before the unintelligible, which is merely privative, is replaced by an affective equivalent, horror. The absence of form, the sheer fact of being when there are no concrete entities, is the *il y a;* the *il y a* can itself be conceived as a metaphor for the Platonic metaphor of the cave from which the light must now be imagined as having been totally extinguished.

The primordial affective encounter with the *il y a* can, according to Levinas, be suspended through sleep. Unconsciousness as sleep is not enacted beyond the sphere of waking life, but is a participation in life as nonparticipation. Sleep is the suspension of psychic and physical activity. It can only take place in the act of lying down. To lie down is a mode of limiting life to being in a certain position. Place as the place where one lies down becomes a refuge, a basis for existence as sleep (DEE 119/EE 69–70).

There are, however, times when sleep seems impossible, when

consciousness balks at all of our attempts to suspend it. We stay awake when there is no longer any reason for staying awake. Such wakefulness is a detachment both from objects and from human presence. Consciousness no longer deploys our attention; instead we are held by the naked fact of the *il y a*. Our watchfulness is not directed to anything specific and thus is quite different from the attentiveness of daytime existence. We experience insomnia not as our own wakefulness, but as the wakefulness of the *il y a* itself. We lose our subjectivity and become the objects of anonymous thought: "Insomnia is constituted by the consciousness that it will never finish—that is, that there is no longer any way of withdrawing from the vigilance to which one is held. . . . From the moment one is riveted there, one loses all notion of a starting or finishing point. . . . Only the exterior noises . . . introduce beginnings in this situation without beginning or end, in this immortality from which one cannot escape, very similar to the *il y a*" (TA 27/TO 48).

The mastery of being through the upsurge of consciousness, the submersion of the *il y a* through the emergence of the subject, the act of beginning as constitutive of subjectivity represent for Levinas a reversal of Heideggerian ontology. It is now being itself that gives rise to horror, that bears down upon human existence. Nonbeing toward which anguished care is directed in the thought of Heidegger is understood by Levinas as a secondary and derivative phenomenon. Levinas concludes that for Heidegger being without anguish would be infinite being. His own thought reverses the affective relation with being through the phenomenological investigation of lived states in which the endless continuity of being, being without cessation, is experienced as the foundation of anguish. Levinas raises the question: "Is not the fear *of* being just as originary as the fear *for* being?" (DEE 20/EE 20). Let us turn to some fundamental Heideggerian concerns in order to clarify both Levinas's understanding of Heidegger and the reason for his dissociation from Heidegger's thought.[10]

DASEIN AND HYPOSTASIS

The traditional view of ego from Augustine to Descartes has presupposed a stable and persistent substratum that underlies every experience. From this point of view, no experience can posit itself as more fundamental than the substratum that undergoes it. While the idea of a subject who experiences remains basic to our everyday conception of the self, the positing of such a subject is according to Heidegger a merely ontic interpretation of human being that results from the finitude of our comprehension in our engagement with our world and other beings.

It is peculiar to human being (Dasein) that its ontic excellence lies in the fact that it is ontological. Dasein does not create being; it discovers it. The everyday life of Dasein that keeps it immersed in quotidian concerns forces Dasein to lose this extraordinary prerogative, the discovery of being. This prerogative is Dasein's transcendence. The task of ontology, according to Heidegger, is to uproot Dasein from its moorings in the everyday. This enables Dasein to recollect itself, to assume itself; on the other hand Dasein may lose itself once more in the fallenness of inauthenticity. In choosing authenticity, Dasein is deliberately engaged, faithful to itself.

Levinas notes that Dasein's self-understanding is achieved through certain affective dispositions. Affectivity becomes a primary source of self-understanding for Dasein because of its thrownness (*Geworfenheit;* DEHH 68/MHO 24). Human existence is abandoned to possibilities inflicted upon it by the very fact that it is let go in the world. This gives to it its character of facticity (*Faktizität;* DEHH 69/MHO 24). But in its self-understanding, Dasein also exists outside of its facticity. To be outside of oneself is to be one's possibilities. Dasein projects its possibilities. Either Dasein can understand itself in its fundamental possibilities as being-in-the world and delivered to anguished "care," or it can flee its authentic possibilities by "dispersing itself" in an understanding of secondary possibilities (DEHH 69/MHO 25). Dasein does this by falling into everydayness. It begins to understand itself from its social role. It knows only "*das Man*"; its authentic silence becomes idle chatter.

According to Levinas, one of the fundamental insights of Heidegger lies in Heidegger's critique of the idealist understanding of time. Levinas points out that for the neo-Kantians time is reduced to an unclear perception: it is not implicated in the being of the subject. For Kant time is a "phenomenal form which conceals from the subject precisely its true subjectivity" (DEHH 53/MHO 13). In the thought of Hegel, time is something into which Spirit is hurled but which nevertheless is separate from Spirit at the outset. Levinas maintains that the destruction of time by the idealists leads to the insight that the subject is something that he is not, for being outside of time he can never be what he is. How can the subject be present, be there, be what he is, if his mode of being always places him behind or beyond being? According to Levinas, Heidegger shows us that an ontology of the subject is impossible for idealism (DEHH 53/MHO 12).

Instead of pondering, as Hegel did, how Spirit fell into time, Heidegger claims that "Spirit does not fall *into* time; but factical existence 'falls' as falling *from* primordial, authentic temporality."[11] Time in Heidegger, Levinas claims, is not a skeleton to which human existence is accommodated. In its authentic form, human existence *is* a temporalization of time; temporalization constitutes the very event in which being is comprehended. An analysis of the comprehension of being will reveal the fundamental nature of time (DEHH 58/MHO 16).

Man exists in such a way that what is at stake for him is his own existence. Being does not appear to man as a concept or theoretical notion; man is not the being who contemplates existence. Rather it is revealed to him in the care that he has for his own existence. This mode of existence is itself a way of comprehending existence. According to Levinas, authentic understanding *is* taking care (DEHH 60–61/MHO 18). The fact that our existence is at stake, that we care for our existence, is a characteristic of Dasein's finitude.

Levinas notes that, according to Heidegger, the fact that things appear to us begins with the existence of a world. This notion of world determines the notion of space rather than the other way around: there is space because there is world, and world is more than bare spatiality because it refers to the existence of Dasein. The things amid which Dasein exists, which are Dasein's world, are objects of care. They offer themselves to manipulation, are good for something. In short, they are utensils (*Zeuge*) (DEHH 62/MHO 19). Manipulation is not the result of representing the object to oneself but is an absolutely fundamental manner of relating to objects. The useful is not merely present but manipulable. An understanding of the useful is possible only in the context of an anterior understanding of Dasein's structure. The useful is "in view of something," that in view of which the useful *is* is ultimately Dasein (DEHH 63–66/MHO 19–22).

Levinas sees in the work of Heidegger more than a recovery of authentic temporality, of primordial relations to the world that lie outside the sphere of cognition and reflective consciousness. He maintains that Heidegger's achievement is to reinstate into the mainstream of the history of philosophy elements that Levinas designates as "pathetic," elements refractory to philosophical speculation. Heidegger brings together affective states that have always been suspect to philosophical thought with categories more familiar to cognitive analysis. Levinas raises the question: "In re-ascending towards the categories—towards the ever-renewed light which emanates from these intellectual myths—one must ask: In what does the category of Heideggerian existentialism consist which casts its particular illumination on all those notions whereby the existentialists describe man, and transforms the old notion into new philosophy" (D 49)? The answer that Levinas gives to this question is crucial to an understanding of his view of Heidegger:

> Well, I think that the new philosophical "twist" originated by Heidegger consists in distinguishing between Being and being (thing or person), and in giving to Being the relation, the movement, the efficacy which until then resided in the existent. Existentialism is to experience and think existence—the verb "to be"—as event, an event which neither produces that which exists, nor is the action of what exists upon another object. The fact of existing, until then pure and reticent and tranquil; the fact which, in the Aristotelian notion of the act, remained quite serene and equal to itself among all the adventures that befall a being; the fact which was transcendent to all *being*, but which was not itself the event of transcending; this fact appears in existentialism as the adventure itself, containing history in itself. (D 50)

Levinas concludes that the meaning of existentialism derives from taking the verb "to be" as transitive. The categories of potentiality and act cannot express this new notion of existence. The reason for this, Levinas argues, is that for Heidegger power constitutes being. Being is the power of being. If this is the case, power must be defined in a way other than by reference to the act, for when potentiality passes into act, its existence is its realization; it loses in existence the very power that made it a possibility. Levinas argues from the premise that power belongs to potentiality and not to act. Act can never express the power of being, since act is itself a loss of power, the power of potentiality. For Levinas "the realization of power is an event of neutralization."

The event of existence must also differ from the realization of a previously existent goal. The single event that meets this quali- fication, an event that has no *telos*, is death (D 52): "To realize the possibility of death is to realize the impossibility of all realiza- tion." Heidegger needs the notion of death, Levinas claims, so that possibility can be grasped as possibility. Death preserves pure possibility because through it that which destroys possibility, namely realization, is itself destroyed. All other possibilities save that of death are realized as acts, but death alone is pure nonbe- ing (D 53).

Levinas interprets Heidegger as having correctly understood being as the power of being. But it is precisely this insight that leads Levinas to write in his first major work: "If . . . our reflec- tions are in large measure inspired by the philosophy of Martin Heidegger, where we find the concept of ontology and of the relationship which man sustains with Being, they are also gov- erned by a profound need to leave the climate of that philoso- phy" (DEE 19/EE 19). I believe that the point of divergence from Heidegger's thought is lodged for Levinas in the very insight with which he credits Heidegger, for if being is the power of being, it cannot, in Levinas's view, ever become the source of values. It can only give birth to the political and economic relations founded upon violence to which Levinas devotes considerable attention in his later work.

Heidegger is interpreted as continuous with the stream of West- ern metaphysics, beginning with Plato. The heart of Plato's world- view, according to Levinas, lies in accepting the dominance of reason. For Levinas reason is the faculty for maintaining identity through all the variations of becoming; it therefore finds nothing alien to itself. Levinas concedes that Heidegger contests the su- premacy of reason but that he too fails to undermine the suprem- acy of the same; that is, he fails to undermine the self's reduction of all alterity through the process of comprehension, the finding of what is identical beneath seeming diversity. Levinas contends that Heidegger is guilty of this failing insofar as he abandons Dasein to its mortality. He argues that the very principle that is constitutive of Dasein, its mortality, is the principle that maintains its ipseity, for only we alone can undergo our own death. No one can substitute for us. Genuine alterity is therefore absent from Dasein in its most fundamental engagement in being: "The supreme moment of resoluteness is solitary and personal" (DEHH 169/CPP 51).

Levinas contends that, for Heidegger, being is an illumination; it converts into intelligibility. *Being and Time* sustains one major point: being is inseparable from the comprehension of being. Being hardens the will so that consciousness of our finitude does not make us ashamed, so that we do not experience as the foundation for our being-in-the-world our imperfections and limitations. Through being we can never approach the idea of the infinite, an idea that is for Levinas, as I shall try to show, fundamental in the understanding of the Other. Heideggerian thought is for Levinas only the culmination of a long history, of an attitude "in which the finite does not refer to the infinite," a tradition of "pride, heroism, domination, and cruelty" (DEHH 170/CPP 52).

For Levinas there is still another issue at stake in the rejection of Heidegger's thought. The injunction to heed the voice of being opens for Levinas the possibility for human existence to be lived as pagan existence. To heed the voice of being is to leave natural existence unquestioned and unjustified. It is for this reason, according to Levinas, not difficult for Heidegger to be drawn to political conclusions that in the contemporary world are the natural outcome of what Levinas regards as a repristinization of human existence, the call of blood and soil. In his view, National Socialism is the inevitable culmination of Heidegger's philosophy.[12] In my view Levinas operates upon strictly Hegelian assumptions: a concrete historical moment is the embodiment of an abstract moment of thought, which so long as it remains abstract remains one-sided and unfulfilled:

> When Heidegger calls attention to the forgetting of Being, veiled
> by the diverse realities it illuminates, a forgetting for which the

philosophy developed from Socrates on would be guilty, when he deplores the orientation of the intellect towards technology, he maintains a regime of power more inhuman than mechanism . . . (It is not sure that National Socialism arises from the mechanistic reification of men, and that it does not rest on peasant enrooted-ness and a feudal adoration of subjugated men for the masters and lords who dominate them.) This is an existence which takes itself to be natural, for which its place in the sun, its ground, its *site,* orient all signification—a pagan *existing.* (DEHH 170/CPP 52)

It is precisely the notion of mother earth that has led, in Levinas's view, to the tyrannical forms of life assumed by Western civilization. He interprets Heidegger's work as an exaltation of the already present antireligious tendencies in Western thought. For Levinas, Heideggerian atheism is paganism; it predates the Socratic worldview, for it is rooted in pre-Socratic texts. It is as such antibiblical. Heidegger shows, according to Levinas, "in what intoxication the lucid sobriety of philosophers is steeped" (DEHH 171/CPP 53).

What is crucial for Levinas is that re-collection can never provide access to genuine alterity. While it is true that the everyday life of Dasein implicates it in relations with others, the being-with-others of Heidegger is a tangential relation of beings who exist alongside of one another. Their association centers around a common term, truth. For Levinas, the understanding of solitary being itself depends upon a proper comprehension of the mode in which we relate to Others. Although, in his view, we are in sensory contact with the Other, we experience ourselves as not being the Other. This is what makes solitude such an acute experience. It is possible to interpret every other relationship as one of transitivity and exchange, as basically an economic relation, except for the relation of oneself to oneself, since our own existence can never be exchanged for another. Despite our sophisticated powers of communication, we remain essentially monads. Monadic existence is not the consequence of the incommunicability of the contents of consciousness, but of the unity of existence with the existent. It may be recalled that Levinas suggests the possibility of an egress from self in his analysis of the *il y a.* Ecstatic experience in the life world of "primitives" enables the self to get out of itself. But if the self is indeed out of itself in this situation, the very phenomenon of merging reinstates a monistic system in which the polarization of terms has disappeared (TA 22/TO 43).

If human being does not find itself thrown into the world as being-with-others in accordance with the Heideggerian analysis, how does it arise as solitary being? For Levinas the basic phenomenon of thrownness as the condition of Dasein is replaced by an event that transpires at the heart of the *il y a* itself, within the anonymity of being. This event constitutes the mastery of being. It is, as we can already guess from the analysis of the act of beginning, the upsurge of consciousness. Consciousness ruptures the anonymous vigilance of the *il y a*. In this situation the existent is put into relation with his existence. Levinas makes it clear that he does not proffer his understanding of the birth of consciousness as a genetic explanation but as a phenomenological account. The appearance of a something that *is,* is designated as hypostasis and constitutes a real reversal at the heart of anonymous being. This something now carries being "as an attribute, is master of this existing as the subject is master of an attribute" (TA 31/TO 52).[13] Being is now experienced by the subject as belonging to him. What makes consciousness what it is is the possibility that there be a departure and a return to self. This is the meaning of the existent's identifying of himself. Through the process of identification, the existent renews his existence as solitude. The *event* of hypostasis, at which our analysis of beginning has enabled us to arrive, is the present (TA 32/TO 52).

In my view, Levinas's critique of Dasein can be seen to rest upon the same foundations as the critique of Dasein[14] set forth in Sartre's analysis of the immediate structures of the for-itself. According to Sartre, Heidegger is caught between the Scylla of Kantian idealism to which a strict adherence to the Husserlian doctrine of essences would hold him and the Charybdis of denying consciousness to Dasein. In Sartre's view, Heidegger falls victim to the latter. Sartre writes: "Dasein has from the start been deprived of the dimension of consciousness; it can never regain this dimension."[15] The restoration of consciousness, its noncoincidence with itself, provides for both Sartre and Levinas a common point of divergence from Heidegger's Dasein. For both, the self is an ideal distance that prevents us from coinciding with ourselves.

Levinas differs in his conception of consciousness from Sartre in the ontological primacy that Levinas gives to solitude. Not only does solitude occur first in the order of description, but it appears without positing any previously given relations with others (TA 35/TO 54). It emerges directly against the ground of the *il y a.* Solitude is required for there to be the freedom of beginning. A pervasive motif developed throughout Levinas's work is the notion that solitude is not despair, abandonment, loss of the Other. He contends that in its break with Romantic psychology, existential thought, with its focus upon despair, has lost the truth of solitude that was correctly understood by Romantic psychology (TA 35/TO 55). The solitary subject wrenched from the anonymity of the *il y a* (unlike the negativity of *pour soi,* which is in its upsurge and remains pure nonbeing) is the appearance in the world of the substantive. Hypostasis designates the activity of transforming that which has been expressed as a verb into a substantive. This is not the upsurge of a new part of speech but the obliteration of anonymity. A being, the one who is, becomes the subject of the verb "to be" and thus exerts a mastery over the fatality of being. Consciousness comes into being with itself as a starting point and finds in itself a refuge from being. At the outset consciousness is not existent but event; this event is then transformed, hypostatized, into a substantive. What defines our existence as such is solitude; the world, the objects within our world, are all given as though coming from us for we bestow meaning upon them. Their existence is founded in our solitude (DEE 144/EE 84–85).

Need, Desire, and the World

While consciousness founds the present, it does not account for our relationship to the world of things. Being in the world is a hunger for things. Our relationship to things is affective; we desire them. Desire is always the desire for something; it has an object. In desiring, we want what can be fulfilled by the object of our desire. In desire we do not care about being but are absorbed in the desirable (DEE 56/EE 37).

Since the advent of psychoanalytic thought, can we say that the desirable posits only its object? Must we not also assume that desire posits an unconscious content, desires more than its object? Levinas maintains that the unconscious is a contradiction in terms, for if it is unconscious it must remain so in order for the term "unconscious" to be applicable. We could not possibly discover the unconscious, for then it would cease to be what it is. According to Levinas, philosophy has always interpreted the unconscious as a second consciousness, failing to recognize the ontological function of the unconscious and its specific relation with conscious illumination, with "sincerity," which is detached from the depth and equivocacy of the unconscious. He concludes that either the conscious has been interpreted in terms of the unconscious, or the unconscious in terms of the conscious. How then are we to interpret the unconscious? "Consciousness is precisely a sincerity. In taking being-in-the-world as an intention, one is above all affirming—and the history of our civilization and of our philosophy confirms this—that the world is the field of a consciousness, and the peculiar structure that characterizes consciousness governs and gives meaning to all the infiltrations of the unconscious in the world" (DEE 57/EE 38). For Levinas the unconscious is present only before there is world.

The theme of the unconscious is not a major focus in Levinas's work. He wishes only to eliminate from consideration the possibility of that which is *eo ipso* closed to the illumination of consciousness as being in any sense part of what can be termed the world. His intensive study of Husserl, to which I shall turn shortly, has made him fully aware of how impossible it is to fulfill the Cartesian desideratum of clear and distinct ideas in all realms of knowledge. Some regions of being, by virtue of the kinds of being that they are, give themselves to consciousness in ways that cannot live up to the visual model. But these opaque regions of being are in no sense the equivalents of an unconscious; they simply give themselves differently to illumination. While Levinas's remarks on the unconscious are suggestive, they cannot in my view be said to constitute a fully developed critique of classical Freudian doctrine.

Once more the fortuitous similarity to Sartre's view is too striking to overlook. Sartre writes that Freud has "cut the psychic whole into two" by distinguishing between id and ego and endowing the ego with the identity of an "I." The hypothesis of a censor establishes a regional division, one in which our drives are reified so that they become entities rather than consciousness, and the other, the consciousness that operates upon them as though they were entities foreign to this consciousness. The subject has split himself into two, into a deceiver and a deceived. The function of interpretation, according to Sartre, is to reattach the deceiver to the deceived. The "I" is deceived for identity lies in the ego and not in the alien consciousness that has deceived us. For Sartre, "psychoanalysis substitutes for the notion of bad faith, the idea of a lie without a liar; it understands how it is possible for me to be lied to without lying to myself since it places me in the same relation to myself that the other is in respect to me."[16]

Levinas does not conclude that there is a fundamental project of human consciousness to deceive itself that we can otherwise designate as unconscious existence and that provides the true explanation for otherwise inexplicable behavior.[17] But he does concur with Sartre in rejecting the notion of a double set of consciousnesses. Both Levinas and Sartre maintain an insight that is fundamentally Husserl's: wherever there is world there is consciousness. World as world can only be the understood world. For Levinas it is consciousness that commands and gives meaning, in much the same way as reason dominates and gives meaning to the irascible and appetitive elements in the Platonic scheme. Thus, we see that there is no unconscious region at which desire aims, either with clarity and precision, or dimly and obscurely.

While in his mature work the term "desire" is always used to designate an affect inadequate to its object, to the other person that it intends, in the early work the term "desire" refers to a want that is satiable, "knows" what it intends. While it is true that the desideratum does not issue from man, that which is desired is given as being at man's disposal. There is nothing that desire intends that lies beyond what can theoretically be given. Since desire in the early work is satiable, it already carries joy within it. It is not an emptiness waiting to be filled but belongs to the very fact that the world is given. World *qua* world is for Levinas happy. Happiness is not a quality incidental to the possession and presentation of objects but belongs to the fact that the world is revealed to us, that the object is for us. There are two aspects under which desire can be considered. One involves a representation of the desirable anterior to its acquisition and in which there is a distance between oneself and the acquisition of the desirable. This distance is expressed as "time before me." The other involves simultaneous possession and representation (DEE 59/EE 39).

Need, on the other hand, seems to aspire to satisfaction, to direct us toward something other than ourselves. Need's own insufficiency is then interpreted as an insufficiency of being. For Levinas the proof that need is not a simple lack belongs to the fact that the satisfaction of a need does not do away with it. Need is a dead weight that satisfaction cannot destroy and that expresses a pressure of being and not a lack of it. The primary phenomenon of the satisfaction of need is pleasure. Pleasure does not move to an end; it has no end. It merely seeks the expansion of its amplitude. Pleasure is concentration in the moment. In pleasure the moment loses its solidity; it is the process of getting out of being. Need is not a nostalgia of being but a mode of egress from it. Pleasure can only break down because there is no escape from being, no evasion of its pressure (DE 74ff.).

The analysis of need in this very early essay already uncovers some fundamental structures of what Levinas designates in his later work as desire for the Other. While fundamentally capable of satisfaction, a persistent restlessness is attendant upon the fulfillment of need. Thus, Levinas is actually contending that need is insatiable since what is given does not assuage the sense of lack still present after the need is "satisfied." Levinas has not yet clearly dissociated two categories of lack, one in which satiety is theoretically attainable and the other in which the desideratum so exceeds the desire that intends it that all possibility for the fulfillment of desire is precluded. The phenomenology of need in this early work is still envisaged within the framework of ontology. Thus, the inherent insatiability of need is tied not to a transcendent object but to pleasure itself, which is an insatiable hunger. The reason for the insatiability of pleasure is not yet understood as the result of desiring the Other whom one can never possess.

Once Levinas links need and desire to the world as world, he is compelled to conflate them, to think them as inherently capable of satiety. Thus, the early writings, in my view, reveal two contradictory standpoints. The first assumes that need is not demolished with the satisfaction of need, that there is a pressure that we experience when need is satisfied, a pressure whose source remains inexplicable; the second assumes the adequacy of intention to what is given, of desire to the desirable, and therefore presumes genuine satiety. Objects so long as they belong to the world lack mystery, are tied to a form, are stable and finite, can fulfill the intention that is directed at them. This peculiar contradiction compels Levinas to affirm either that there are some things that we can think that are totally formless (something that Levinas refuses to do as our investigation of the *il y a* has shown), or to claim that there are objects of need and desire that transcend ontology and therefore do not have to meet the requirement for all thought, namely, the requirement that they have form in order to be thinkable. Levinas will choose the latter alternative. The other person will emerge as an object of desire, as lacking form, as being beyond ontology.

A phenomenological analysis of love brings to light the difficulty inherent in this early ambiguous view of desire. The hunger of love is inextinguishable; there is always something left over in love, something unexpressed, not amenable to formalization. Food is consumed, but the gesture of love cannot fully express love: "The bush which feeds the flame is not consumed" (Ex. 3:2). The disturbance experienced in the presence of the loved one is not a simple feeling that precedes possession of the loved object but a disorder basic to possession itself. In a sense, Levinas claims, love apes eating. Desire and hunger are confounded in the phenomenon of love itself. But the promise of desire is always beyond the possibility of fulfillment. There is no end or object possible for love since satisfaction is simply a return to self (DEE 66/EE 43–44). Eating, on the contrary, "is peaceful and simple; it fully realizes its sincere intention: 'The man who is eating is the most just of men'" (DEE 67/EE 44). In our being in the world, Levinas contends, there is an exact conformity of object to desire. A feeling of malaise is not a residue of such basic acts as breathing, eating, or drinking. These acts are not undertaken in order to live; they constitute the very act of living. In desire where form and content are adequate to each other, consciousness describes a circle in which satisfaction is not merely possible but constitutes the meaning of the world. The world is the possibility of such adequation, and adequation is what we mean when we speak of satiety (DEE 67/EE 44). But the reason for the lack of conformity of the object to desire in the case of love, to which the present work calls attention, is left unexplained.

Levinas, even before the synthesizing operation of *Totality and Infinity,* anticipates the objection to the legitimacy of the use of cognition, that is, of the adequacy of form to object, as the model for phenomena such as desire that are essentially activities. Does this not imply a confusion of theory and practice (DEE 71/EE 46)? What enables Levinas to legitimate the cognitive model as the paradigm for action as well as for all knowledge is the idea of intention. I shall try to show subsequently and in some detail how Levinas understands this key term in Husserl's thought. Suffice it to say for the moment that in his earliest analyses of activities and of prereflective states—in the phenomenological analysis of world—theory and practice need not be separated in Levinas's view since both require an activity of the subject (DEE 72/EE 46). What Levinas argues is this: the intention that directs itself upon the object when I know the object is an *activity,* so that there is really no difference in kind between the sort of operation that knowing is supposed to be and the kind of operation that life *qua* life implies, for example, eating, drinking, and so on. This scheme, which is elaborately developed in *Totality and Infinity,* enables Levinas to show how affective states, life-sustaining processes, and cognition are activities directed to reducing the alterity of the Other by reducing it to an intentional act of the subject.

What differentiates our relation to the object in desiring from our relation to it in cognition is a certain distance that, in cognition, we maintain with regard to it. This distancing belongs to intention in the strict sense, that is, to intention directed upon an object. The world given us in intention leaves us with a certain freedom with regard to it. The self while directing itself toward a thing also retreats from it. It cannot penetrate the thing itself; it can merely glide across the surface of a thing. Intentionality, since it cannot go through the object, withdraws from it, becomes interiority (DEE 73/EE 47).

Since intentionality is not a merging with the object, the outside of the self must somehow be adjusted to what is interior to it. This act is the bestowal of sense as meaning. Sense does not involve the reduction of a perception to a concept, for then we would have to seek the meaning of the irreducible principle (the concept) itself: "sense is permeability for the mind, and already characterizes what we call sensation. Or, we can say, it is luminosity" (DEE 74/EE 47). Light is what makes *any* phenomenon possible. For this reason, vision, which is born in light, is the paradigmatic sense; it gives not only the object but also our relation to it. It is the only one of the senses that opens a "horizon" so that the object coming to us from without is already within our purview welling up from the horizon that precedes it. Yet the object is given as though coming from us, as though commanded by our freedom.

For Levinas this world that is given to us is not the sum total of the objects within it. The world is what it is, a totality, because there is "someone" who encompasses it: "There is a totality because it is referred to an inwardness [*intériorité*]" (DEE 76/EE 49). Knowledge is a way of knowing while retaining the power to refrain from becoming involved in the known; to be subject is to have the "power to withdraw infinitely" (DEE 79/EE 50). The subject can always, so to speak, "get behind" what is happening to him. The subject is free with regard to every object in the relation of knowledge. Knowledge is the very condition upon which freedom is based. The act of knowledge as an abstention from involvement in the world constitutes a decision to remain outside the world. Thus, I believe that Levinas's understanding of knowledge itself without any further operation required puts into effect what Husserl calls a "bracketing," a putting out of operation of the activities of existence. Knowledge suspends involvement in the totality of existence. We are thus enabled to achieve an identity as being what we are by not being one with the world (DEE 74–75/EE 48).

A number of crucial elements are left undecided in the early work of Levinas. We are told that intentionality is an activity just as desire and eating are activities. Are these also, strictly speaking, intentional? Are certain affective states such as indolence and fatigue "intended"? Does Levinas wish to show that when we reduce alterity in cognition by intending the given, that is, by already determining the given through an activity of the subject, that we are performing a radically different operation from activities in which we consume the given because the consumption of the given is nonreflective? Is it not one of the fundamental insights of phenomenology that the satisfaction of vital human needs is always humanly undertaken and not biologically determined? Are not complex human intentions involved in the simplest activities: walking, standing, eating, and the like? Is Levinas trying to show that there are different sets of intentions for these activities, or is he maintaining that intention, which is an activity like the aforementioned activities, belongs strictly to those operations in which distancing of the subject from the given is involved?

One thing, however, is clear. Levinas's approach to world as world even in his early writings will have significant repercussions from the theological standpoint, a standpoint that underlies his later thought. The world of the everyday is not a fallen world. The ontological adventure is a necessary moment in the trajectory of human consciousness. It is de rigueur for there to *be* an everyday world, since only through the upsurge of an existent, who enjoys, who reflects, is the separation from the anonymous vigilance of the *il y a* possible. Man belongs in history. He has not fallen into it: "In the ontological adventure the world is an episode which, far from deserving to be called a fall, has its own equilibrium, harmony, and positive ontological function: the possibility of extracting oneself from anonymous being. . . . To call it everyday and condemn it as inauthentic is to fail to recognize the sincerity of hunger and thirst" (DEE 69/EE 45).

NOTES

1. According to Jacques Derrida, "Violence et métaphysique: Essai sur la pensée d'Emmanuel Levinas," in *L'écriture et la différence* (Paris: Seuil, 1967), 120, n.2 (translated by Alan Bass as "Violence and Metaphysics: An Essay on the Thought of Emmanuel Levinas," in *Writing and Difference* [Chicago: University of Chicago Press, 1978], 312, n.4), the term "Western philosophy" is tautologous since for Levinas philosophy is Western (Greek) in its very being.

2. Plato, *Timaeus* 34b, trans. Donald J. Zeyl in *Plato: Complete Works*, ed. John M. Cooper (Indianapolis: Hackett, 1997).

3. According to Aristotle (*Metaphysics* 998b21), being cannot be a genus since one cannot predicate the genus, taken apart from its species, of its differentiae. One cannot, for example, claim that if mammal

is a genus, cat a species, and four-footedness a differentia, that the genus mammal can be predicated of four-footedness. Similarly, if being were a genus, it could not be, a manifest absurdity.

4. In one of his earliest writings, a review of Leon Chestov's "Kierkegaard et la philosophie existentielle" in *Revue des Études Juives* 1, nos. 1–2 (1937), 139–41, Levinas concludes: "Shestov interprets the philosophy of Kierkegaard as a combat undergone by a soul abandoned to despair in a world ruled by reason and the ethical." (Leon Chestov is also known as Lev Shestov.) He sees in Shestov's interpretation a Kierkegaard who proclaims the supremacy of Jerusalem over Athens. This interpretation, he notes, is made explicit in Shestov's book *Athens and Jerusalem*. What Levinas writes of Shestov's analysis of Kierkegaard might well be taken as a program for his own future work.

5. Søren Kierkegaard, *Philosophical Fragments*, trans. David Swenson and Howard V. Hong (Princeton: Princeton University Press, 1962), 15–16.

6. Ibid., 16.

7. Levinas understands Marxism as being continuous with historical expansionist movements of a messianic character. He speaks sympathetically of Marxist fervor, if not of Marxist programs, as late as 1957 in an essay entitled "Freedom of Speech," which appeared first in *Les Lettres Nouvelles* 51 (1957) and was reprinted in DL 287–90/DF 205–8. He writes: "The uninterrupted growth of the Communist party, its conquest of the world, which was more rapid than the spread of Christianity ·or Islam, its catholic range, the faith, heroism and purity of its youth . . . have accustomed us to hearing in this movement the very footsteps of Destiny" (DL 287/DF 205).

8. Georges Bataille, in "De l'existentialisme au primat de l'économie," *Critique* 4 (1948): 140 (translated by Jill Robbins and Marcus Coelen as "From Existentialism to the Primacy of Economy," in Jill Robbins, *Altered Reading: Levinas and Literature*, 178f. [Chicago: University of Chicago Press, 1999]), in an analysis of anguish from the economic point of view, sees the affective encounter with being as the absence of subject and object and notes that Levinas's analysis is incomplete because it lacks a quantitative basis. It therefore is, for Bataille, thought from which nothing can follow.

9. Bataille comments that Levinas's discussion of the *il y a* creates the problem of attempting to communicate an ineffable experience, an experience without content: "The *il y a*, from the very fact that it is not *this* which I can relate to *that* (as to a genus of which it is the example), cannot exist in me . . . except in the form of ignorance. At the same time, supreme ignorance necessarily reveals the nudity of *that which is*,

reduces it to an unintelligible presence in which all difference is destroyed" (ibid., 134 [French]; 172 [English]).

10. While it is my view that Levinas's interpretation of Heidegger is sometimes debatable, a critical discussion of the merits of this interpretation lies outside the scope of this book. It is my purpose merely to elicit what that interpretation is since an understanding of the grounds for the rejection of ontology will show why an ontological foundation is precluded for Levinas's ethical metaphysics. For extended analyses of the merits of Levinas's interpretation of Heidegger, see Derrida, "Violence et métaphysique," esp. 161–228 ("Violence and Metaphysics," esp. 109–53), and Rudolf Boehm, "De Kritiek von Levinas op Heidegger," *Tijdschrift voor filosofie* 25, no. 3 (1963): 585–603, including a German summary.

11. Martin Heidegger, *Being and Time,* trans. John Macquarrie and Edward Robinson (New York: Harper and Row, 1962), 486. Cited by Levinas in DEHH 55/MHO 14.

12. For a related view, see Hans Jonas, "Heidegger and Theology," in *The Phenomenon of Life* (New York: Harper and Row, 1966), 235–61.

13. Levinas makes a number of claims concerning the nature of being that are difficult to adjudicate. In contrast to the passage quoted, he writes: "[Being] is not a quality which the object supports, nor what supports qualities. Nor is it the act of a subject, even though in the expression 'this is' Being becomes an attribute—for we are immediately obliged to state that this attribute adds nothing to the subject" (DEE 17/EE 18). What kind of attribute is it that adds nothing to the subject? It would seem that Levinas wishes to maintain the Kantian view that existence is not a predicate while insisting that consciousness in its upsurge from the *il y a* masters being and thus takes being on as an attribute.

14. A long captivity in Germany during World War II prevented Levinas from reading *Being and Nothingness* before he had finished writing *Existence and Existents.* See Bataille, 127. Therefore, despite the similarity of view, no direct influence need be assumed.

15. Jean-Paul Sartre, *Being and Nothingness,* trans. Hazel E. Barnes (New York: Philosophical Library, 1956), 74.

16. Ibid., 51.

17. Levinas writes: "There is then a regrettable confusion in contemporary philosophy when it situated within the world the events which it has the incontestable merit of having discovered and designated by the purely negative term of the unconscious, and when it denounced as a hypocrisy . . . behavior in the world, whose secular nature and contentment are simply counterparts of the very destiny of the world" (DEE 63–64/EE 42). The intention to deceive is absent from Levinas's interpretation.

II

Husserl and the Problem of Ontology

IN A TERSE AUTOBIOGRAPHICAL ESSAY that coordinates personal data with the intellectual perspectives opened for his own life and thought by the work of Edmund Husserl, Levinas assesses the value of Husserl's method:

> Husserl will be remembered for having brought to philosophy a method. It amounts to the analysis of "intentions" that maintain the irreducibility of the various experiences of the real, delineates the unsuspected horizons in which this reality situates itself when one "heeds" the "intentions" that apprehend the real, and fixes the original standing of the being thus approached. But the method consists especially in recognizing a dignity of experience and of apprehension in the attitudes of the mind (and of the body) that until now were not supposed to play a part in discovering being. These experiences of a new type, totally strange to the subject-object archetype, sometimes are foundations of the contemplative thought that fixes things and ideas and are prior to the technique that handles them and fashions them. The structure of the contemplated object does not serve at all as a norm for the correlate of nontheoretical experiences.[1]

This comment supports a point of view maintained in Levinas's introduction to his early but major critical study of Husserl, *The Theory of Intuition in Husserl's Phenomenology*. There Levinas insists that his interest lies not in tracing the evolution of Husserl's thought, which in any case could not be effectively undertaken in our time since Husserl is too close for judicious historical appraisal, but in phenomenology as a living philosophy. For this reason Levinas feels justified in interpreting Husserl's work by taking into account the perspectives provided for the understanding of phenomenology both as a method and a philosophy of life in the thought of Heidegger. In so doing, Husserl's concern with questions of philosophical method need not be separated from questions of ontology (TIPH 15/TIH lvi).[2]

PHENOMENOLOGICAL METHOD AND ONTOLOGY

In *Ideas I*, Husserl claims that transcendental phenomenology is concerned with the constitution of the world for pure consciousness. Husserl adds that this introduces a genuinely philosophical "dimension" into phenomenological thought. The genuinely philosophical dimension to which Husserl refers is, according to Levinas, the problem of ontology (TIPH 15/TIH lvi). He contends that "Phenomenology as a revelation of beings is a *method of the revelation of their revelation*. Phenomenology is not just the fact of letting phenomena appear as they appear; this appearing, this phenomenology, is the essential event of being" (DEHH 117/DEH 97). Phenomenology can be understood to be ontological rather than methodological only if methodology is narrowly construed to mean an instrument for the exploration of some domain of the real, if it is severed from the region of being in which it is operative. But, Levinas maintains, we must first be able to anticipate the region of being where a method will be put into operation in order to arrive subsequently at the method itself. The method of the natural sciences, for example, shows itself to be inadequate to investigations in psychology because its application involves a prior intuition of the region of being in which the method is grounded. Levinas maintains that Husserl had an intuition of his philosophy before creating a philosophy of intuition. We cannot infer from this that we must have a full-fledged science before we can seek its method. But Levinas wishes to point out that the science of the meaning of being is not the same study as an understanding of the properties of being, that the former is in some sense a priori and is presupposed by the latter (TIPH 11/TIH liii).

Levinas interprets Husserl's quest for apodicticity, for a foundation upon which to base the sciences that would be self-evident and unquestioned, as an ontological quest. Husserl found in the science of logic a *mathesis universalis,* "the science of science" and the basis for such a foundation. While Husserl's quest for an absolutely certain grounding for the sciences is essentially that of Descartes, Husserl's solution to the problem of certainty is, however, non-Cartesian. Levinas maintains that "the problem is less that of guaranteeing the certainty of propositions than that of determining the *meaning* which certainty and truth can have for each domain of being" (DEHH 8/DEH 47). Husserl, according to Levinas, refuses to construct a single model of truth whose variations would be approximations of truth; rather he treats the alleged uncertainties of any given mode of consciousness as appropriate to the region of being that is revealed in that consciousness. The possibilities for "error" in sense experience, for example, constitute the character of sense experience and are only designated as "erroneous" when models foreign to it provide the criteria for truth. The being that is revealed in sense experience can only be grasped by the "fallible" type of consciousness that sense experience is. Husserl seeks the positive significance of the truths to which the alleged uncertainties of particular states of consciousness give us access, rather than an ideal of certainty, which these states of consciousness could not even approximate and which would undermine their character as truth. Phenomenological method understood in this way deepens our consciousness of the being of things. Levinas claims that for Husserl phenomenology is a vehicle of spiritual destiny, a mode of existence for man whereby he fulfills his spiritual end.[3] It serves as the basis not only for the physical, but for the moral sciences as well. It brings with it "a discipline through which the mind takes cognizance of itself [*Selbstbesinnung*], assumes responsibility for itself and ultimately for its freedom" (DEHH 8/DEH 48).

According to Levinas, what confers upon Husserlian ontology this peculiar quality of deepening the meaning of being belongs, as I have suggested, to Husserl's development of the notion of regional ontology, to the view that every region of being is to be thought differently.[4] This does not mean that we cannot speak of objects and of relations as universally applicable to all regions of being. These concepts are, however, purely formal. The formal structure is not to be understood as a genus; the universality of the form goes beyond all generality (TIPH 21/TIH 4). The categories that express the material structure of being are not merely specifications of the formal structure. Material categories differ according to the domain of being that they describe. The concept of regional ontology opens, for Levinas, the perspective in view of which he establishes one of the most significant conclusions of his major work on Husserl, *Theory of Intuition:* the regions of being differ in their modes of existence, "*to exist does not mean the same thing in every region*" (TIPH 22/TIH 4). The fact of "being found there" (in one region rather than another) is not an empty and uniform characteristic added on to essences but belongs to the difference among the essences themselves. Thus from an essentially eidetic science that unites a group of ontological disciplines, Levinas feels justified in proceeding to a new question: what is meant when we say that the object *is*. Moreover he understands this question as arising naturally from the philosophy of Husserl (TIPH 22/TIH 4).

NATURALISTIC ONTOLOGY AND PSYCHOLOGISM

Being is the object of the natural sciences, which presupposes certain basic notions that the sciences themselves ultimately fail to clarify, such as memory, perception, space, and time. These concepts underlie the different domains of being. They are the determinants of the necessary structure of being. A theory of being should study the nature of being as being in terms of the categories that provide the conditions for its existence. Such a study *is* ontology (TIPH 20/TIH 3). Levinas maintains that even in his critique of psychologism, Husserl is attacking the theory of being that underlies it, its ontology: "At least implicitly, psychologism is itself founded on a more general philosophy which has a definite way of interpreting the structure. It is founded on an ontology, and this ontology is naturalism" (TIPH 18/TIH lviii).

The error of naturalism is its confusion of the being of nature as it is revealed in the physical sciences with absolute being, reducing the latter to the former for the sake of consistency. The natural scientist envisions everything as nature and therefore falsifies every other region of being that cannot be thought of in terms for which nature provides the model (TIPH 30/TIH 10). The Husserlian understanding of naturalism is, according to Levinas, absolutely original. According to Husserl, naturalism is not a doctrine that separates matter from spirit, a doctrine that is in fact often materialistic. Instead it is a point of view concerned with the type of existence intended by the naturalistic attitude with its particular interpretation of being. According to Levinas, Husserl claims that when naturalism speaks of psychic phenomena, the very objectivity of these phenomena is presumed to "imply the physical world." In light of these reflections, being for naturalism means being there in the same way as the material world, "being on the same plane" as the material world. Naturalism conceives of existence as modeled upon the material thing (TIPH 31/TIH 11). The success of modern physics, according to Levinas is the result of the fact that the ontology of nature was discovered (correctly) to be founded in the mathematics of classical antiquity. What is appropriate for one region of objects is, however, inadequate for another: "According to Husserl, the fact that Galileo saw the ontology of nature in the geometry and mathematics elaborated in antiquity has made possible the great progress in modern physics. The great mistake of the other sciences—psychology, for example—is to see, in the ontology of nature the ontology of all regions, or else reject all ontology" (TIPH 167/TIH 114).

It is indifferent for naturalism whether it is interpreted within a framework of idealism or realism since being remains in both psychophysical in nature. If the mode of being of consciousness and matter is the same, consciousness is reified. Whether the physical world is reduced to the contents of consciousness or whether consciousness is conceived as a complex physical entity, both are situated in nature and reveal themselves in identical terms. Psychologism is the consequence of the naturalization of ideas (TIPH 33/TIH 12; DEHH 137ff./DEH 122ff.). Levinas claims that only a new understanding of the mode of existence of consciousness has enabled Husserl to escape from this dilemma.

In what sense is consciousness understood as naturalized consciousness? It is assumed that the same categories that apply to the being of nature—time, space, causality—also apply to consciousness. This is possible since consciousness is constructed on the model of the body to which it is linked. My experience of nature is translated in naturalism into the terms of the being that is experienced; that is to say, the *experience* of nature is itself seen as belonging to the realm of nature not as "material nature" but as "psychic nature." The connection between the subjective phenomenon and the objective reality is explained as a causal relationship (TIPH 34/TIH 13). Alongside of the naturalization of sensations and perception, naturalism "naturalizes" all ideal reality, number, and so on. In order to attribute reality to these ideal entities they are reinterpreted as being individual since naturalism situates objects in nature as individuals. This is accomplished by situating them in consciousness as contents of consciousness and attributing properties to them like those that we attribute to objects in nature. Ideal objects are perceived subsisting in the same way as objects in the world of nature. The conclusions of logic and mathematics are seen to follow from their premises as "water from the union of hydrogen and oxygen" (TIPH 36/TIH 15). Objects of whatever type can be converted into psychological experience: for the English empiricists, for example, the law of contradiction is a psychological law based on generalizations from experience.[5]

If naturalistic philosophy addresses itself to the question of consciousness, if consciousness becomes the object of its investigation, philosophy becomes psychology. The subject and the object of consciousness are now situated in one world: nature. Their relation to one another is apprehended as a causal relation. The problem of consciousness is understood in terms of the organs of, for example, sense perception and reflexes. When the naturalistic attitude is incorporated into an idealistic framework, knowledge is interpreted as a causal sequence operative within a stream of consciousness. It is then a purely subjective feeling devoid of all objective value that confers certainty upon knowledge (TIPH 36/TIH 15).

When the naturalistic attitude persists, logic itself can be understood as being founded in a psychology that has as its object the laws of thought. But Levinas insists that according to Husserl "the psychology of thought understood as a science of psychological facts cannot serve as a foundation for logic" (DEHH 12/DEH 51). Husserl does not oppose the idea that logic reverts to subjectivity; what he does oppose is the notion that the *content* of logic is subjective. Important in this connection is that subjectivity must not be approached as a content of consciousness, but as that which itself thinks some objective unity. In the *Logical Investigations* Husserl asserts that "one ought not to confuse the psychological presuppositions or components of the *assertion* of a law [of logic] with the logical 'moments' of its *content*."[6] The object of logic is not determined by the content of the domain in which it is operative since its laws are the same for all domains of being. The something in general that it thinks and that transcends all genus is not abstracted by generalizations based on observations of concrete objects: "Pure science is the logic of this lawfulness" (DEHH 12/DEH 51). Pure logic is the condition of truth insofar as truth is the adequacy of thought to its object. The laws of logic are not the result of psychological forces; they belong to consciousness as "unities of meaning." According to Levinas, "psychologism is not a failure to recognize logical truths; it is a false interpretation of their meaning" (DEHH 16/DEH 54).[7]

THE PROBLEM OF INTENTIONALITY

The operations of logic themselves tell us nothing about the spiritual horizons from which they emerge.[8] Logical forms possess their own objective meaning, but the logician does not focus his attention upon the complex network of intentions or the "horizons" in which these objects appear. The method of phenomenology is to analyze not the content of logical thought but the intentions that "animate" it. We compare what was intended with what we have attained; we analyze the very activity by which thoughts are thought (DEHH 15/DEH 54). Formal logic must be completed by transcendental logic. In the first volume of the *Logical Investigations* Husserl sets out to show, as I have already indicated, that the laws of logic are independent of psychological laws. The a priori truths of logic cannot be reduced to the a posteriori truths of psychology. What must be emphasized is the fact that the psychology to which Husserl's critique refers is the naturalistic psychology of nineteenth-century British empiricism in which consciousness is an object in the world. Such a psychology tacitly or explicitly understands the investigation of an object in the world, even though that object be consciousness, as a science of facts (TIPH 143ff./TIH 97ff.).

In the second of the *Logical Investigations* Husserl establishes, in Levinas's view, that it is impossible to reduce ideas to facts, or essences to properties of individual things. This is the investigation addressed to the problems raised by the English empiricists (TIPH 145/TIH 98). In the third and fourth of the *Logical Investigations* Husserl is concerned with ideal laws founded in universal essences. These sections of his work, intended to free consciousness from the science of psychology, give rise to the persistent accusation that his views represent a resurrection of Platonic realism (TIPH 145–46/TIH 99). Levinas, however, insists that this erroneous interpretation arises from a failure to incorporate the final two of the *Logical Investigations* in which Husserl initiates a new trend to be continued and elaborated in the *Ideas* and in the *Cartesian Meditations,* the trend of transcendental idealism (TIPH 146/TIH 100). In these *Logical Investigations* the experiencing subject and his relationship to the ideal objects of logic is stressed rather than the ideality of the objects. To understand such a relationship, according to Husserl, the structures of the subjective act and of the object must be understood as correlatives (TIPH 151ff./TIH 103ff.). This relationship is possible because consciousness is intentional.

We must then carefully study the acts that reveal the presence of things:

> *The true return to things is the return to the acts in which the intuitive presence of things is unveiled.* This is certainly the great shock given by the *Logical Investigations*—particularly because the first volume of this work, the *Prolegomena,* and all that is said in the second and third Investigations in favor of the object and its essence, blocked giving a psychologistic interpretation to this recourse to acts of consciousness. Thus, as early as the *Logical Investigations* we find the affirmation of what appears to us to dominate the phenomenologists' way of proceeding: *access to the object is a part of the object's being.* (DEHH 115/DEH 95)

The object cannot be psychologized as in British empiricism, nor is it the object of Platonic thought, for in Husserl's view, according to Levinas, only in uncovering "access" to the object is the being of the object disclosed.

What can we hope to accomplish by uncovering the intentional structure of formal logic, since the self-evidence of formal logic is sufficient to guarantee the truth of its laws? According to Levinas the meaning of the propositions of pure logic can themselves be falsified by situating them in a domain in which they have no place. As the error of psychologism has shown, locating the meaning of purely logical propositions in the empirico-psychological realm would represent a falsification of the ontology of an object, of the realm in which the object could be said to belong. Phenomenology will extend to all possible objects the method of delineating the content of any realm of being within the perspective of intentions within which we think it (DEHH 17/DEH 55–56). To say that intentionality is the fundamental characteristic of consciousness is to say (TIPH 69/TIH 40) that "all consciousness is consciousness of something." We distinguish in intentionality an animating act that bestows upon what Husserl calls the hyletic phenomena a transcendent meaning (TIPH 68/TIH 39). Hyletic elements are those that are deprived of intentional structure and that underlie all domains of consciousness: "Intentionality is, for Husserl, a genuine act of transcendence" (TIPH 69/TIH 40). It is not a property added on to consciousness but consciousness' very mode of existence. Levinas sees intentionality as consciousness' way of being in the world. It is the very subjectivity of the subject (TIPH 70/TIH 41).

Husserl has shown that the subject is not something that exists prior to its relation with an object. There is no mental object that is the subjective representation of real being. The mental image is not the portrait of a reality that is its original. According to Levinas, Husserl sees consciousness itself as substantial because it is intentional: therefore the idea of a self as a substance is rejected by Husserl since such a self would only have intentionality as a property (TIPH 70/TIH 41).

Intentionality is not always an identical act. It differs according to the sphere in which it is operative, practical or aesthetic, for example. Not only do the objects differ from one another, but the acts that intend them also are dissimilar (TIPH 73/TIH 43). The real world is not a world of things correlative with my perceiving them. It is a world in which things matter to me or are indifferent to me, in which fear or desire arises. These characteristics cannot, according to Levinas, be excluded from my constitution of the world, since they are given not as personal reaction to the world but as objects of intention. Thus they too belong to the objective sphere. Predicates that refer to value and to emotions belong to the existence of the world. Levinas emphasizes that these notions have an ontological status (TIPH 76/TIH 45). Intentionality is present even in those acts in which attention is lacking. Attention is a *possible* mode of all acts but is not identical with intentionality. Attention is "a subjective modification of it" (TIPH 77/TIH 46).

An understanding of intentionality is the foundation of Levinas's interpretation of language as expression. Turning to the first of Husserl's *Logical Investigations,* Levinas asserts that we find posited there a relationship between verbal signification and intentionality. To understand the fact that words mean something leads to a grasp of the nature of intentionality. The meaning of words is not to be confused with the mental image of an auditory or visual experience. Nor is it a sign of something else, of that which is signified. The word is expression; it is nonsymbolic (DEHH 21/DEH 59). For Levinas, the symbol is opaque, perceived first for itself and only then as referring to something else, whereas the word insofar as it is expression is "like a window" through which we see at once what is meant. The meaning of a word is neither the relation between two psychological facts nor that between two objects, for in these relations the word becomes an object standing for something else. It is rather a relation between "thought and what it thinks." What is thought is ideally present to the thought that is not itself. This is not only what we mean when we speak of the word; it is also what is meant by intentionality. The relation "between thought and what it thinks" is an act; it is the act of bestowing a meaning (DEHH 22/DEH 59).

Intentionality *is* meaning-bestowal in which the apparent exteriority of the object is the consequence of the exteriority of what we think in relation to the thought that thinks it or intends it. The object for Husserl serves as a pole of identity that is determined by the very structure of thought and without which the phenomenon of meaning would be impossible. Identification of a unity (the object) through multiplicity is what Husserl means by thought. Levinas maintains that the objectifying act is a "synthesis of identification" and that this synthesis of identification is not opposed to representation once we see that, as such, representation is active. It is true that intentionality does not belong exclusively to representative thought. Affective states are not superimposed upon objects of contemplation; in their inner dynamism they too harbor intentions. Indeed, this is according to Levinas one of the most fertile ideas to spring from Husserlian phenomenology.

But for Husserl, in Levinas's opinion, it is nevertheless also true that representation plays a crucial role. Husserl maintains in the fifth of the *Logical Investigations* that intentionality is either an objectifying act or supported by an objectifying act. In the *Ideas* he asserts that the positing of values or the expression of a wish "harbors . . . a doxic thesis, the positing of the object which is the pole of the synthesis of identification" (DEHH 23/DEH 60). This means that the valued, the wished-for can become in their turn theoretical notions. The desirable and the wished-for can always become the objects of theoretical intentions even though when we speak of a desirable object we mean one that appears as possessing the attribute of desirability as belonging to it intrinsically and not as the consequence of my reflections upon it.

What Levinas finds significant in this analysis of intentionality is the model that it provides for the life of mind. The work of intentionality, the process of identification, terminates in certainty. All intention is the obvious in search of itself. But certainty with regard to the clarity of what is brought to light is not just a feeling we happen to have; rather, "it is the very penetration to the true" (DEHH 24/DEH 61). For Husserl, mind is identified with intellect and intellect with light. Mind in its clarity is not merely at the mercy of the given; it is also the origin of what it receives. We are free with regard to the given. The matter-of-factness of the world is, according to Levinas, "the positive fulfillment of freedom." The lesson taught by Husserl is that man is knowledge, consciousness, freedom.

Levinas insists, while still remaining within Husserl's framework, that the result of intentionality is the disappearance of the exteriority of the object. Intelligibility for Husserl is, according to Levinas, characterized by the mystery exerted by thinking over thought; it presumes the adequacy of thinking to thought. Thus, the act of bestowing meaning makes us the creators of our thoughts in the sense that the object gives itself as though deter-

mined by us (TeI 96/TI 123). Levinas insists that since the underlying structures of representation and intelligibility are the same.
Intelligibility, like representation, is in its clarity free from any
jarring elements. What can be represented gives itself to us in all
its being, is totally present. It becomes possible for that which is
represented, that which is other than ourselves, to become
through representation part of the same, that is, part of our projects, the consequence of our intentions. The object represented
is designated "the same" because the distinction between subject
and object is obliterated. In representation the object is presented to thinking, indeed, determines it but does not touch it,
think it, weigh it down.

Representation is a project; it invents the end of an act still in
progress as though the end were already achieved a priori (TeI
97/TI 125). The refusal of the other by the same in representation belongs to the temporality of representation: representation
refuses what is exterior to its own instant in time. Representation
is the present that because of its refusal of the other interprets
itself as eternity (TeI 98/TI 125). Thus representation is a present
that refuses to assume itself as such. The self that represents grows
older in time, is enmeshed in the process of becoming, but this
becoming that is the process of aging of the self does not appear
on the plane of representation, is extrinsic to the representing
act: representation is activity, and to become is to undergo. The
self that grows older is not marked by its past when it represents
it; rather it uses its past as an objective element in the project of
representing.

The subject who represents is, for Levinas, the subject who is
attuned to himself. He coincides with his own thought. In so
doing he coincides with universal thought: "the I of representation is the natural passage from the particular to the universal.
Universal thought is thought in the first person" (TeI 99/TI 126).
The self that understands is lost in the task of understanding,
loses his temporality; he enters the realm of the eternal. Representation, in Levinas's view, is idealism. The very being of the existent is reduced to the noema.

To make intentional thought universal thought as Levinas does
somewhat cryptically is, in my view, to introduce a dialectic into
Husserl's notion of representation that requires comment. I be-

lieve that what Levinas has effected is a Hegelian transformation of the Husserlian subject. The self that represents, that takes what exists for it to be a universal, is for Hegel consciousness as perception, a consciousness that supersedes the truth of sense certainty in *The Phenomenology of Spirit.* The latter (the consciousness of sense certainty) wishes to deal with the particular, the truth of the "this," the "here," and the "now." Yet the "this," the "here," and the "now" are themselves universals: they can never yield being in its original concreteness. With the failure of sense certainty to provide knowledge of particulars, consciousness emerges as consciousness of perception. In perception the "I" as well as the object is a universal.[9] The existence of the thing that was originally set up as a unity, as an independent existence, is undermined in the consciousness of perception, for the object is seen to contain properties, that is, diversity. The one behind the properties and the properties themselves have, in Hegel's view, become the responsibility of consciousness itself. In distinguishing between the one and the many, consciousness passes into unconditioned universality so that, as Levinas maintains, universal thought is thought in the first person. Thus it is Hegel rather than Husserl for whom perception marks the passage of the particular to the universal in representing objects to itself. The idealism attributed by Levinas to representation as such is, in my view, derived from the idealism of Hegelian dialectic.

THE MEANING OF ESSENCES

How, according to Levinas, does Husserl understand the mode of the existence of essences? The existence of the essence must be distinguished from that of the individual object. It is atemporal and cannot be localized in space. Yet its ideality is subject to descriptive modification; it is not undifferentiated. This ideality is not a real predicate; it is not the property of an object. It is rather another "mode of being." Husserl rejects any translation of the ideality of essences into the properties of things, a rejection that reflects his attack upon British empiricism. The general cannot be understood as an undetermined individual, as Locke had asserted, but is ideal in its very way of being. Nor does Husserl wish to identify the essence "with a characteristic trait or moment of the individual object that has been isolated by an effort of one's attention." The genus "red" is different from my focusing upon the red of an object, thus throwing its redness into relief: "The genus is ideal." Nor should ideality be confused with an absence of clarity; there is no necessity that there be anything vague or indeterminate in the essence (DEHH 19/DEH 56). Essences can have truth or falsity predicated of them. An example of a false essence would be that of a regular decahedron that does not exist but that is merely meant (TIPH 154/TIH 105).

Husserl maintains, in Levinas's view, that an examination of the consciousness that intends the ideal enables us to determine precisely the ideality that it uncovers. We can, for instance, establish the difference between the essential structure of an object, its *eidos,* and its empirical concept in which the essential and the accidental are mixed. How do I intuit the ideal? How is my intuition of the ideal related to the sensible object? Can I have an intuition of what Husserl calls "the categorical," a collection of formal elements in the object? Since intuition is defined by characteristics that are not appropriate to sense perception alone, there can be an act that fulfills for categorical elements of meaning what sense perception can fulfill for material elements. But since it is the essential point of all phenomenological analysis to consider the meaning of the object and of its existence as accessible to a determined type of thought, categorical forms cannot be grasped in the same way as colors and sounds. The intuition of the categorical object fulfills what is common to all intuition: that the intention confer the fullness of presence of the intended object, but like all other objects it has its own mode of being given (TIPH 155/TIH 106).

What characterizes sensible intuition is the instantaneity and directness with which its objects are present. It does not follow that the object in sensible intuition need be given in all of its perspectives at once, since it is one of the commonplaces in Husserl's thought that perception can never exhaust all possible perspectives of the object that are infinite. Perception in that sense, by its very nature, remains unfulfilled. What we designate as the object is the pole of identity of its many aspects whose multiple facets are given in a synthetic unity. But the synthesis that takes place on the level of perception is given at the same time as the facets of the thing. The multiple aspects of the object alone with the acts that tie them together are experienced as one. In contrast, intellectual intuition is what it is in accordance with the meaning of its object. While grounded in sense perception, we see the processes of conjunction and disjunction. Relations are not instantaneously perceived together with the object or given all at once as they are in sense perception. This is essentially what makes categorical objects to be what they are: objects "of the second degree" (DEHH 29/DEH 65). It must be emphasized that the categorical object is inconceivable without the sensible object; its relationship to the sensible object is nonreciprocal. The sensible object does not require the existence of the categorical object for its own existence to be fulfilled. Categorical functions do not change the sensible object; while forming the sensible object they leave it essentially intact (TIPH 155/TIH 106).

While still ideal, Husserl separates the intuition of material essences from categorical intuition. What are material essences? With the material object as our starting point we focus our attention not upon the individual object (e.g., this red flower) but upon the object in general (e.g., red in general). The individual object provides only a starting point for our intuition of essences but it remains indispensable. Examples of material essences adduced by Levinas are such essences as red, triangle, and man in the domain of consciousness, "the essences of memory, intentionality and the like."

Levinas considers it a matter of fundamental importance for Husserl to distinguish between objects in general, objects that depend upon empirical generalization and pure essences. It is of importance for the following reason: we are compelled to ask how can we postulate an intuitionist theory of truth (and Husserl does) while simultaneously upholding the possibility of a priori knowledge (which Husserl also does). We can posit both if we can show that the intuition of pure essences in no way depends upon empirical generalization. In order to do this we must distinguish between objects-in-general and pure essences. Had Husserl failed to make this distinction, Levinas contends, he might have been confronted with the following objection:

If you have the concept of a swan in general, you would say "all swans are white," and claim that this is a truth based on the intuition of the essence swans. But your concept of swan comes only from induction, and your alleged intuition of the essence of swan may be false. There are indeed black swans. Hence, if there is no distinction between "ideal objects" and "pure essences," the truths revealed by the intuition of essences are either mere tautology (in the essence of "white swan there is whiteness") or they include inductive truths. (TIPH 157/TIH 108)

The distinction between the general essence and the a priori essence is not elaborated in Husserl's own work, but it is clear that Husserl rejects the notion that the essence is the individual object raised to the level of the ideal. It is important to note, according to Levinas, that "in the determination of the object there is a hierarchy, and some objects are required for the others to be possible" (TIPH 159/TIH 109). This leads directly to the meaning of the essence: "the essence of the object thus is its necessary structure." The essence is that before which each empirical trait of the object becomes comprehensible. It is a nexus of characteristics that reciprocally invoke one another, as in the case of sound, where pitch and intensity invoke one another. These constitute a necessary structure delineating what it means for sound to be sound (TIPH 160/TIH 109).

What is meant when a structure is spoken of as being necessary? The necessity intended is one that belongs to the dependence and independence of certain contents of consciousness. A house is, for example, an independent content requiring nothing but itself for its existence; a color is a dependent content requiring that it be extended in order to exist. The important characteristic of dependency is not that we cannot conceive a dependent content to be other than it is, but that it is "an objective and ideal necessity" in the realm of existence (TIPH 161/TIH 110). There is no other way in which this content could exist. This necessity is independent of all logic since the laws of logic do not depend upon any material content. The laws of dependence are "material laws." The intuition of material essences such as tree, house, and sound make it possible to have *necessary* and *material* cognitions: "For Husserl, direct vision of the necessary structure of essences seems to be the primary phenomenon of intellection" (TIPH

162/TIH 110–11). Moreover the necessity involved in the laws of deduction is itself a *consequence* of the intuition of essences:

> The necessity of the conclusion of a syllogism is founded on the formal essence of its premises, in which this necessity is grasped with evidence. Each "link" in a deduction is an intuition of essences although, in this case, an intuition of *formal* essences. The role of deduction consists in providing evident intuition for a truth that is not evident by itself, by means of a series of steps that are themselves evident. It is evidence, not deduction, which is the rational element in knowledge. Deduction is an act by means of which certain truths are reduced to the evidence of first principles. (TIPH 162/TIH 111)

Moreover deduction is characteristic not of all rational thought but only of a specifiable domain of objects. Clearly analytic or synthetic logic cannot provide the models for all intelligibility.

The "independent content" to which Husserl refers (and which he calls "concrete" as opposed to "dependent content," which is "abstract") does not require any specific content other than itself to make it what it is. Those contents that can be separated from the object vary freely. Such content remains what it is despite the destruction of any number of concomitant contents. Thus we are enabled to vary the form of any material content without limit. If, however, we vary the content in such a way that the object loses its forms, is no longer itself, then the object ceases to exist: "The essence of an independent object determines the limits between which we may vary its contents. A variation which steps over the limit imposed by the essence takes away from the object its concrete character, its independence, its capacity to exist. The essence of an object seems to express the conditions that must be realized to make its existence possible" (TIPH 164/ TIH 112). Or to put the matter somewhat differently, "essences are made up of a set of predicates that an object must have in order to have other predicates" (TIPH 164/TIH 112). The essence is what makes the object to be what it is.

This analysis of essences is of fundamental significance for Levinas's own thought in that what emerges from it is the ontological value of eidetic science without which the object would not be what it is.[10] What is investigated by eidetic science is the very condition, the sine qua non, of the object's existence as object. It is an investigation of that which all other knowledge, such as the knowledge of the natural sciences, already presupposes. It is, Levinas claims, really Husserl himself who makes eidetic science ontological.

THE PHENOMENOLOGICAL REDUCTION

For Husserl the life of mind is a conferring of meaning. But we are also the ones who bestow meaning as beings among other beings with whom we are involved in transactions. Intentionality, or the directing of thought upon objects, is an activity that takes place in a context, the context of being in a world. The life of mind becomes a technique that confers meaning without taking into account the meaning of its own mode of being (DEHH 35/ DEH 72).

The attitude that does not probe its own mode of existence as the positing of the existence of the world is characterized by Husserl as the natural attitude. It is not so much an attitude of "realism" as of "naive realism." The failure of consciousness to interrogate itself as to the meaning of its own objectivity characterizes both perception and the natural sciences, which posit objects without reflecting upon the structures of consciousness enabling them to do so. It lies behind the crisis of meaning undergone in the naturalization of consciousness when consciousness becomes reified and is interpreted on the plane of things. The naturalization of logic that is psychologized, as I have already indicated, by reducing the objective truths of logic to laws of the mind is also a consequence of the natural attitude. In order to resolve these crises the natural attitude must be abandoned. We must recover the original thought in which this situation is constituted and suspend our engagement in the world. This suspension is the phenomenological reduction. For Levinas the suspension of the natural attitude actually does violence to man but must be put into operation in order that we may discover ourselves as pure thought.[11] It becomes necessary not to suppose the world: "All truth which implicitly contains the 'thesis of the existence of objects' must be suspended." The result of this operation is the discovery of the existence of consciousness as such. This consciousness lends a meaning to things although things themselves are independent of the bestowal of meaning. For Levinas, we suspend the thesis of the existence of objects in order to ascertain the true meaning of the consciousness that posited it (DEHH 36–37/DEH 73).

Levinas claims that the phenomenological reduction is introduced because the existence of the world is never fully guaranteed; it always remains open to doubt and question. Since consciousness of the world can never be perfectly certain we put it between parentheses, bracket it, put it out of play. The consciousness with which we are left is now distinguished from the world. Only the immanent perception of reflection gives us full and certain consciousness of the world. This transcendental consciousness alone is apodictic. As in the case of Cartesian doubt, we must locate certainty in the *cogito* itself (DEHH 38/DEH 73).

Husserl does not *deduce* the world after the *epoche* (the bracketing of the existence of the world) has suspended our judgment as to its existence. The world recovered after the phenomenological reduction is now "constituted by thought." Levinas stresses that the recalcitrance of the object now appears as an outgrowth of mind. This is why bracketing is not a mere technique to be abandoned but a decisive point of view (TIPH 213ff./TIH 150ff.). Levinas is emphatic in this regard: bracketing is not so much a quest for apodicticity but the mind's expression of its "vocation."[12] It is for Levinas a way of being free with regard to the world, for the newly constituted world that results from the *epoche* is not relative to anything; it is free insofar as it is consciousness. It is consciousness as freedom (DEHH 38/DEH 74).

INTENTIONALITY AS MOVEMENT

For Levinas, one of the major consequences of phenomenology has been to prevent a confusion between psychic life and its "intentional object." The structure of thought is not confused with the structure of things. This is the meaning of the struggle against psychologism. When we say that consciousness is intentional we mean that it reaches being; it is not a mere projection of its own states. Phenomenology concludes that being is transcendent as the very objectivity of the object. Yet Levinas claims, despite the fact that phenomenology goes beyond scientific positivism, that such a notion of transcendence makes being into a scientific object. It becomes a fact that resists the subject. In order for being to be comprehended by the subject an adjustment is made so that the being of the object is accommodated to the "a priori of the subject" (DEHH 137/DEH 122). The crucial question for Levinas's own thought is whether there is any phenomenon that enables me to transcend objectifying consciousness. For Levinas, Husserl's enterprise reveals that the encounter with an object confirms or deceives the empty intention that precedes it; the experience of the object completes the thought. Thought thus retains a degree of immobility, as if "there were reflected in it—like a monad enclosed within itself—the whole universe." Is there for Husserl, in Levinas's view, a level of experience that is given without being sought? Can it be that the sensible, what Husserl calls the hyletic datum, while not without intention, is given at once? "The subject bathes in it, before thinking or perceiving objects."[13] There is still no distinction between sensing and sense, but an element of "anticipation" is missing. Consciousness of the sensed coincides with the sensed thus undermining the subject-object distinction (DEHH 139/DEH 124–25).

According to Levinas, the sensible is characterized for Husserl by its essentially kinesthetic character. The sense organs open as movement upon the sensible. Movement is not added on to the sensible: it "is the very way in which sensing senses the sensed." The intentionality of feeling is movement. For Husserl the constitution of space begins with this perception of movement. The perception of movement is anterior to the perception of objects because objects already presuppose place. Place and its forms (space) are already idealizations of the lived life of kinesthesis. This idealization enables us to arrive at identifiable points that are localized in infinite space (DEHH 140/DEH 125).

Kinesthetic perceptions are bodily sensations of movement. Movements that are perceived in the world as exterior to ourselves, to the lived body, go back to these kinesthetic sensations of the body. It is even possible to speak of the kinesthetics of keeping still. Levinas observes that the "kinestheses of repose are not the same as the repose of the kinesthetic sense." He is thus careful to point out that rest is a positive phenomenon. Space and place are the incarnation of consciousness. Space is constituted through different modes of corporeality: visual space, oculomotor space, and so on. The references to which our intentions refer are no longer object poles of identity but enmesh us in situations that can no longer be reduced to representations. To walk, to push, to pull, to resist are movements that are nonobjectifying (DEHH 141/DEH 126).

What is important for Levinas's own thought is that consciousness as kinesthetic transitivity marks an end to idealism without involving a return to naive realism. Realism identifies being with the object. The idealistic critique of this position claims that the appearance of the object is always understood through the structures of consciousness. It implies the adequacy of the self to the not-self, of the same to the Other. In representation the Other is made an equivalent of the same. Idealism is tautologous in the sense that to be anything an object must be for a consciousness; anything that oversteps the limits of consciousness and therefore is not anything for a consciousness is not anything at all: "Intentionality as an act and as transitivity, as the union of the soul with the body, that is, as the *inequality between the ego and the other*, means a radical overstepping beyond the objectifying intentionality that sustains idealism. The discovery of intentionality in praxis, emotion, and valuation, which was seen to constitute the newness of phenomenology, in fact derives its metaphysical strength from the transitive intentionality of incarnation" (DEHH 143/DEH 127). Kinestheses are the original mobility of the subject (DEHH 169/CPP 47). Thus, the philosophy that introduced eidetic structures, in Levinas's view, ended by radically undercutting the idea of immobile structures and the fixity of consciousness by introducing movement into the subjectivity of the subject: "The body, zero point of representation, is beyond this zero, already within the world it constitutes" (DEHH 160/DEH 148).

THE BREAK WITH HUSSERL

It is the primacy given to theoretical consciousness that leads Levinas to break decisively with Husserlian phenomenology. Nevertheless, Levinas is sensitive to the complexities of theoretical consciousness, to what complicates and enriches its primordiality. It is true that the *Logical Investigations,* according to Levinas, grants a privileged place to theoretical life. Acts of will and valorization are understood on the model of representation, and this bias, which Levinas finds objectionable, has, in his view, never been denied by Husserl. Yet Levinas concedes that Husserl's position is modified in *Ideas I* insofar as we find affirmed there the principle that nontheoretical acts can constitute objects of new and irreducible ontological structure. These acts as well as those of judgment and representation are objectifying. Levinas sees phenomenology enriched by these inclusions. Husserl writes: *"Any acts whatever—even emotional and volitional acts—are 'objectivating,' 'constituting' objects originaliter* [and therefore] necessary sources of different regions of being and their respective ontologies. For example: valuing consciousness constitutes the unique 'axiological' objectivity in contrast to the mere world of things, a 'being' of a new region."[14] These new characteristics introduced into being are not simply the added properties of an object that is still theoretically constituted; they transform the plane of existence of the object. We encounter specific intuitions that are not acts of theoretical contemplation: "It follows that, in addition to theoretical truths, there can be 'practical and axiological truths.' . . . The existence of a value—its mode of presenting itself to life, does not have the same ontological structure as theoretically represented beings" (TIPH 191/TIH 133).

But what is crucial for Levinas is that even if the constitution of these objects differs from that of theoretical objects, it is the constitution of theoretical objects that serves as the model for all objectifying acts. The material thing plays a privileged role in founding the notion of constitution itself. What underlies the primacy of theoretical consciousness is this: while the meaning of objects differently constituted is indeed different according to their manner of constitution, the act that posits these differently constituted objects as existents, the doxic thesis, is common to all. The doxic thesis intends the object as existing. For Levinas this ties existence irrevocably to consciousness. The primacy of the objectifying act, in his view, cannot be maintained simultaneously with the irreducible originality of nontheoretical consciousness.[15]

The ontologizing direction of Levinas's interpretation of Husserl is, as I have already indicated, influenced by Heideggerian thought. We have seen that Levinas argues that the problem that transcendental phenomenology poses, the problem of the constitution of the world for pure consciousness, is directed by an ontological problem in the sense that Heidegger gives to the term "ontological." Levinas criticizes Husserl for his "intellectualism" despite the fact that Husserl had raised the concrete world, the world in which science itself is embedded, to prominence. Heidegger's worldview provides a corrective to this Husserlian intellectualism, for his is a world in which vision is no longer primary. For Levinas, Heidegger's world is a field of activity:

> Even though Husserl maintains the profound idea that, in the ontological order, the world of science is posterior to and depends on the vague and concrete world of perception, he may have been wrong in seeing the concrete world as a world of objects that are primarily perceived. Is our main attitude toward reality that of theoretical contemplation? Is not the world presented in its very being as a center of action, as a field of activity or of *care*—to speak the language of Martin Heidegger? (TIPH 174/TIH 119)

Levinas accepts Heidegger's view of Dasein's historicity against Husserl's ahistorical theory of consciousness. For Levinas, Husserl had merely destroyed a naturalistic view of history without an awareness of the essential historicity of human existence. In this connection Levinas writes: "It is in life that we must search for the origin of reality, for the origin of the objects of perception as well as of the sciences. This life has the historical character in the sense in which it is said that 'all men have a history.' . . . [T]his historicity is not a secondary property of man as if man existed first and then became temporal and historical. Historicity and temporality form the very substantiality of man's substance[16] (TIPH 220/TIH 156). While Levinas dissociates himself from Husserlian phenomenology as founded in theoretical contemplation, he still maintains, as we have seen, a loyalty to what can narrowly be termed phenomenology as a method, to the analysis of intentions. The question must be raised: can phenomenology as a method be isolated from what the method actually intends? Can it not be said that Levinas retains more than an attentiveness to the life world, a fidelity to descriptive accuracy? He retains the structure of intentionality itself to which Husserl had given primacy. Desire, which becomes central in the relation to the Other, is an affective intention, a supra-ontological transcendence toward the Other. Husserl's failure is, according to Levinas, as we have already seen, to assume the adequacy of the intending to the intended, an assumption that traduces alterity by interiorizing the Other. For Levinas, the underlying structure of all intentionality presupposes an intention in which the intended goes beyond intention: the idea of the infinite is "preeminently non-adequation" (TeI xv/TI 27).

If the Husserlian *cogito* could think the infinite, it would, for Levinas, think it as an infinite object, "something" lacking alterity. It could be argued against Levinas that Husserl himself insisted that the extended thing could never be perceived in all of its multidimensionality, and that therefore the dimension of the infinite belongs to the thing itself. Objects well up from a lived world that can never be grasped as a whole. Levinas could reply that theoretically there is no facet of the object that we cannot make ours by placing ourselves vis-à-vis that facet of the object, by going around it, so to speak, that there is no absolute necessity that occludes any one object from our purview. There is no object that inherently, by virtue of the kind of object it is, or any facet of the object that cannot theoretically become an object for representation, cognition, and so on. The inadequation thought through by Husserl can never, for Levinas, be radical enough. Nor does the concept of the horizon provide an idea of that which exceeds any idea we may have of it, that is, an idea of the infinite, because the horizon is precisely that which we can never make the object of a constitutive act. Indeed, it is the horizon that makes the work of objectification an endless task. Husserl writes: "But not even with the added reach of this intuitively clear or dark, distinct or indistinct *co-present* margin, which forms a continuous ring around the actual field of perception, does that world exhaust itself which in every waking moment is in some conscious measure 'present' before me. It reaches rather in a fixed order of being the limitless beyond. . . . The zone of indeterminacy is infinite."[17]

But the fundamental disagreement between Levinas and Husserl is lodged in the notion of the other person that prevails in Husserl's thought. For Husserl, the other person can never be given to us in an original way, but only through analogical appresentation. Husserl insists that if what belongs to the other's own essence were directly accessible, he would merely be "a moment of my own essence; ultimately, he himself and I myself would be the same."[18] What does Husserl mean by appresentation? In the experience of a physical thing the seen aspect of the thing (the front) "appresents" an unseen aspect (the rear) and prescribes for it a specific content. But the difference for Husserl between such appresentations (which occur in nature) and the appresentation of the other person lies precisely in the fact that I can verify the former. For Husserl, the other who is appresented is another ego (alter ego). In the sphere of perception a body is presented. Since our own body "is the only body that is or can be constituted originally as an animate organism," the other's body "derives this sense by an apperceptive transfer from my animate organism" in a way different from a direct showing of it in perception. This "analogizing apprehension" is not understood by Husserl to mean that there is an inference from analogy. The apperception of which Husserl speaks is specifically disavowed as being a thinking act.[19] It is clear that however complex the process through which the other is given to us, he is given through a prior understanding of ourselves, through an irreducibly mediate intention: he can never be given to us in person. Husserl recognizes in the other a modification of ego in general.[20] But for Levinas the Other is never an alter ego but the one whom we are not. It is true that we often see the other as known by sympathy, as another self, but this is precisely where we are mistaken.

NOTES

1. Levinas, "Signature," trans. William Canavan, *Philosophy Today* 10 (1966): 31–33. This version of "Signature" is a translation of the version that appeared in the first edition of *Difficile liberté* (Paris: Albin Michel, 1963), 321–27. The version that appears in the third edition, the basis for the English edition of *Difficult Freedom*, is quite different. Notably, it does not emphasize quite as succinctly the manner in which Levinas

sees phenomenology as a path that opens up a way for thinking about experiences in a manner irreducible to the language of subject and object.

2. Pierre Thévanez, *What Is Phenomenology?* trans. James M. Edie (Chicago: Quadrangle, 1962), 54, ontologizes phenomenology in much the same way. He writes: "To the degree that phenomenology developed it became increasingly clear that it had been from the beginning an ontology which, because of its very novelty, needed time to recognize itself as such. By this continual movement of going-beyond and of progressive explication, phenomenology very naturally discovered and uncovered the ontology which sustained it and toward which it was tending. This was already apparent in Husserl; it became fully explicit in Heidegger."

3. Paul Ricoeur, *Husserl: An Analysis of His Phenomenology* (Evanston: Northwestern University Press, 1967), also concludes that Husserl's method is a spiritual vehicle. In his analysis of the existential sense in which he believes Husserl's reduction ought to be understood, he argues that reduction is not a "negative moment" but rather a way in which limitation is removed. Reduction then frees the "whole sweep of consciousness" (19). Phenomenology is for Ricoeur a discipline, a radical ascesis, a *rite de passage* transforming man in the natural attitude into a transcendental subject (15).

4. Edmund Husserl, *Ideas Pertaining to a Pure Phenomenology and to a Phenomenological Philosophy, First Book* (hereafter *Ideas I*), trans. F. Kersten (The Hague: Martinus Nijhoff, 1982), 18, writes: "Any concrete empirical objectivity finds its place within a *highest* material genus, a 'region,' of empirical objects. To the pure regional essence, then, there corresponds a *regional eidetic science* or, as we can also say, a regional ontology." Regional ontology differs from the science of fact in the following way: eidetic science or science of essences has in it "no experience qua experience." (Experience is for Husserl "an act that supplies grounds.") The science of essences studies not actual but ideal possibilities. It follows (17) that the "*sense* of eidetic science necessarily precludes any incorporation of cognitional results yielded by empirical sciences." Husserl summarizes this position in what has become an apothegm of phenomenology: "From facts follow always nothing but facts."

5. Herbert Spiegelberg, *The Phenomenological Movement* (The Hague: Martinus Nijhoff, 1960), I:94.

6. Husserl, *Logical Investigations,* trans. J. N. Findlay (New York: Humanities Press, 1970), I:106.

7. It is interesting to note that Levinas does not invoke some familiar criticisms of psychologism: (1) if logical laws are generalizations from

experience, as Mill had claimed, then they enable us to do no more than make probable inferences for the future, and (2) if logical laws are really psychological laws, they become relative to the thinkers who hold them, thus denying the possibility of certain knowledge. These criticisms are discussed by Spiegelberg, I:93–95, though not in connection with Levinas, who is interested in distinguishing the fact that there are logical laws at all and in asserting that the fact that there are such forms has a meaning. He is interested in what I believe can be called the "situation" of logic. See DEHH 15/DEH 53.

8. Levinas's interpretation of intentionality seems to be drawn mainly from Husserl's *Ideas I.*

9. G. W. F. Hegel, *The Phenomenology of Spirit,* trans. A. V. Miller (Oxford: Oxford University Press, 1977), 67.

10. Merleau-Ponty maintains that essences are the expression of a thing's style of existence. Husserl is wrong, he claims, in conceiving essences as the primordial objects of thought. They are rather secondary expressions of our existence; our experience underlies essences rather than the reverse. The necessity we attribute to them stems from the original experience itself. See Remy C. Kwant, "Merleau-Ponty's Criticism of Husserl's Eidetic Reduction," in *Phenomenology,* ed. Joseph C. Kockelmans (New York: Doubleday, 1967), 402ff.

11. This view contrasts with that of Merleau-Ponty, who writes in *Signs,* trans. Richard C. McCleary (Evanston: Northwestern University Press, 1964), 163: "The natural attitude really becomes an attitude—a tissue of judicatory and propositional acts—only when it becomes a naturalist thesis. The natural attitude itself emerges unscathed from the complaints which can be made about naturalism, because it is prior to any 'thesis,' because it is the mystery of a *Weltthesis* prior to all these. It is, Husserl says in another connection, the mystery of a primordial faith and a fundamental and original opinion . . . which . . . gives us not a representation of the world but the world itself." Merleau-Ponty's analysis assumes the veridical character of the natural attitude. Levinas stresses the suspension of the natural attitude as definitive. This suspension is nonprovisional, a new mode of interiority, of being free before the world. See DEHH 38/DEH 74.

12. Ricoeur in *Husserl* also interprets the phenomenological reduction in an existential sense as the mode of being in which freedom becomes possible. The phenomenological reduction is a liberation from mundane illusion. It is consciousness's first act of freedom. Ricoeur regards the world of doxic positing as a "trap" through which man is enmeshed in things and ideas: "The thesis of the world is a blindness in the heart of seeing" (20). The thesis is not genuine believing; it is, on

the contrary, an attitude that contaminates belief. Phenomenological reduction is thus not a "negative" movement but one that removes a limitation by freeing the whole "sweep" of consciousness (18).

13. This interpretation of the sensible is brought into an existential perspective in Levinas's analysis of life in the elemental, in which the distinction between feeling and the felt does not arise. The subject is said to "bathe" in the elemental. While I believe that Levinas has Husserl's analysis in mind, sensuous intuition is understood in a new way. In an unpublished paper entitled "The Elemental Background," Alphonso Lingis claims that the elemental is not sensuous because of inert hyletic matter within consciousness itself. What is absent from Husserl's notion of consciousness and its relation to hyletic matter is the notion of enjoyment. Enjoyment is the modus vivendi of the elemental. In addition, the sensuousness of the elemental does not wait for the shaping influence of theoretical intentions.

14. Husserl, *Ideas I*, 306.

15. See also Jacques Derrida, "Violence et métaphysique: Essai sur la pensée d'Emmanuel Levinas," in *L'écriture et la différence* (Paris: Seuil, 1967), 130–31 (translated by Alan Bass as "Violence and Metaphysics: An Essay on the Thought of Emmanuel Levinas," in *Writing and Difference* [Chicago: University of Chicago Press, 1978], 87).

16. The substance of these remarks is modified by (1) the development of the notion that man, while thrown into history and himself historical, stands under eternal judgment, and (2) the progressive dissatisfaction with the Heideggerian bias reflected in these comments. See "Heidegger, Gagarin and Us" (DL 323–27/DF 231–34).

17. Husserl, *Ideas I*, 282.

18. Husserl, *Cartesian Meditations,* trans. Dorion Cairns (The Hague: Martinus Nijhoff, 1960), 111.

19. Ibid.

20. Derrida, "Violence et métaphysique," 181–82 ("Violence and Metaphysics," 123).

III

From Self to Same

THE METHOD of phenomenology makes possible, as we have seen, an analysis of what is present to consciousness by revealing the structure of consciousness in its various spheres of operation. The work of thematization presupposes existing entities, a world; it presupposes "consciousness-of," the relation with an object, with what is posited. Levinas does not question the methodological adequacy of phenomenology, its power to uncover the structure of cognition, the relation of consciousness to all positing. But at the heart of Levinas's thought is the question: Does thematizing consciousness exhaust the data of all experiencing?

To discover the answer to this question we must not only identify thematizing consciousness but also uncover it in its primordiality. To do so we must investigate what is accomplished in thematizing, and what is distorted when brought into its purview. As I have tried to show in the preceding chapter, a method arises naturally from a particular region of being and is a powerful instrument for the uncovering of the meaning of the being from which it derives. But the misapplication of a method falsifies the ontological realm into which it may be transplanted but from which it does not originate. For Levinas, thematizing consciousness is exercised in a particular way; it is not activated neutrally to do its cognitive work, but as power, dominance, and egoity. When the self is identified exclusively with the work of reason, when the noetic-noematic relation is invoked as the paradigm for all experiencing, some domain of actuality may be falsified. Particularly when the relation in existence between the self and other persons is assumed to be only a variant, differing in object but not in kind from the cognitive model, the experience of other persons is distorted. There are for Levinas certain experiences that contain more than consciousness can hold at any given moment. These are the metaphysically rich experiences of the infinite, of transcendence as that which is alien and strange.[1] The task of metaphysics is to attest the reality of these experiences that resist intentional analysis and bring them into relation with the totality of existence.

Contrary to the Heideggerian philosophy of existence, Levinas refuses to ground the existence of the existent in care; instead he grounds metaphysics in social relations. What is the standpoint of thematizing consciousness, its project that makes it inherently improper for thematization to be the mode for apprehending the realm of intersubjectivity? To answer this question we must first distinguish (phenomenologically rather than genetically) the moment of its upsurge and the infracognitive structures anterior to it. The purpose of this chapter will be to investigate the modes of being of the separated self, the self that detaches itself from being, that exists apart from being. We have seen how in Levinas's early work the emergence of consciousness is tied to the activity of beginning, the assumption of the instant such that the dynamic taking on of temporality is itself the mode in which a self comes to be. The self arises not as an *ekstasis* toward the end, but as the very event in which being posits itself (DEE 18/EE 19). In *Totality and Infinity* and related shorter essays dating from the same period, Levinas develops phenomenologically the life world in which this event transpires.

THE SELF AS LIFE

Psychic life, even in its infracognitive structures, apprehends itself as totality. Consciousness is totalizing consciousness. Just as Husserl had affirmed the integrity of a particular species of consciousness in relation to the realm of being in which it is operative, Levinas maintains that since there is no model of correctness for all consciousness, infracognitive consciousness is not a consciousness in error. It does not think badly; it is simply consciousness that does not think at all, consciousness as life. Consciousness as life exists as if being radiates around it and experiences the forces encountered in life as already related to its needs and joys. The being who perceives what is exterior to itself as soliciting work or appropriation understands exteriority as that which is con-substantial with itself, as essentially immediate, as milieu (EN 25/CPP

25). Consciousness as life, the vital self, has no knowledge of the world and does not think its own sensation. It is the consciousness of instinct without problems and without exteriority; it determines Others without being determined by them. If another disturbs the life of this consciousness, it kills or is killed. It is characterized by the alternative of freedom or death.

Thought begins when consciousness reflects upon its particularity, when what is extrinsic to it is conceded to lie beyond it. The one who thinks is one for whom the outside world exists. Thought represents to self what is extrinsic to it as an exteriority strange to its interiority. Thought becomes the mode in which the alien existence is incorporated into the inner life of the thinker (EN 26–27/CPP 27). Consciousness as life is also forced to take account of what is unassimilable, of what cannot be integrated into the structure of life. This refractory element is death—not the knowledge of death, death as represented to it, or as the end of its own possibilities—but death itself, that is, paradoxically, lived death. Through death the vital self enters the totality but thinks nothing.

How is the transition effected between life and thought? In order for life to become thought, exteriority must somehow overflow the possibilities of vital consciousness without at the same time destroying it. A partial system, the vital self, must be penetrated by a total system, exteriority, the sensible manifold, to which the vital self is invulnerable. This penetration into the appropriative but partial system of the vital self is expressed by the vital self as wonder. Wonder possesses ontological status; it lies between what is purely lived and the beginning of thought. It is consciousness in transition (EN 28/CPP 28). Levinas may well have had in mind the Aristotelian dictum that philosophy begins in wonder. Wonder finds itself before the fact as something distinctive, as different from the idea.

It is not difficult to perceive the vital self as rooted in the anthropology of the Hobbesian state of nature or even more clearly in the *homo homini lupus* psychology of Hegel's analysis of consciousness as life. Hegel's self as life is totalizing, takes its first step toward self-certainty; when convinced of the nothingness of the other, it obliterates what stands in its way, what presents itself to the self as another life. The self thus gratified becomes self-assured but not yet self-conscious. In Hegel's scheme individual forms appear against a continuous fluidity that constitutes the medium of life as process. But consciousness of self as instinct, impulse, or desire while recognizing its distinctiveness from the universal flux does not yet know genuine alterity as a particular. All it is capable of effecting is the sublation of alterity.[2] It is interesting to note that for Hegel when desire experiences the loss of its object, desire itself is transformed. It learns the necessity for maintaining the other as life in order that desire itself might well up again and find an object rather than the void left in the wake of the depredations of the appropriating self.

Through this other that desire finds, the appropriating self becomes a self-consciousness. To be self, a self must have before it another self-consciousness: "Only so is it in fact self-consciousness."[3] Levinas refrains from taking this final step of the Hegelian analysis, since for Levinas mutual recognition can never establish the alterity of the Other. Alterity is established only in the nonreciprocity of relation.

While the vital self, the self of enjoyment, is independent vis-à-vis the being from which it has emerged and stands out from being, it is not an independent consciousness. It requires content, "lives on" something. What the enjoying self lives on is not, for Levinas, a means for maintaining the biological continuity of life, not a means toward an end, life. The content of what is lived on is never experienced as biologically indispensable. What we live on is useful but its utility is a derivative feature of a more fundamental ontological mode of existence. Phenomenologically "living on" is the experienced modality of transforming the Other into the same. This is what is essential to enjoyment. An energy foreign to our own has become incorporated into vitalistic existence, is now our energy (TeI 83/TI 111).

Eating is the paradigmatic act of the vital self. It is not undertaken to stay alive except in extreme cases but as a way of feeling invigorated. The human *telos* of an act is never rooted in the simple biological status of the act. Eating is never mere replenishment but a way of feeling reinvigorated, of enjoying one's own vitality. Hunger is need, the most fundamental of deprivations, yet its satisfaction transcends its physiological purpose.

Through enjoyment we relate to objects dialectically; we relate to things as though dependent upon them, yet the pleasure we experience through them is independent of the particular content of what is lived on. The consciousness of pleasure is lived not reflectively but as joy. Pleasure is not accidental to separated being but its ontological foundation. Even if continued existence is guaranteed by what is lived on, the means for keeping us alive are always more than strict necessities. Through "living on" we express not only the needs of life but the love of life as well (TeI 84/TI 112).

Levinas develops the phenomenology of "living on" far beyond a mere sharpening of Hegelian perspectives, beyond consciousness as life; the phenomenology of "living on" functions in Levinas's thought to break the primacy of Aristotelian ontology through a thoroughgoing analysis of noncognitive consciousness. "Living on" lies outside the sphere of representation. It does not depend upon the categories of potency and act (TeI 84/TI 112). Why is this the case? Within the Aristotelian framework, human nature is fulfilled by functioning, by fulfilling itself such that the act accomplishes the purpose envisioned; the act has a *telos*. In the case of eating, for example, the purpose is to sustain life. This purpose is attained through the act of nourishing oneself. It is true, Levinas acknowledges, that Aristotle claims human nature is fulfilled by putting itself into relation with things and that "living on" in his thought also presupposes a similar relation with things. But for Levinas the advantage of "living on" to account for such phenomena as eating, breathing, and the like belongs precisely to the fact that the act of eating, for example, does not *exhaust* our relation to things. For beyond theory and practice is the enjoyment derived from "living on." It is the welling up of the lived quality of the act that remains absent in the Aristotelian account of potency and act. If the act is fulfilled, nothing remains in excess of the exhaustion of potency, no indefinable quality that the scheme of adequacy of potency to act fails to take into account. It is precisely "life" that is absent from this picture.

"Living on" is a reflexive act. There is a human experience of need beyond the submission to the simple experience of lack and repletion. Man acts by virtue of need but simultaneously experiences himself, at the same time and in the course of the same activity, as enjoying, as powerful, as free.[4] While "living on" is reflexive, it is a noncognitive reflexivity. Enjoyment of the act must be distinguished both from the perception of it and from an affective coloring that clings to it; enjoyment is rather the modus vivendi of the very act of "living on." Pleasure is a human triumph beyond the fullness of being. We do not merely satisfy a need; we remember the need itself in the very act of satiation such that enjoyment wells up in recollecting the need now in process of being satisfied. Levinas maintains that in enjoyment the act remembers its potency. The human fulfillment of need is never simple repletion uncomplicated by memory and accompanying pleasure.

It could be argued against Levinas that the self as need is *enslaved* to the cycle of need and satiety, that unfulfilled need provides the ontological foundation for suffering rather than enjoyment. This essentially Platonic point of view is rejected by Levinas. He argues that need is the precondition of all gratification, that without need pleasure itself is occluded. Need does not prevent pleasure from arising, does not prescind from pleasure the sense of well-being that belongs to it. On the contrary, pleasure is what it is because of an anterior need. Thus, need does not corrode an already preexistent state of satisfaction but founds that state by making it possible for there to be satiety and the possibility of pleasure beyond mere repletion.

Thus, against the Heideggerian philosophy of a primordial anxiety as the affectivity anterior to all other human experiencing, Levinas posits a self at home with itself, satiable and happy. Suffering is understood against the background of prior satiety and is experienced as the destruction of satiety. Levinas introduces into contemporary existential analyses of primordial affective states a radically new understanding of being-in-the-world, a view that upholds human satisfaction within the framework of ontological plenitude. If Heidegger asks, "Why is there something rather than nothing?" the quandary for Levinas might well be expressed as "How can there be nothing if there is not first something?" The absence of need, if it could be imagined, would for Levinas produce only a kind of ataraxy, an undialectical and absolute tranquillity that precedes the upsurge of a self.

The phenomenology of natural man sustains two points that become critical in the development of Levinas's ethical metaphysics. The first is the fact that there is a relation to being such that it bypasses the cognitive scheme of reducing alterity to the same through representing alterity. Need is an immediate and original relation to being, a lack that nevertheless transcends the repetitive and universal machinery of sheer emptiness and repletion. In need Levinas uncovers a way of relating founded upon an absolutely primordial structure of being in the world, a structure that bypasses the unveiling of being, the bringing to light of truth. It is effectively lodged, prior to any transformation of it that may be accomplished by bringing it before the scrutiny of thematizing consciousness; thus need wants what is other than itself and is shown capable of acquiring what it desires. Levinas has been extremely careful to show that the *pleasure* of "living on" does not lie outside of the cycle of need but is phenomenologically included within it. Pleasure is not the residue of the act of repletion but belongs to repletion as such.

While Levinas establishes a relation to being that bypasses cognition it is a relation that cannot allow for transcendence. It transpires entirely within the framework of ontology. Once need is established phenomenologically as belonging to natural man, Levinas has prepared the ground for *homo religiosus*, who remains man as need but who cannot fulfill his need in natural existence. It is the need for transcendence that characterizes fully human ethical existence. This transcendence as we shall see subsequently is founded in the experience of other persons.

The second point of importance for ethical metaphysics that is grounded in the phenomenology of need involves, in my view, a radical thinking through of the universality of need. Levinas does not say that some are "natural" men and others "ethical" men. The gnostic distinction, for example, of psychic/spiritual (pneumatic) men as crosscutting existing men in existing societies is foreign to Levinas's point of view. *All* men are natural men before they are ethicized; it is only upon this background in this context of ruthlessness, self-containment, and domination that *homo religiosus* can arise. The totalizing aspirations of natural man are destroyed only through the encounter with other persons. Then and only then can totalizing propensities be enhanced and reinforced by some or rejected by others, because then and only then does ethical life begin. In acknowledging man as need Levinas is maintaining dialectically that from the point of view of a developed ethical consciousness man is hopelessly guilty, but from the point of view of natural man he remains innocent. Natural man thus behaves no differently from fallen man, but natural man simply has not experienced the conditions that make his behavior be nonethical behavior. He has not yet encountered the upsurge of the Other.

I have already suggested that what separates genuine desire from need is its insatiability. But this distinction alone does not suffice to explain the difference. Desire for the Other is not what it is without undergoing a dialectical process that, in my view, includes and presupposes not only need but also contemplation, that is, all the modalities of highly inflected cognitive processes. To desire is to need without consuming. Not to consume what we find outside ourselves is to represent it, to intend it cognitively. Thus, desire is not a mere modification of need but a complex process in which ideation is presupposed.

Simone Weil points out that the desire of religion is a desire that cannot be sated. She makes this distinction in a context that distinguishes eating from metaphysical desire. What separates the one from the other is, she contends, the fact that eating demolishes the object of desire; eating is an act of violence whereas metaphysical desire is contemplative, looking at what is desired without ingesting it. Weil writes:

> The great trouble in human life is that looking and eating are two different operations. . . . Children feel this trouble already, when they look at a cake for a long time almost regretting that it should have to be eaten and yet are unable to help eating it. It may be that vice, depravity and crime are nearly always, or even perhaps always in their essence attempts to eat beauty, to eat what we should only look at. Eve began it. If she caused humanity to be lost by eating the fruit, the opposite attitude looking at the fruit without eating it, should be what is required to save it. "Two winged companions," says the Upanishads, "Two birds are on the branch of a tree. One eats the fruit, the other looks at it." These two birds are the two parts of the soul.[5]

It is true that Weil speaks of the desire for beauty, the desire for something outside of cognitive grasp. This distinction in her work takes on in Levinas's thought an ethical rather than an aesthetic dimension. But Levinas does not fail to recognize the distinction between the consciousness that nourishes and sustains life by consuming what it lives on, and contemplation. While contemplation itself does not yield genuine alterity, it is, in my view, one necessary dialectical stage, for it permits us, as Weil has shown, to look without demolishing, to interiorize without touching. Thus, Levinas disavows the Platonic metaphor of *Phaedrus* 246e in which Plato speaks of feasting upon the truth. The desire for truth is beyond life, so that one cannot even speak of satiety in connection with it.

HUMAN CORPOREITY AND NEED

Once need is established as the mode of existence of the separated self it is not difficult to see that the notion of corporeity will become central for a genuine understanding of need. Levinas writes:

> The body appeared not as an object among other objects, but as the very regime in which separation holds sway, as the "how" of this separation and so to speak as an adverb rather than a substantive. It is as though in the vibration of separated existing there would by essence be produced a node where a movement of interiorization meets a movement of labor and acquisition directed toward the fathomless depth of the elements whereby the separated being is placed between two voids, in the "somewhere" in which it posits itself precisely as separate. (TeI 137/TI 163)

Man is now a being detached from the world that he feeds on. Freed from the ceaseless pressure of world as environment, he has become man at a distance. Levinas maintains that this distance is converted into time, since an interval is now interposed between any given need and its satisfaction. In the new situation of separated being, sheer animal need is replaced by the ability to enjoy pleasure. The situation of separated being is not without its difficulties. While freedom is enjoyed by the separated being, this very freedom is invaded by uncertainty, by anxiety for the future. The need of the beast cannot be separated from struggle and fear. The world from which consciousness has liberated man looms up as threatening man's very existence. The being who lives in terror of the world has conquered the world by subjugating the Other through the brute exercise of power.

In the primordial paradisiacal state of enjoyment the other that separated being enjoys is neither friend nor foe; separated being is merely determined by what it is not. It experiences itself as the milieu in which it bathes. The autochthony of separated being is not undialectical; it dominates the being from which it has severed itself but submits itself to the environment in which it is enclosed. Freedom is the consequence of this original equivocation, an equivocation lived as body (TeI 138/TI 164). The body is both the master and slave of what it lives on. The body can become an encumbrance through which the primordial harmony established between separated being and environment is established. Health can become sickness, and so on.

Levinas's view of body is profoundly anti-Platonic and anti-Gnostic. Consciousness has not fallen into a body, is not "trapped" by matter, but rather represents a suspension of the body's corporeality. It is produced as consciousness of time: "To be conscious is precisely to have time—not to exceed the present time in the project that anticipates the future, but to have a distance with regard to the present itself, to be related to the element in which one is settled as to what is not yet there" (TeI 140/ TI 166). The present is consciousness of peril emanating from the elemental. The sheer fluidity of the environment, its lack of contour and the resultant insecurity of life within it, becomes consciousness as the possibility of using time. It now becomes the task of the terrified creature to arrange time so as to ward off the threat to his imperiled contingency. This use of time is the upsurge of human freedom.

In the essay "Freedom and Command"[6] Levinas notes that human freedom must experience the order in which it finds itself alien to itself in order to know itself as freedom. Once the alien order is completely interiorized so that it is experienced as emanating from the self, the self has lost its freedom. This, Levinas claims, is precisely the situation that is presented in the Platonic view of the will,[7] where the will of the one who commands is in advance, in accordance with the will of the one commanded, and the one commanded experiences the command as something discovered but that preexisted its discovery as something resident within himself. This is why, in my view, Levinas develops the notion of separated being as an upsurge of ipseity in an alien environment. Separated being is free and freedom requires the tension of exteriority, a noncoincidence with an anterior state of will. Decisions in an alien environment are then genuinely free because they do not represent foregone conclusions.

It might be contended that there is then a genuine exteriority apart from the alterity of other persons that belongs to the nature of freedom itself. But I believe Levinas could meet this objection by arguing that this externality is still the object of an intentional system that attempts to interiorize what it finds outside of itself. The given offers itself as novel in the sense that it wells up from an inexhaustible and previously untrammeled exteriority. But any particular given upon which the will exerts itself is still the object of an intention to reduce it to the same. Ever new horizons of possibility may unfold before the transforming will of separated self, but the *project* of the will is to reduce these novel aspects of environment to the same. The point is, however, that the given upon which the will operates is not one with the will before the operation of intentionality; were this not the case there would be no given at all but simple undifferentiated unity.

We begin to experience our existence as freedom in the sensuous manifold as body. Body for Levinas is the organ that can seize the world. It is as body that we insert ourselves into the world; it is as body that separated being works, carries out its tasks. The body establishes our position on earth. It gives us a point of view; to posit oneself corporeally is to "touch ground." It is through body that the intentional structure of enjoyment clings to exteriority. It is this cohesion that distinguishes the intentionality of enjoyment from that of representation, that suspends exteriority, puts it out of play. Exteriority is maintained not simply by affirming a world but by an act of corporeal positing. Body, naked and indigent, identifies the center of the world. It is irreducible to thought (TeI 138ff./TI 164ff.). Its being as lack confirms exteriority as nonconstituted, as ontologically prior to all affirmation. While such an observation may seem trivial, the act of constituting itself could not begin prior to the act of eating. In the domain of need unlike that of representation, exteriority persists. Such acts as work and destruction presume the exteriority of the world just as the exteriority of the other person is confirmed in such acts as wounding and killing.

The relevance of the preceding analyses to ethical metaphysics can now be brought to light. Levinas shows in the elaboration of body, of need, of "living on" that not all modes of reducing alterity are the same. In need the Other is reduced to the same and is profoundly altered by this reduction. Need confirms the nonconstituted nature of the alterity that it consumes, the nonself in which the self is suspended. Levinas writes: "This sinking one's teeth into things which the act of eating involves above all measures the surplus of the reality of the aliment over every represented reality, a surplus that is not quantitative, but is the way the I, as absolute commencement, is suspended in the non-I" (TeI 101–2/TI 129). Representation reduces the Other to the same but leaves the Other unaffected. Yet for Levinas, in another sense, eating is innocent, for it is necessary to sustain life, whereas representation that addresses itself to the alterity of the other person traduces alterity at its most vulnerable point, by reducing the Other to the same. Both need and representation fail to found religious existence; both in different ways are aggressive, violent, self-aggrandizing modes of being in the world.

LIFE AND THE ELEMENTAL

In enjoyment things are not comprehended in terms of ends; they are embedded in an environment from which we are compelled to loosen them. This environment cannot be reduced to a system of operational references. It is thus distinguishable from the intertwining nexus of *Zeuge* to which Heidegger's Dasein is open and that themselves are open pathways to one another (TeI 106/TI 133). Since the environment is not a referential system, it can never be understood as a totality. It is thick, lies in wait, lies in abeyance, cannot be possessed. This is what distinguishes the elemental background from things: it is earth, sea, sky, light. The elemental envelops things without itself being contained in anything else. It is the sine qua non for possession: "Every relation or possession is situated within the non-possessable which envelops or contains without being able to be contained or enveloped. We shall call it the elemental" (TeI 104/TI 131).

The elemental can be dominated or used but remains essentially what it was before. It does not become something else as the materials with which we work are transfigured into things that have utility. We cannot know the elemental, for although we may know the precise rules that govern its operation as the navigator understands the sea, we fail to seize it as object. The elemental is characterized by its nonutility, its noncognizability. It is as imprecision that the elemental appears, as being without form. Yet the elemental has a content that appears without being enclosed. It is unidimensional, having only a single facet or surface: "the surface of the sea and of the field, the edge of the wind" (TeI 104/ TI 131). It is not as if an alteration of our own position could yield new perspectives, another surface, another face of a multifaceted object. The elemental has no other face hidden beyond the one revealed. It has depth but no length or width. It is extended throughout its depth and lost in earth and sky. Amorphous, spread out, it offers no privileged vantage point. Things give themselves to us as soliciting encounter through the sheer fact of their multifaceted appearance through which we identify their unity. But the fundamental quality of the elemental is that it is being without support. It offers itself as being without origin as though, in Levinas's terms, one were in the "entrails" of being.

While it is important for Levinas to distinguish the elemental from things that are the objects of representation, it is equally important to distinguish it from the indeterminacy of the infinite. The source of the idea of the infinite that I shall examine at some length subsequently lies elsewhere. Indeed, the elemental separates man from the infinite (TeI 105/TI 132). Its indeterminacy is of a different order, for it does not lack qualities although its qualities cannot be represented. The elemental precedes the distinction between finite and infinite; it is the backdrop for instinctive biological needs and drives that in their satisfaction are lived as joy; it is the setting for an existence entirely without concern for the Other. It can in a sense be called the a priori structure of pleasure, for pleasure is the return of things to their elemental quality. No value underlies the quest for the satisfaction of need save satisfaction itself (TeI 107/TI 134). This according to Levinas is what moral hedonism understands correctly.

Since in pleasure things are not enmeshed in technical ends, not organized into a system but laid out in a milieu, they are there, so to speak, for the taking. The milieu is common territory. What is freed from it refers exclusively to our pleasure. Even if things freed from the elemental are used, they refer to utility only in a derivative and secondary way: essentially they are submitted to our pleasure. Indeed, Levinas remarks that "pleasure is the universal category of the empirical." It is as pleasure that we relate to the substantial fullness of being (TeI 107/TI 134).

Being in the elemental is for Levinas a midpoint between "blind and deaf participation in a whole" at one extreme, and "thought" that is directed toward exteriority at the other (TeI 108/TI 135). Feeling is the way in which the elemental is lived. Feeling is not mutilated representation or thought that lacks clarity and distinctness. From Levinas's point of view, Husserl had definitively undermined the Cartesian and Spinozist ideals of apodicticity, ideals that denigrated affective life because it lacked clarity and precision. Feeling is the modus vivendi of living as a self. In affectivity, sensible qualities are not known; they are lived. Feeling puts us into relation with the pure quality of the elemental.

The elemental as Levinas describes it is Janus-faced: it both gives itself and escapes through its very insubstantiality in the giving. What is offered by the elemental disappears without explanation. The future is thus lived as insecurity, an insecurity that is expressed concretely in the mythical divinity of the elemental gods (TeI 115/TI 142). But for Levinas these gods are without face; one therefore cannot address them: they lack the fundamental prerequisite for *religio*. They stand as the nothingness that marks the limit of enjoyment.[8] Consciousness as separated being is pagan consciousness. This nothingness that marks the limit of enjoyment has in Levinas's early work been designated as the *il y a* (TeI 116/TI 142). It may be recalled that Levinas distinguishes the *il y a* as the return to nothingness of all things, beings and persons, a return that already presupposes a world. The *il y a* is not the *apeiron* that precedes being, but that to which all things return. In *Totality and Infinity* the *il y a* is that into which the elemental is extended so that it represents the possibility of the withdrawal of enjoyment through the obliteration of the elemental itself. But Levinas's *il y a* is not radical chaos. It implies the possibility of obliterating all things, beings and persons, but not the withdrawal of the preconditions for their upsurge. It is, in my view, closer to apocalyptic thought in Judeo-Christian religion than to the nihilistic possibilities of contemporary thought. The former portends the possible retrenchment of benevolent cosmic forces so that apocalypse is a prelude to a new existence rather than the final collapse of ontology.[9] But chaos that cannot be overcome, so radical that there is absolutely nothing, is a chaos from which separated self could not, in Levinas's scheme, emerge.

We have already seen that life in the elemental is the love of life. The *tedium vitae* that rejects life wallows in the love of the very life that it rejects. Even in despair there is no break with the ideal of enjoyment (TeI 118/TI 145). Pessimism is thus not primordial but built into an economic infrastructure that expresses the anguish for the next day and the pain of work. Levinas can envisage the limiting case in which need is imposed beyond all possibility of satisfaction and poverty does not allow the self to be at home with itself. This case of poverty *in extremis* may, in unusual circumstances, be the condition of the proletariat. But Levinas does not stress the exceptional case since this would weaken the edifice so carefully constructed of a happy natural man for whom distress supervenes only upon an anterior enjoyment.

Levinas's analysis of the limiting case where need is imposed beyond all possibility of enjoyment so that human existence cannot be at home with itself is closer to Weil's analysis of affliction than to classical Marxist doctrine. Weil stresses not the alienation of the laborer from the products of his labor and the ensuing distress of the proletariat as a class, but the exceptional condition of human existence when it is so degraded as to find the satisfaction of human need impossible. In Weil's account affliction is inseparable from physical suffering, which, while not the same as bodily pain, is inseparable from it. If affliction is genuine, it uproots the life that it attacks in all its parts, the psychic and the physical, but most especially the social. It is a "more or less attenuated equivalent of death."[10] Need that is beyond all satisfaction attacks not only biological life but also the very phenomenon of enjoyment, yet this possibility does not for Levinas overthrow the preceding anthropology.

Apart from a striking analysis of the sensuous manifold extraordinary in its revelation of the phenomenality belonging to environment, Levinas's discussion of the elemental is of strategic importance in the development of his ethical metaphysics. The concept of the elemental that provides need with a content, so to speak, affords an absolutely novel approach to the life world conceived by Husserl in terms of horizon and object. The elemental is not a horizon, for it is itself content. Yet as we have seen its content lacks form, distinctiveness, multifaceted appearance. It is a content that cannot be represented. I hope to show subsequently how important it is for Levinas to have established two points: (1) human existence is in its very foundation lack, and (2) it is possible to speak of a content that cannot be represented. The infinite that, as we shall see, is the object of *religio* is apprehended both as lack and as content that cannot be represented. Need, "living on," life in the elemental establishes at an infracognitive level the possibility of phenomena that will recur in the life world of *homo religiosus*.

HABITATION

The being inside of the elemental is not destined to remain as the pristine being that is first presented. Man appropriates some aspect of it for himself. That which he appropriates confers upon him a species of extraterritoriality, for what was previously undifferentiated, unifaceted, all-enveloping background is now distinguished as humanized. For example, what was formerly the sea becomes the locale where we fish, the earth, the field where we plow. According to Levinas the single form of possession anterior to all other manifestations of it is habitation, the domicile or place where we dwell. The home is the presupposition for all property, the place in which we are inside as opposed to being thrown into a hostile exterior. Ensconced in its domicile the self is at home with itself. Not only is the domicile the condition of all property, it is also for Levinas the condition for all inner psychic life (TeI 130/TI 156).

Meditation and representation are produced and lived concretely as dwelling. Being in a dwelling establishes extraterritoriality at the heart of the elemental. The interiority of the house is produced as intimacy. This intimacy or gentleness comes to separated being not from itself but from the upsurge of another, of femininity. In an essay devoted to the feminine element in Judaism, Levinas writes:

> To light eyes that are blind, to restore to equilibrium and so overcome an alienation which ultimately results from the very virility of the universal and all-conquering *logos* that stalks the very shadows that could have sheltered it, should be the ontological function of the feminine, the vocation of the one "who does not conquer." Woman does not simply come to someone deprived of companionship to keep him company. She answers to a solitude inside this privation and—which is stranger—to a solitude that subsists in spite of the presence of God; to a solitude in the universal, to the inhuman which continues to well up even when the human has mastered nature and raised it to thought. (DL 55/DF 33)

Woman occupies a unique place in the history of spirit as intimacy within the natural sphere rather than as the ethical upsurge of the Other. But Levinas's thought deviates from a strictly Hegelian analysis, which it might in that regard seem to resemble. In Hegel's system, woman as woman seduces man from his proper place in the political arena, subverts political life in the interest of her private ends. Hegel writes: "Womankind—the everlasting irony [in the life] of the community—changes by intrigue the universal end of government into a private end, transforms its universal activity into a work of some particular individual, and perverts the universal property of the state into a possession and ornament for the Family. Woman in this way turns to ridicule the earnest wisdom of mature age, which [is] indifferent to purely private pleasures and enjoyments."[11] From Levinas's point of view woman offers serenity and repose rather than the dark turbulence of passion and the gods of the nether world as in the Hegelian analysis. She represents rooted existence in a particular place. What is necessary for man to live on is wrenched from nature by work, which attests the break with spontaneous existence, an end to the instinctive life of man in its intimacy with nature.

This separation from nature is lived as the beginning of the life of mind. But although reason recognizes itself through the world of work, the world remains essentially uninhabitable. Woman represents the transformation of existence as work into serenity, the transformation of place into home. Feminine existence *is* in Levinas's view habitation (TeI 128/TI 155).

Dwelling can be interpreted in terms of utility, but its usefulness is only an ancillary function. It is true that dwelling is both shelter from the elements and a place of concealment from some hostile presence, but the essential function of dwelling is to provide a place for meditation or contemplation. Nature, according to Levinas, does not become a world until it is either worked on or represented: the house is the precondition for these activities. We maintain ourselves in the world as coming forth from a private domain, from the home. The world comes toward us as toward persons whose bearing in the world is that of persons who occupy homes (TeI 125/TI 152). The house provides the possibility of a retreat from the world. Because we dwell in a place we are not abandoned to the outside.

The dwelling is a building and as such belongs to the world of objects; but dwelling as such is an original phenomenon. Because there is dwelling there can be objects. The house is not situated in relation to an objective world; rather the world is situated in relation to dwelling: "The whole of the civilization of labor and possession arises as a concretization of separated being effectuating its separation. But this civilization refers to the incarnation of consciousness and to inhabitation—to existence proceeding from the intimacy of a home, the first concretization" (TeI 126/TI 152). For Levinas we do not first represent dwelling to ourselves and then, afterwards, dwell. Dwelling is the precondition of all representing even though subsequent representation engulfs all dwelling after the fact. Dwelling does not magically evoke the contemplative attitude according to Levinas, but meditation, which is the meaning of life as separated being, is concretized as dwelling. Levinas maintains that meditation is not exhausted in the lived state of dwelling but that dwelling opens up new states of existence not analytically contained in the notion of dwelling itself.

The house has a dual function of looking out onto a street and of maintaining an interiority, which provides for us a secret recess. Its original purpose that was to allow a break with the elemental does not cut us off from the elemental from which we can now separate ourselves. We see from the window the world from which we have been separated without ourselves being seen. This vantage point allows us to dominate the world from which we are secluded. The elemental still remains at our disposal, but we are free to reject it (TeI 129/TI 156).

The domain of work also changes the elemental by transforming nature into a world. Work begins when satisfaction can be delayed. It therefore establishes a new nonhedonic relation with the elemental. It is important, I believe, to distinguish Levinas's point of view from psychoanalytic theories that maintain that work is a sublimation for pleasure-seeking impulses whose satisfaction is blocked and whose energies are then channeled elsewhere.[12] In Levinas's thought there is no dark realm of the unconscious that serves as the repository for hidden desires that cannot surface because the consequence of satisfying these desires would destroy the social structure. Indeed, for Levinas the fabric of the society itself incorporates all the self-aggrandizing impulses of natural man; the corrective for this situation must be sought in something other than work, in ethical life with the Other. The phenomenon of work is understood by Levinas as one whose very conditions are embedded in the nature of man's primary relation to the elemental. The elemental threatens him with an uncertain future. While Levinas would agree with certain psychoanalytic approaches that claim that the gratification provided by work is delayed and therefore different from the instantaneous gratification of need satisfaction, the resemblance is only superficial. For Levinas the repression of instinctual life is not the consequence of social restriction but essentially ethical in nature. The social structure cannot serve this function since it only reflects the brutality of instinctual life. Work, is for Levinas, an original task in which one "seizes" and "carries off" the uncertain future of the elemental. Thus, the *telos* of work is not oriented to the far-off past of infancy for whose gratifications we maintain an ineradicable longing, as it is in classical psychoanalytic doctrine. Work is oriented toward a future about which we are anxious and whose dangers we can effectively forestall only through work.

Work makes possible the secondary phenomenon of possession. It is true that in the elemental we also possess what we desire, but what we possess is consumed. When our needs are sated, we no longer have the commodity that satisfies. That which is possessed in enjoyment is confused with the feeling of enjoyment itself; no activity precedes our enjoyment. But Levinas points out that such possessing is to be possessed. Possession that begins with dwelling must be distinguished from possession without acquisition, for now we not only take what we enjoy but we also hold on to it (TeI 81/TI 109).

In possession that is the consequence of work we distinguish the act of possession from the content possessed. We also distinguish what we possess from the enjoyment of it. Work, in laying claim to something, in establishing ownership, suspends the elemental without "carrying off" the enjoying self. Possession neutralizes being; it is only in the light of this neutralization that the thing wells up as a thing. The ontology that grasps the being of the existent demands the suspension of the being of the elemental. We do not think this suspension; its ontology is prereflective and pretheoretical; it is lived by us as work. The hand grapples with the elemental and even in its first groping gestures subjugates the elemental to the *telos* of the thing. It constitutes things only through wresting them from the elemental (TeI 81/TI 109).

I believe that for Levinas there is a prereflective mode of living the Husserlian *epoche;* it is lived as work. The true emergence of the thing occurs only against the ground of a suspension of the being of the elemental. Thus, in my view, dwelling that makes work possible is the concretization of the *epoche,* so to speak, in the context of existence; it keeps out the elemental. Levinas preempts what is for Husserl a device for establishing the foundations of cognition as a fundamental structure of human existence. Bracketing is no longer an instrument invented for understanding consciousness in its primordiality but a fundamental structure of human existence. Thus, Levinas engages in more than an exercise in descriptive phenomenology in his analysis of habitation; he brings the *epoche* into the life world itself.

Work in its original intention is not yet a mode of transcendence. The elemental that becomes city, field, countryside as soon as work transforms its surface returns to its elementality as soon as work ceases. While work transforms the anonymity of matter it nevertheless fails to define or to comprehend the fruits of its effort. Matter is for Levinas the "darkness" that presents itself as the resistance to effort. Work is the first attack upon the pagan faceless gods for it destroys the nothingness that they represent. It masters and suspends the undetermined future of the elemental, for possessions endure and affirm human power over time. The product of work remains through time as substance (TeI 133–34/TI 159–60).

Work precedes intelligibility, for it grasps the thing before it forms a concept of it. The hand fulfills its function before the plans and projects of intelligence take shape. The hand is no longer a part of one's sensory apparatus, ceases to be the tactile instrument for sensory enjoyment and becomes the means by which we dominate. The hand that acquires is weighed down by what it possesses. It might be argued that the body already establishes possession before dwelling and work (TeI 135/TI 161–62).

Possession of the thing establishes more than the human power over time. It establishes the substantiality of the thing, while other relations to objects attain only their attributes. But the substantiality of things, what confers upon them their permanence, is undermined through the possibility of exchanging things for one another. The thing is not refractory to such transactions. Resistance to possession of the thing is offered by other persons who themselves are not subject to possession. We are then confronted with the face of the Other in his alterity for the first time as the one who resists us. This resistance is the first indication we have of the Other as commandment and as word. Once this confrontation has taken place murder as a human possibility is born (TeI 136/TI 162).

ART AND THE ELEMENTAL

It might be argued that the relation to things as possessions, the foundation of economy, ought not to make us aware of the alterity of the Other, for economy is not language; rather art as language ought to reveal the being of things, to unveil alterity. Levinas, however, expressly dissociates himself from this view. In an early article on the nature of art Levinas shows the discontinuity between art and the ethical. He separates the function of art from the quest for truth that belongs for Levinas to philosophy and action.[13] In its attempts to generate a world, art succeeds only in achieving the "pseudo-presence" (RO 773/CPP 3) of a world. The view that he rejects is the fashionable but erroneous dogma that assumes that the function of art is to "express," to convey the ineffable, to bypass the vulgar perceptions of everyday life in order to rescue language from banality. This approach to art assumes, Levinas asserts, that art is more real than reality, that art coincides with metaphysical intuition.

For Levinas art for art's sake is simply wrong. It situates art above reality. To go beyond reality is the function of understanding, whereas the function of art is precisely not to understand. Obscurity is its mode of being; art is a commerce with darkness. It is not the mode of comprehension of any particular type of consciousness but "cuts in on consciousness." Levinas considers it "the very event of obscurity." It is a "fall of night" or "an encroachment of shadow." This early insight is reaffirmed in *Totality and Infinity* where Levinas declares that the aesthetic orientation that man confers upon his world is a return to the elemental, a return now organized at a new level of existence (TeI 111/TI 137–38).

What is art? The thrust of Levinas's analysis depends upon three points: (1) that art substitutes the image for the object, (2) that the image can never become a concept, and (3) that only concepts belong to the realm of intelligibility (RO 774/CPP 3). According to Levinas the image neutralizes any relation to the object, and since the image can never give rise to the concept, art can provide us only with images; we can never bring them into clear and distinct rational thought. This would seem to be fairly obvious, but its importance for Levinas lies in the fact that the concept represents an activity of consciousness, whereas in the case of the image we are gripped by it, remain passive to it. The artist is inspired or possessed; the image is related to magic rather than to genuine *religio*.[14]

The most fundamental level of art is represented in rhythm where something, sound and interval, is imposed upon us. We are carried away by it, we give up the self to anonymity. The incantatory quality of poetry is basically sorcery. Thus, art at its most rudimentary level (rhythm) is for Levinas not a form of consciousness since consciousness is in his view an activity, the assumption of a task. Nor does art belong to the world of the unconscious since images, even if obscure, are present. In art consciousness plays (RO 775/CPP 4). We have already seen in Levinas's early work a careful distinction between the game and the assumption of a task. In light of this distinction it is clear that art is for Levinas the absence of seriousness and commitment. One is in the world of things as a thing, as a participant in a spectacle.

Art is a peculiar doubling of reality. The thing is both what it is and its double. When I gaze at the image of an object I am conscious of the object's absence, but unlike the act of representation that takes place in the absence of the object, I am confronted with a tableau. This tableau does not carry me beyond myself, for the world of art does not symbolize an actual world. On the contrary, the artist moves in a realm that precedes the world of creation that he as a person has already superceded in his everyday existence (RO 778ff./CPP 7ff.).

It is not difficult to discern the Platonic bias in Levinas's point of view. The creative work of the artist belongs to the Dionysiac world of seizure, of transport that is at the furthest remove from the world of a metaphysics based upon the discernment of other persons. The ontology of the sensible is an ontology of shadows cast by being, of the resemblance that being bears to itself. Levinas's analysis of the image is in my view best comprehended through the myth of Narcissus, who gazes upon his own image reflected in a pool and makes it the object of his love. The image could be termed the narcissistic work of being in Levinas's thought; it is being imitating its caricature, recovering its shadow. For Levinas every image is a caricature that aspires to life but remains inert.

The work of art is for Levinas locked into present time. Powerless to alter its future, it remains fixed within the present, which it establishes. The persons of a novel are prisoners with all of their possibilities fixed by the work in which they are embedded. Yet the time of art is not eternity; it is the entretemps that belongs neither to the realm of life nor to the realm of the concept that is truly eternal (RO 784/CPP 10). It is for this reason that Levinas insists the proscription of images is the supreme command of monotheism (RO 786/CPP 11). The temporality of the image is the interval of death.

For Levinas as for Sartre, art is an evasion in a world that calls us to responsibility. Both seek a way of constructing a link between the game of art and the seriousness of life.[15] For Levinas art belongs to the prehuman milieu of the elemental and can therefore never be the ultimate value of any civilization. Only criticism in his view can call art to responsibility. The critic treats the artist as a worker. In seeking to discern the influences in an artist's work he reattaches the artist to the realm of history. The work of art is to be interpreted as we interpret myths whose nontruths become true only when opened up by the understanding of the critic (RO 788/CPP 12–13).

While it is true that Levinas upholds a Platonic view, since he interprets the work of art as the substitution of an image for being itself, I would argue that Levinas does not legislate a corrective for deficiencies inherent in the work of art itself. He does not maintain that art become didactic. In this respect he is a thoroughgoing phenomenologist. Art is inherently unable to teach and cannot be forced within the confines of its own endeavor to become the tool of ethical imperatives. Levinas recognizes that art is what it is and cannot be required to be what it is not. He therefore ascribes great value to criticism that restores the work to its historico-cultural nexus from which, as art, it has been isolated.

Art belongs to a lower world of dream, of fantasy of noncognitive and necessarily obscure vision. It is experienced as a liberation. It is for Levinas the realm of pleasure and dark threat as separated being experiences their alternation in the elemental. Art conjures up a feeling of joy and power to both artist and spectator.

The work of art is the very opposite of teaching and commandment, which are explicit and unambiguous. Indeed, it is the function of the teacher to wrest experience from the aesthetic realm. Criticism is the word of one living creature to another; it is the language that makes us leave our dreams. The living word appears where criticism becomes teaching.

While the devaluing of art gives to Levinas's work a tone of unrelieved austerity, it is perfectly consistent with his subsequent, more developed views on the philosophy of language. I shall subsequently examine in detail how Levinas regards the problem of language in its relationship to ethics. Suffice it to say for the moment that Levinas develops a theory of language in which all terms are understood metaphorically; the metaphor belongs to language in its very upsurge. Terms are already characterized by a duality of meaning, by an allusive character. Language even at its most abstract is not without the interposition of images. Meaning is conveyed only as something other than the vehicle that conveys. The thinker resolved upon the most abstruse language can only speak in terms of inside and outside, of substance and form, and so on. He cannot evade spatiality in his language, cannot convey precisely what is intended. So long as ideas are put into language, spatiality is simultaneously given. Every metaphor points to another term having a somewhat different meaning. Thus, language is necessarily equivocal. There is no meaning that does not already imply another meaning. The duality of language, however, is spurious; it lacks the radical alterity implicit in authentic experience, that is, in the upsurge of the other person. Genuine experience is without metaphor.[16]

The work of the writer Michel Leiris, the subject of an early article,[17] generates an analysis of language that presages the later view of language just sketched. Levinas finds that Leiris uses a form of double entendre that derives from free-association techniques. The power of the *biffure* lies in the ability of thought to deflect its movement from the path along which it was proceeding to follow another quite different course. What Levinas discovers is that language is equivocal to begin with and that this is why free association is possible rather than the converse. All thought is originally equivocal. One idea is buried in another, and no thought is an isolable unit that crosses over into another thought.

These reflections on the nature of language put Levinas's view of art into proper perspective, for now we can see that language as such fails to express immediately, to give both itself and its meaning unequivocally. There is, I believe, in Levinas's view of metaphor an implicit understanding of all language as conveying something of the same duplicity that he finds in the realm that we designate as art. The more abstract the language, the more precise it is. The closer language comes to conveying what is intended (but insofar as language as such intends indirectness) it cannot do otherwise than circumvent the self-evident. It becomes less and less a window through which the real appears and more and more visible as an entity in itself. It is in this context that art can be seen as something opaque that overwhelms human consciousness rather than as the upsurge of transparency and self-evidence that we shall see is found in the human face.

NOTES

1. According to A. Dondeyne, "Inleiding tot het denken van Emmanuel Levinas," *Tijdschrift voor Filosofie* 25 (1963): 555–81, the philosophical importance of Levinas's work lies in analyzing the traditional themes of phenomenology while at the same time putting their ultimacy for metaphysics into question.

2. Hegel, *Phenomenology of Spirit,* trans. A. V. Miller (Oxford: Oxford University Press, 1977), 105ff.

3. Ibid., 110.

4. See also Jean Catesson, "Une philosophie de l'inégal," *Critique* 21 (1965): 642.

5. Simone Weil, *Waiting for God,* trans. Emma Cranford (New York: G. P. Putnam's Sons, 1951), 166.

6. Levinas, "Liberté et commandement," *Revue de Métaphysique et de Morale* 3 (1953): 264–72; translated by Alphonso Lingis as "Freedom and Command," in CPP 15–24.

7. It might be argued that there is no doctrine of the will in Plato, but that is precisely the conclusion to which Levinas's analysis points since, according to him, there is no clear distinction in Plato between the will of the one who commands and that of the one who is commanded.

8. The *il y a* is for Levinas no mere hypothesis of conditions in the time of origin. One can always revert to the mythical level of being. The distinction between individuals can disappear; a return to primitive mentality can destroy the primacy of representation. The value of Levy-Bruhl's studies of nonliterate societies is, in Levinas's view, that they show that representation is not the original way of being in the world but already represents a choice of being in the world as *mens.* For primitive mentality the world is experienced in participation, which is "the condition of existence. To exist is to participate in a mystical reality." See Levinas, "Levy-Bruhl and Contemporary Philosophy," EN 53–67/ENT 39–51.

9. It has been noted that apocalypse is not just a collapse but precedes a new time. Mircea Eliade, *Cosmos and History,* trans. Willard R. Trask (New York: Harper, 1959), 126–27, writes:

> A series of calamities will announce the approach of the end of the world; and the first of them will be the fall of Rome and the destruction of the Roman empire, a frequent anticipation in the Judeo-Christian apocalypse. . . . "It will be a time," writes Lactantius (*Divinae Institutiones,* VII, 17, 9), "when justice will be rejected and innocence odious, when the wicked will prey as enemies upon the good, when neither law nor order nor military discipline will be observed, when none will respect gray hairs, or do the offices of piety, nor take pity upon women and children; all things will be confounded and mixed, against divine and natural law." But after this premonitory phase, the purifying fire will come down to destroy the wicked and will be followed by the millennium of bliss that the Christian chiliasts also expected and Isaiah and the Sibylline Oracles had earlier foretold.

D. S. Russell, *The Method and Message of Jewish Apocalyptic* (London, SCM Press, 1964), 106, writes: "The triumph of God's predetermined purpose will provide the key to all God's mysteries and problems. This triumph will come, not by a gradual transformation of the universe and not by a whittling down of the power of evil, but by a supernatural and catastrophic intervention."

10. Weil, *Waiting for God,* 118.

11. Hegel, *Phenomenology of Spirit,* 288.

12. Philip Rieff, *Freud: The Mind of the Moralist* (New York: Viking Press, 1959), 245, writes in reference to Freud's *Future of an Illusion:* "Men must work. Freud makes the old scourge a test of maturity and independence. Take the fact that 'men are not spontaneously fond of work,' add to it 'that arguments are of no avail against their passions'— and you have the 'two widespread human characteristics' which make a coercive society inevitable." Rieff's citations of Freud have been updated to the Strachey translation (New York: W. W. Norton, 1961), 8.

13. An editorial note preceding the original version of this article ("La réalité et son ombre," *Les Temps Modernes* 38 [1948]: 771) points to the similarity in this regard between Levinas and Sartre.

14. It would seem that Levinas interprets all art as Dionysiac in its foundations in accordance with Nietzsche's description in *The Birth of Tragedy* (New York: Doubleday, 1956) of enchanted man through whom a supernatural power speaks. The artist "feels himself to be Godlike and strives with the same elation and ecstasy as the gods he has seen in his

dreams. No longer the *artist,* he has himself become a work of art." (24).
For Levinas, art is a savage impulse that in Nietzsche's theory of tragedy
is mitigated by Apollonian influence.

15. For elaboration of Sartre's view, see *What Is Literature?* trans. Wallace Fowlie (New York: Harper, 1965).

16. Catesson, "Une philosophie de l'inégal," 652–53.

17. Levinas, "La transcendence des mots: à propos des biffures," in
Hors sujet (Montpellier: Fata Morgana, 1987), 215–22; translated by Michael B. Smith as "The Transcendence of Words: On Michel Leiris's
Biffures," in *Outside the Subject* (Stanford: Stanford University Press,
1993), 144–50.

IV

The Foundation of Ethical Metaphysics

IN THE PRECEDING CHAPTER I tried to show that separated being is no longer one with the totality of being; it is a being that has a locale, dwells, works, exists within an economy. To dwell, to work, to exchange, to meditate are the lived modalities of separated being. Its life world is the domain of economy; within its confines the products of man's labor are subject to exchange and thus to usurpation. Yet inner life persists although it cannot recognize itself in that economy. The life of economy is therefore more than precarious; it is experienced as tyranny.[1] This tyranny is represented by the state; the persons we are, our interiority, is betrayed rather than expressed in the political domain. It is precisely this network of functional relationships with others that Levinas designates as totality. The totality is the whole into which the observable lives of individuals are incorporated. It devours individuality and fails to recognize genuine alterity and the meaning of inner life.

All work is symbolic within totality; it conceals the original intention of the work in question. In this sense, work is as deceptive as the dream of Freudian psychology. But from Levinas's point of view, when we have penetrated the concealing façade of work we have revealed only the intention of the work but not the inner self, which remains absent from it (TeI 151/TI 176). Thus Levinas remains consistent with the insight of his early writings: where there is world, there is also the possibility of making it manifest in its totality. Work is not a devious project of concealment but the modus operandi of totality. What is not at once obvious can be brought to light. But the realm of work can never reveal the interiority that transcends totality. Only the word in its pure function as a calling forth to responsibility can break into totality. It is the purpose of this chapter to examine the break with interiority, which, we have seen, resists totalization but remains self-aggrandizing in its egoity.

What Separated Being Means

To be as separated being is to be in such a way that life has a meaning apart from its integration into the historical order. The work of history is to establish a chronological arrangement in which being-in-itself is transformed, articulated into the order of history as though the order of history were the order of nature. To create a totality is the function of history; history is the chronicle of what no longer lives. The historian is the survivor, the chronicler of what is defunct. The being who lives only becomes part of history, is totalized after his death. Life itself is a suspension of history, or to use Husserlian language, brackets history, suspends it, puts it out of play. The living individual has a private destiny that cannot be totalized. Separated being exists as interiority. It inaugurates a dimension in which everything that has been closed to history remains open. The destiny of the individual is distinct from historical destiny (TeI 25–26/TI 55).

The being of interiority, the being that resists the totalizing historical process, is designated by Levinas as psychism. Psychism is a being such that its being is an absolute beginning. The phenomenology of separated being established in the early work as the severance of the individual from the *il y a* is now elaborated as an antihistorical dimension impervious to the temporalization of universal history, as a resistance to incorporation into collective temporality. From the point of view of history it is ridiculous to speak of absolute beginning, which is the modus vivendi of separated being. Universal history can be thought only as a sequential continuum whose smooth continuity is invaded by psychism. Psychism breaks into history as memory allowing us to put into question what history designates as irrevocable, to rescind the past, to master it. Through memory we ground ourselves "retroactively" (TeI 27/TI 56), so to speak; we reverse the irreversible. Memory inverts historical time and as such is the living tempo of interiority as opposed to the inexorable swell of universal history. Memory halts universal time, reverses it, prevents our existence from being engulfed in its flow. In the early work of Levinas we have seen that separated being is an upsurge against being as such, but the lived modality of that upsurge is enriched in *Totality and Infinity* by the addition of the historical dimension. Memory makes possible the triumph over history by bringing into clarity what has already been bypassed in the inexorable flow of historical time.

But if history can be reversed, memory itself is vulnerable to death, to the obliteration of memory and the reinauguration of historical time. Our own time, the time of interiority, again becomes integrated into historical time. The point of *Totality and Infinity* is to show that death is not a final triumph, that the continuity of the self is assured. The lived modality of the triumph over death cannot be understood without prior investigation of the phenomenology of death, of desire, enjoyment, and cognition. Suffice it to say for the present that death is not overcome through the advent of a new possibility after all other possibilities are closed. Death cannot be transcended by a refusal to be caught up in historical time. Such a refusal is merely symbolic; it is expressed theologically as the idea of the eternity of the soul. To posit the eternity of the soul is tantamount to proclaiming that one survives one's own death. This is to deny the reality of death. The survivor can witness another's death, but one cannot stand with regard to one's own death in the relationship of those who survive it. One's beginning and end as they belong to historical time are third-person events to the consciousness that historicizes but remain first-person events to us. We therefore remain without perspective with regard to them (TeI 28/TI 57).

Levinas maintains that we can choose to understand interiority through third-person categories, that is to say, historically, or we can start from the point of view of "inner intention." A number of interesting consequences follow when we begin from the latter standpoint. We see that such a point of view is available only to oneself, that interior life remains private, secret, impervious to the third person. Thus the observer to whom the movements and operations of societies are accessible must recognize that there is an aspect of social reality that falls outside the scope of human history and that complete totalization is impossible. Genuine pluralism, impervious to totalization, begins as a result of interiority:

The discontinuity of inner life interrupts historical time. The thesis of the primacy of history constitutes an option for the comprehension of being in which interiority is sacrificed. The present work proposes another option. The real must not only be determined in its historical objectivity, but also from interior intentions, from the *secrecy* that interrupts the continuity of historical time. Only on the basis of this secrecy is the pluralism of society possible. We have always known that it is impossible to form an idea of human totality, for men have an inner life closed to he who does, however, grasp the comprehensive movements of human groups. (TeI 28–29/TI 57–58)

The natural mode of existence for separated being is atheistic. We have already seen from Levinas's early work that human existence as separated is not a decline from a better state antecedent to it, but the legitimate upsurge of consciousness against the amorphousness of the unlimited (DEE 19/EE 19). Man no longer participates in the being from which he has been severed. He lives beyond God, at home with himself, for to be a self *is* to be at home with oneself. Atheism, from Levinas's point of view, is neither the successor to theistic belief as a revolt from it, nor a process of enlightenment, nor an ontologically secondary phenomenon: it is prior to either the affirmation or denial of God's existence. It is the self's mode of positing itself (TeI 29–20/TI 58).

Some theological repercussions of this point of view left implicit in Levinas's work are, I believe, worth noting. Atheism is a state *prior* to revelation, that is, prior to the break with totality. It is the ground against which revelation becomes possible and is thus inherently innocent. It cannot fall under judgment since it is a prerequisite for the upsurge of the very conditions that will make judgment possible. Since atheism is prior to revelation it cannot constitute a violation of what is commanded. While it is true that natural man requires judgment, before such judgment is possible there must be commandment anterior to judgment; the one judged must be the one already commanded. Atheistic man is natural man before the advent of the Other. The atheism Levinas has in mind is not divorced from theistic belief itself, for theistic belief is the adherence to a set of propositions whose truth or falsity depends upon cognition and merely reflects the totalizing tendency of cognition. Such "theism" reduces the alterity of the other, in this case "God," to the same. Thus theistic belief, if understood as an apprehension of a being among other beings, a being that can be made into an object of knowledge, is itself atheistic. Atheism (in which theism understood as the cognitive apprehension of a being among other beings is included) is prior to theism properly understood. True theism, or in Levinas's terms, the idea of the infinite, as we shall see, arises in the realm of intersubjectivity with the appearance of the other person. It is possible only for separated being as such. Oddly enough this point of view places Levinas within the conspectus of death-of-God theology.[2]

Totality and Exteriority

How is the atheistic self called to responsibility?[3] How is the monadic solidarity of the whole broken? Separated being is the being who inquires, who asks what a thing is. This question already implies that the thing is not what it seems to be. The "something more" that is implied in the question can often be answered in terms of psychology. But no question of quiddity is ever an inquiry such that we ask: Of whom do we inquire? This question is not a psychological question for Levinas but wrenches us free from the domain of psychology (TeI 151–52/TI 177).

The one to whom we address our inquiry is always already presented without ever being understood as a content. We can always discover answers to questions of quiddity even though the answer may not be instantly available. It is, however, impossible to find a satisfactory answer to the question "Who is it?" because the answer to this question lies outside the domain of knowledge. The reply to such a question is always presented as a face and is the answer that precedes every question. What is anterior to the question "Who is it?" is not still another question, not a form of a priori knowledge, but desire: "The *who* correlative to Desire, the *who* to whom the question is put, is in metaphysics, as fundamental and as universal as quiddity, being and the existent and the categories" (TeI 152/TI 177).

It is perfectly true that a reply to the question "Who is it?" can always be given in terms of quiddity, that is, in terms of a person's social role within the totality (it is the French ambassador, etc.), but in that case the genuine intent of the inquiry has been evaded. This question always seeks an absolutely unique individual, a face, as its answer. When we inquire "Who is it?" the answer to the question and the person interrogated are, for Levinas, always identical. The meaning of the sign and the sign that points to it coincide; the face is both sign and meaning. We have already seen that we cannot answer the question "Who is it?" by referring to a person's work; the work is "a manifestation in the absence of being" (TeI 153/TI 178). We may surprise a person through an understanding of his work, unmask him, but then he is merely reduced to a content of the totality. It is only when we have perceived his exteriority that is not the exteriority of things that we have become aware of a human presence beyond ontology.

With the appearance of true exteriority the totality of contentment reveals its phenomenality, its inadequacy with respect to the face of the Other. We do not experience this inadequacy as discontent, for lack of contentment is inherently satiable, and the feeling aroused by exteriority is incommensurable with satiety, irreducible to need. Interiority recognizes its insufficiency not as a limitation within its own sphere of operation but as emanating from an entirely different source. Separated being now acknowledges a double source of lack, the first inherently satiable, the second beyond the reach of all possible satisfaction. Not only are we unable to satisfy the second type of lack, but we are also unable to quash the feeling since its horizons lie altogether beyond the perspectives of satiety. The hunger experienced in the presence of the Other feeds upon itself (TeI 154/TI 179). It is lived as a hunger for the Other that can neither be consummated in pleasure nor bypassed and forgotten:

> Desire does not coincide with an unsatisfied need; it is situated beyond satisfaction and nonsatisfaction. The relationship with the Other, or the idea of the infinite, accomplishes it. Each can live it in the strange desire of the Other that no voluptuosity comes to fulfill, nor close, nor put to sleep. By virtue of this relationship man, withdrawn from the elemental, meditating [*recueilli*] in a home, represents a world to himself. Because of it, because of presence before the face of the Other, man does not permit himself to be deceived by his glorious triumph as a living being, and, unlike

the animal can know the difference between being and phenomenon, can recognize his phenomenality, the penury of his plenitude,
a penury inconvertible into needs which, being beyond plenitude
and void, cannot be gratified. (TeI 154–55/TI 179–80)

What Levinas calls the epiphany of exteriority brings into view the
inadequacy of separated being; it is not an exteriority added on
interiority so that together both form a totality. Each belongs to
a radically different order of existence.[4] Both the sovereignty of
separated being and the relation with the other person are characteristic of human existence.

THE FACE AND THE PROBLEM OF APPEARANCE

The truth of Levinas's contention that the intervention of the
face breaks the hegemony of totalizing forces in human existence
depends upon our acceptance of an absolute distinction between
the way in which the face is apprehended and the way in which
we experience other phenomena within the totality. But, it could
be argued, is not the face given in sense experience just as other
phenomena are given? Is not the face something that we see and
therefore part of the order of representation?

Levinas develops an elaborate and original view of sensuous
intuition that enables us to establish that the real can be apprehended without intermediation of a concept. Once this principle
is confirmed we see that the face too, on an entirely new level,
can also be directly apprehended. We have already learned that
the Husserlian analysis of sensation undermined a purely physiological notion of sensation to which nothing psychological corresponds. The notion that sensation is equivalent to simple free-
floating qualities without anchorage is, for Husserl, an abstrac-   .
tion, for without an object to which the quality relates, the quality
has no meaning as quality. But this critique of sensation is inappli-
cable, as I have already suggested, to experience as enjoyment,
which cannot be interpreted in terms of objectivation. For Levinas enjoyment is inherently a satiety that underlies "all sensations
whose representational content dissolves into their affective content" (TeI 161/TI 187). Indeed, Levinas maintains, the fact that
we are able to distinguish between "representational" and "af-

fective" content in enjoyment shows that the dynamics of enjoyment are quite different from those of perception. We distinguish sight and sound after we have experienced a plethora of sights and sounds in which we "bathe," and in which the individual object is lost. We then live in sensation as in a set of "qualities without support." To some extent this reestablishes the idea of pure sensation prior to the experience of the division into subject and object: "Sensation recovers a 'reality' when we see in it not the subjective counterpart of objective qualities, but an enjoyment 'anterior' to the crystallization of consciousness, I and not-I, into subject and object. This crystallization occurs not as the ultimate finality of enjoyment but as a moment of its becoming, to be interpreted in terms of enjoyment" (TeI 162/TI 188).

Levinas contends that in the domain of enjoyment instead of forcing sensation to function as content, to fill, as it were, a priori forms of objectivity, we must grant it a transcendental function that is sui generis. He is emphatic in this regard:

> A priori formal structures of the not-I are not necessarily structures of objectivity. The specificity of every sensation reduced precisely to that "quality without support or extension" the sensualists sought in it designates a structure not necessarily reducible to the schema of an object endowed with qualities. The senses have a meaning [les sens ont un sens] which is not predetermined as objectification. It is for having neglected in sensibility this function of pure sensibility in the Kantian sense of the term and a whole "transcendental aesthetic" of the "contents" of experience, that we are led to posit the not-I in a univocal sense, to be known as the objectivity of the object. (TeI 162/TI 188)

The result of the tendency to objectify has been to understand objects in visual and tactile terms. We use vision and touch as paradigmatic senses irrespective of the sensation we happen to have in mind. Levinas has consistently sustained the thesis that sensation does not belong to the order of vision insofar as the meaning of sensation is not exhausted by the visible object. Moreover representation itself is not only the simple consequence of looking but of language as well.

What is this looking, this pure seeing apart from representation? Pure seeing presupposes light that remains distinct from the

eye and that which is seen. But Levinas insists that the eye perceives not light itself but objects illumined by the light. Light
makes the thing appear because it disperses shadow; this dispersal
empties space, that is, makes space appear as an emptiness. Touch
is like sight to the extent that the hand traverses the "nothingness" of space to reach its object. But sight, unlike touch, sustains
the object in its nothingness as though the object originated from
this nothingness. Even in the case of touch, the nothingness in
which we find the object situated is palpated by the hand that we
direct through it. The advent of a thing from nothingness in vision and in touch is, according to Levinas, what gives these senses
their primacy in philosophical inquiry. The appearance of things
out of nothingness is the human mode for appropriating origin.

Levinas shows that there are relations in the realm of pure
seeing in which the subject-object relation is subordinated to the
relation of the existent with emptiness (TeI 163–64/TI 189–90).
To understand a particular being is to apprehend it as emerging
from an illumined space that surrounds it but that it does not fill.
Is this space an a priori form of all experience? Can it, in its turn,
be made the object of philosophical inquiry? Illumined space is
in and of itself nothing (although not what could be designated
as an absolute nothing). Yet it is not an object. The emptiness
that is disclosed when light disperses the shadows in space is
something that is there; it is the *il y a*. Light cannot eradicate the
il y a; it merely represents the possibility of forgetting it and of
apprehending objects as though they came from nothingness. We
can look at objects against an emptiness that apes nothingness
and see them as though created ex nihilo. The escape from the
pure horror of the *apeiron,* of the *il y a,* is experienced as enjoyment (TeI 165/TI 191). Levinas is careful to establish the meaning of this emptiness, because it is not across spatial emptiness
that that which is absolutely other, pure exteriority, arises. What
emerges from the emptiness of space is enjoyment and separated
being. Illumined space is not absolute distance but the precondition for relationships sustained within the framework of totality:
"Vision is not a transcendence. It ascribes a signification by the
relation it makes possible. It opens nothing that, beyond the same,
would be absolutely other, that is, in itself. Light conditions the
relations between data [*données*]; it makes possible the significa-

tion of objects that border one another" (TeI 165/TI 191). Vision always implies a horizon against which things are apprehended. It is therefore incapable of encountering a being beyond all being; it is a forgetting with regard to the *il y a*, the unseeable, and is a mode in which contentment within the finite is experienced. Vision needs no recourse to the infinite.

Total alterity presents itself as starting from itself, is given without recourse to form since form conceals rather than reveals. Forms are easily transformed so that what once was the surface of a thing can become its interior. Things have a façade. It is this aspect of objects that is given to us. But the façade guards the secret of things so that we cannot tell what lies behind it. It shines forth but does not deliver the thing itself. That which gives itself in its entirety must renounce the form as the term through which it reveals itself. It must provide an opening into being. The only "given" that fulfills this requirement is the face. Its transcendence cuts through the realm of sense experience. The revelation of the face is not given to us in the mode of sense experience, the mode of seeing, but as language in its authentic sense (TeI 167/ TI 192–93).

We have seen from our previous analyses of need and the elemental that Levinas establishes the possibility of a content that gives itself directly without being clothed in a form. This content, however, is not genuine alterity; on the contrary it most closely approximates a blurring of the boundary between separated being and the elemental. We have also seen that representation is equally incapable of yielding genuine alterity. Our present analysis of sensuous intuition enables us to uncover the source for the illusion of alterity in the operation of representation. Vision is possible because the *il y a* has been dispelled by the light, which in its dispersal of shadows enables us to see objects emerging from emptiness as though born afresh beneath our gaze. The objects seem to be created from nothingness by thematizing consciousness and thus appear to be the products of the structures that intend them. This is the source of their spurious alterity.

THE BREAK WITH ONTOLOGY

If total alterity is neither given in enjoyment nor revealed in the forms of things since things hide beneath their forms, how is the break with totalizing ontology achieved? What is true of the face so that its revelation constitutes a new dimension within the sensible? The face resists our powers to conceptualize it not because the resistance of the face to conceptualization is so great that we cannot overcome it but because the face breaks with the sensible form that appears to contain it by addressing us, by soliciting a relationship with it that cannot be expressed in terms of enjoyment or knowledge.[5]

To say that the face is resistant to conceptualization does not mean that the other person is invulnerable to power but that the nature of the power that we have over him is transformed: we now have the power of life and death over the Other. The face offers the possibility of murder.[6] We are now before a sensible being whose being cannot be neutralized. The Husserlian *epoche* can be effected only if the being of the phenomenon in question can be suspended. The being of the face is such that the negation of its being involves its annihilation. All other forms of destruction, the hunt, the destruction of things, find their *telos* within a framework of utility that reverts to man's activity as work. Only murder is the absolute and total negation of the being of the Other for its own sake (TeI 172–73/TI 198). To kill is to renounce both domination and comprehension. It is still for Levinas the exertion of power, for it is exercised against something sensible, but insofar as the face expresses something outside the sensible, is transcendence, murder is also in that sense powerless (TeI 173–74/TI 199).

The one who is killed is absolutely independent. The phenomenon of separated being is required to establish the possibility of murder, for we can only wish to kill one whom we cannot incorporate into the totality. The interiority of the Other stands in the way of cognition or enjoyment as possible modes for appropriating his subjectivity: "The other is not an object of comprehension first and an interlocutor second. . . . In other words, the comprehension of the other is inseparable from his invocation" (EN 18/ BPW 6). The Other is opposed to us not through the force that he uses to resist us but through the absolute unpredictability of his responses. Force and countervalent force can be measured in terms of the totality. What the Other offers is the transcendence of his being, that can never be totalized.

What we encounter is the infinity of his transcendence; his face is the expression of that infinity. The power of the infinite is stronger than the power of murder. The expression of the Other's face is the commandment "Thou shalt not kill." The infinite paralyzes all power as the infinite resistance to murder, a resistance that we experience in the nakedness of the Other, in his defenselessness. His very destitution is the "opening" of transcendence. The resistance of the Other is the resistance of nonresistance. Against the temptation of murder is posited the infinite resistance of the face (TeI 173/TI 199). As a purely ethical possibility murder is impossible, for if the resistance to murder were not ethical but "real," we would be able to perceive it, and perception would then restore the Other to the realm of the totalizing self. The face would be brought again into the world of objects (TeI 174/TI 199).

For Levinas the "epiphany of the face is the ethical." The relation with the Other may turn into conflict, but such conflict can only arise upon the prior ground of the epiphany of the face.[7] The expression of the face does not convey information about an inner psychological state but is rather an immediate presentation of self. The person is fully present in this self-manifestation. His presence is not only one in which destitution and distress are revealed; it is the revelation of the inequality that subsists between self and others, of the elevation of the Other. The other person always appears as from on high (TeI 174/TI 200).

We cannot refuse to hear the appeal made by the Other, for he arouses our kindness, calls us to responsibility. The link between the expression of the Other and our responsibility to him represents a function of language anterior to every unveiling of being: "It is a question of perceiving the function of language not as subordinate to the *consciousness* that one has of the presence of the other, his neighborliness or our community with him, but rather as the condition of any conscious grasp" (EN 18–19/BPW 6). Language does not serve a thought that precedes it that it somehow "translates" in order to make publicly available the content of our inner lives. Its upsurge is simultaneous with that content. The language of the face is such that it obligates us to enter into discourse (TeI 175/TI 201). The existent who expresses himself is anterior to the being that reveals itself and forms the basis for knowledge.

The event of expression consists in bearing witness and in guaranteeing the witness that it bears. The truth of the face is itself its own truth. All language refers to the face that is its own "word of honor." The one who speaks is the guarantor of what he says even though he may lie or be mistaken. There is no word for which someone is not ultimately responsible, that does not revert to a speaker whose face as such commands (TeI 177/TI 202).

The face that is a manifestation of the Other is nevertheless in Levinas's thought not a denial of the same. It does not vitiate the legitimacy of the same, for if we recall its upsurge, we can see that the same is not the degradation of a more original phenomenon. The call to responsibility does not demand a total upheaval in point of view so that we regard experience within the totality as betrayal of a prior, more original truth. The face of the Other commands, but our recognition of its demands is not the first step of an ascesis that requires a renunciation of life in the world. Such a renunciation is impossible since separated being is rooted in the world in its most basic processes, in its very biological existence. The point is that for Levinas while we are inevitably separated being, we are not *merely* separated being.

It might be argued at this juncture that the radical dualism that Levinas's view of the inequality of self and other establishes—the total alterity of self and other—is unnecessary for the founding of an ethical metaphysics. Why must we reject the world of sensuous intuition, or of cognitive reflection to found a system of values such as those that Levinas derives within his radically dualistic frame of reference? Why could these values not have been primordially given? Had not Husserl and his followers paved the way for asserting that values are just as primordially phenomenal and manifest themselves as a region of being quite as authoritative and self-evident as that of sense experience? I believe that Levinas's originality consists precisely in denying this standpoint; such a view would only distinguish the world of values and the empirical world through their modes of appearing. Both would remain within the realm of ontology as subject to the structure of intentional life. The demand for the radical apodicticity of value that places Levinas in the Kantian tradition can be sustained only by drastically separating the realm of values from the realm of all other experiencing. Yet at the same time Levinas relates values to something found in the world, that is, to a someone who is their guarantor. What appears, the face of the Other, has the form of law, for Levinas tells us that "thou shalt not commit murder" is written on the face of the Other. Yet the authority of the law and its apodicticity lie outside the totalizing structure, do not themselves appear.

Totality *is* structure in Levinas's thought; it can only appear as a series of articulated forms. These forms must be shown to be vulnerable not only in their particularity but as a result of the nature of form as such. Form itself must be demonstrably inadequate to an absolutely certain area of reality that lies beyond it. Yet Levinas is careful to forestall the charge that the face is a *res extensa* behind which something lies hidden, as the physical object in Platonic thought is an imitation of the idea hidden behind it. To appear as the face is to *embody* the law and its authority, which lie outside the totality. The face "speaks" without the intermediation of an image. The form that we see, the physical appearance of the face, is altogether different from the invitation to respond that we experience.

THE IDEA OF THE INFINITE

The face of the Other conveys the idea of the infinite; this idea is the pivotal point of Levinas's ethical metaphysics. Only the idea of the infinite transcends the self that contains it. We have already seen that Levinas sustains the Socratic epistemology as Kierkegaard understands it: we can never learn anything that we do not already know; yet the impasse created by this position is unacceptable. Levinas cannot refute this view by arguing from the standpoint of empiricism that the data of sense experience are other than the consciousness before which they appear since he has already argued that the alterity of the given is undermined because of the totalizing nature of the consciousness that intends it.[8] The empirical world is thus interpreted by Levinas as belonging to totality as if what is given originates with the thinker. On the other hand, Levinas does not argue from the standpoint of an unreflective idealism that the being of the object originates in the mind of the perceiver (*esse est percipi*). What he does maintain is that that which is given is present to consciousness as the given that it is as a result of the meaning bestowed upon it by consciousness. Nothing is the way it is without reference to self.

What are the characteristics of a self that seeks alterity through a route other than empiricism or the ego of idealistic metaphysics? How is this self, the primary phenomenon of identity from which all other relations of identity are derived, first given? We are not ourselves because we identify some aspect of our being, some trait of character, with a preceding trait in order to find ourselves the same as we were before. We are instantly given to ourselves as selves. It is only because we are thus given that we are then able to predicate identity with regard to objects of conciousness. Self-identity is not understood by Levinas as repetition of the self by itself as when we say that "A is A": "The 'A is A' that characterizes the I is an 'A anxious for A,' or an 'A enjoying A,' always an 'A bent over A.' The *outside of me* solicits it in need: the *outside of me* is *for me*. The tautology of ipseity is an egoism" (DEHH 187/TrO 345).

Thematizing consciousness does not identify what we are not with what we know, for consciousness of the object soon ceases to disturb us by its alterity as soon as we bestow a meaning upon it. Every experience, however passive, becomes a "constituting of being" as if what is given originates with the thinker. The existence of the self unfolds as an identity-making process, as the unification of what is diverse.[9] The passage of time and the movement of events do not strip the self of its recognizable character. The self's mode of remaining the same is not characterized by an invulnerability to change but rather by its mode of weaving together different events into a narrative: "The ego [*le moi*], the oneself [*le soi-même*], the ipseity (as it is called in our time), does not remain invariable in the midst of change like a rock assailed by the waves (which is anything but invariable); the ego remains the same by making of disparate and diverse events a history—its history. And that is the original event [*fait*] of the identification of the same, prior to the identity of a rock, and a condition of that identity" (DEHH 166/CPP 48).

The self that is thus held together resorts to what Levinas calls the "neuter" in the understanding of what is not itself. We gain access to the other through that which both is and is not oneself, a principle of mediation between self and other. The singularity of the Other no longer stands over against us. His alterity disappears in the generality of the concept or in the network of relations in which it is enmeshed. It loses its uniqueness in the a priori categories through which it is given. Levinas sees the alterity of the Other victimized in this mode of apprehension. Individuals exist; cognition yields only generalities. The operations of the understanding are in and of themselves tainted with guilt (DEHH 168ff./CPP 50ff.). It is not difficult to detect the biblical origin of the view that the appearance of knowledge portends a loss of innocence.

How can the self for whom all knowledge is guilty, know the Other? In a brief essay on the idea of the infinite Levinas maintains that there is a truth that the self can know that lies beyond the everyday world so vulnerable to the reductive powers of the self. Philosophy itself opens up this inquiry, for it seeks what transcends the everyday. Philosophy properly understood means, according to Levinas, metaphysics, an inquiry into the question of the divine. Levinas does not mean that the object of our inquiry exists because we inquire about it.[10] I believe that what he does intend is this: when we inquire into the truth we want more than the results of our inquiry, for these results can be expressed in categories only already familiar to us. The very notion of truth affords us at least a possible relation with a reality distinct from ourselves. This does not yet mean that this reality exists. Levinas's philosophy is a quest for heteronomy, but the other will not be found to be analytically contained in our idea of it (DEHH 165/ CPP 47). Levinas does not reinstate the ontological argument. Rather we will find the other whom we seek in the sphere of intersubjectivity. But the alterity we find will always exceed the idea we can have of it.

It is the formal structure of the Cartesian analysis of the idea of the infinite that provides Levinas with the means for a break with ontology. He argues that for Descartes the self who thinks maintains a relation with the infinite. This relation is not one of that which contains to the content contained since it is impossible for the self to contain the infinite (DEHH 171/CPP 53–54). The content is not attached to or united with the containing since for the infinite to be what it is, infinite, it must be separated from the self. It differs radically from other objects of consciousness in that the "ideatum" exceeds any idea we can have of it. Consciousness that intends the infinite differs from all other intentional structures insofar as it intends more than it can encompass; indeed, it intends precisely what cannot be encompassed: the infinite. The alterity of the infinite is never canceled since there is not thought adequate to think it. The infinite is not grasped by the idea of the infinite since it is necessarily beyond the grasp of thought. The self in thinking the infinite "thinks more than it thinks." The fact that the infinite transcends the self who thinks it is the sign of its infinity (DEHH 172/CPP 54).

The idea of the infinite is, in Levinas's view, placed in us; it does not arise from any structure of the self (DEHH 172/CPP 54).[11] It is experience in the most radical sense since we can never bring to it a structure of intentionality adequate to it. It is therefore a genuine relation with what is other than ourselves. We cannot reintegrate its alterity into the same. The thinker who has an idea of the infinite goes beyond himself, exceeds himself, is more than himself.

How can we prevent ourselves from abandoning our selfhood to what is greater than us? Was not the philosophy of the same a struggle against a reintegration of the self into being? Radical experience, that is, the idea of the infinite, emerges in social relations. In our relation to the Other we are addressed by a being who is absolutely exterior to our own. The infinity of this Other assures us of his exteriority. The exteriority of the infinite is attested as an opposition to our powers, which we experience at the appearance of the face of the Other. We do not experience the face as form but as an absolute negation of our powers. Levinas is aware that we may enter into relationships with others based upon power, chicanery, deception, and physical violence. But if we do so, then the face has not appeared as face; we have not discovered the Other in his alterity. We have then not experienced the nudity of the Other's look, the primary phenomenon upon which all other forms of shame are based. True exteriority lies in the look that prohibits appropriation and conquest not as a result of a lack of power, but because our powers are paralyzed before the appeal of the Other's defenselessness. We abandon the will to power; we will not will. What resists us is nonresistance, an "ethical resistance." The face is that which appears before us as unmediated; it is an epiphany, a direct and true presentation of the nonself (DEHH 173/CPP 55).

We experience the Other as being closer to God than we ourselves, as being above us. His proximity to God confers upon him rights that we do not have with regard to our own conduct. Desire is the mode in which we experience the Other, in which we think the infinity of the infinite. It is distinguished both from eros and need; it is beyond all satisfaction.[12] The reason for the insatiability of desire is that it expresses a lack in that which lacks nothing, in being itself. The myth of Poros and Penia, the parents of eros, in Plato's *Symposium* 203bc expresses this idea, for there, in the need of each for the other, we find wealth that is still indigent and the poverty of fulfillment. The desire for the other does not express a lack as when we feel an emptiness that can be filled, for such desire is experienced by a completely independent being who is already fulfilled: "It is the lack in a being which *is* completely, and lacks nothing" (DEHH 174–75/CPP 57). The relation with the other does not make us happy; it puts the self into question, empties the self of itself. It calls upon all of the resources of the self, which we have no right to withhold from others. The desideratum does not fulfill an appetite but calls forth our generosity. It fulfills only in the sense in which it increases our hunger by adding new hungers to it (DEHH 193/TrO 351).

The face of the Other reveals the injustice of the totality and of all the phenomena that derive from human freedom. One's own freedom is ashamed of itself before the Other, for it has discovered in itself the possibility of murder and usurpation. It discovers itself as injustice. Moral consciousness is always dissatisfied with itself; this is not the overzealous scrupulosity of the neurotic but belongs to the very meaning of moral consciousness.

Ultimately, Levinas argues, there is a being such that its being cannot be represented. The significance of such a being cannot be its being brought to light because its being is always in excess of what can be represented. It is a being that exceeds its appearance, an infinite goodness that belongs to the Other by virtue of his alterity and is inherent in the ethical order. Levinas does not deny that there is an intentional structure that can be brought into clarity with regard to our relations with others, but he depicts that intentionality as a structure that always falls short of itself. This intentionality intends more than the given can fulfill. Consciousness that intends radical exteriority in the etymological sense is metaphysics, beyond process, beyond nature, beyond the possibility of appearing. Levinas writes: "If . . . ethical relations are to lead transcendence to its terminus, this is because the essential of ethics is in its *transcendent intention* and because not every transcendent intention has the noesis-noema structure. Already *of itself* ethics is an 'optics' " (TeI xvii/TI 29).

It might be argued that it is strange for Levinas to speak of ethics as an optics when he so clearly rejects the visual model as appropriate for relations whose meaning lies outside the realm of appearances. What he means, I believe, is this: the ethical relation that is commanded in the epiphany of the Other is not a preliminary to a theoretical exercise. It is in and of itself a command to action without intervening theoretical structures. It breaks down the distinction between theory and practice. Action no longer rests upon illuminating knowledge, upon preliminary reflection. Now, Levinas maintains, both theory and practice can be understood as (TeI xvii/TI 29) "modes of metaphysical transcendence."

Levinas maintains that the relation with the Other that is preceded by neither representation nor comprehension can be termed "invocation" or "prayer." The essence of such invocation is *religio,* but *religio* of a very special order, for it arises, as in the case of Kant, within the framework of ethical relations: "If the word *religion* should, however, announce that the relation with human beings, irreducible to comprehension, is itself thereby distanced from the exercise of power, whereas it rejoins the Infinite in human faces, then we accept the ethical resonance of that word and all its Kantian echoes" (EN 20/BPW 8).

METAPHYSICS AND JUSTICE

We have seen that metaphysics is the aspiration for radical alterity that cannot be thought, yet we also know that theoretical thought is the form that metaphysics has traditionally taken. What then unites metaphysics to *theoria?* Both metaphysics and *theoria* allow the being of the Other to be; they leave the being encountered unscathed. But in the case of *theoria* the alterity of the being that appears is lost. The being that is encountered does not present itself as a limit to consciousness. The being that is known is deprived of its alterity, as we have seen, through the intermediation of a neutral term that is not itself a being. The force of the collision between the same and the other is mitigated through the intervention of this mediate neutrality, which appears as the concept that is thought (TeI 14/TI 44). The neutral term can also appear as sensation, in which affect and quality are confused, or it can appear as being when we distinguish being from existence, a being that *is not* since it is not given as an existent (TeI 13/TI 42). The realm of intelligibility is one of neutral terms lacking the "thickness" of existence. This realm belongs properly to ontology, which deprives the Other of his alterity by reducing it to the same.

Metaphysics is a critique of the *logos* of being, a critique of ontology. It puts into question the freedom that is the mode of existence of intelligence. The critique that metaphysics launches against ontology lies outside the realm of ontology itself. It cannot be a theoretical attack since the standpoint of such an attack would itself belong to the same. The same cannot be put into question from the point of view of the same. This can only be done by the Other. In fact, Levinas defines ethics as the putting into question of the same by the Other; the strangeness of the Other puts everything that we are into question. This putting into question undermines ontology: that is, metaphysics takes precedence over ontology (TeI 18/TI 47–48).

We are confronted in this analysis with a puzzle that concerns the meaning of the neuter itself. What sense does it make to introduce "the neuter," a mediatory theoretical structure, when it could be argued that the notion of intentionality alone is sufficient to account for the reduction of alterity to the same? I would suggest that Levinas's emphasis upon the freedom of consciousness leads him to see in consciousness an activity and spontaneity far more radical than what is implicit in Husserl's original analysis of intentionality. Thus for Levinas, what consciousness does in its usual operations—that is, without the artificial intervention of the Husserlian reduction—is to "bracket" the otherness of the not-self. The Other is neutralized from the moment he becomes theme or object; that is, existence or particularity is neutralized. The clarity with which another emerges before us is the result of making inoperative two factors, the first that the Other is not one-self, the second that the Other limits the self. There is thus an automatic spontaneous operation of consciousness to deactivate existence so that existence becomes a mere shadow of itself. It is only across this neutralized existence, across a neutered particularity, that cognition can take place. How is this accomplished? As we have seen, to illumine the Other is to make him appear as though against the ground of empty space, as though the Other had been created ex nihilo by thematizing consciousness.

The phenomenological approach to the Other continues the tradition of ontology by substituting the idea of a horizon for that of the "concept" in classical idealism. The existent wells up against a backdrop that extends beyond him. Against an illumined horizon, as though from nothing, he appears not as a face but as dark faceless figure silhouetted against a bright ground.

Metaphysics reverses the self-aggrandizing structure that prevails in the ontological realm. Power, the destroyer of the Other, becomes vis-à-vis the face of the Other the reverse of what it was: it becomes the impossibility for murder; that is, it becomes justice. The situation in which the Other maintains his alterity is the upsurge of authentic language. Levinas maintains that such discourse is not prephilosophical. The ethical relation is the fulfillment of rationality, for we do not stop asking questions; but in every question that we ask concerning the being of the Other, the authority of the Other as existent is already assumed. Such questions do not ask about the Other but interrogate the being of the Other himself (TeI 18/TI 47). The understanding of being cannot dominate the relation with other persons since we cannot wrench ourselves free from the society of others in order subsequently to consider the being of the existent before us. The presence of the Other precedes our comprehension of him. The Other becomes an interlocutor whose alterity puts our own being into question.

It is critical for an understanding of Levinas's thought to realize that the Other is always posited as the poor and the stranger. It is in and through our relation with the Other thus understood that our relation with the divine begins. There can be no relation with God apart from the relation with men. Levinas cannot emphasize sufficiently the social origin of the human encounter with God: "The dimension of the divine opens forth from [*à partir de*] the human face. A relation with the Transcendent free from all captivation by the Transcendent is a social relation. It is there that the Transcendent, infinitely other, solicits us and appeals to us" (TeI 50/TI 78).[13] The nearness of the other person, of the one next to us, is a decisive moment of revelation in being. His epiphany is an appeal; it solicits because it is destitute, without recourse. Its appeal compels without the intermediation of a tertiary principle, of a concept or a relation apart from himself and from us. The modality of the Other's presence is conceived by Levinas in biblical terms: the Other is "the stranger, the widow, the orphan."

The relation with the absolute through the alterity of the Other means for Levinas that we are not violated by it as in pagan or mythic religious consciousness. Only when we are separated from the sacred, when it appears as the dimension of height, is it possible for us to look at the infinite, as Levinas terms it, "without burning our eyes." The absolute is purged of sacred violence; it does not captivate, it speaks. The absolute no longer gives itself in its mythic dimension, as that which we cannot address; it is no longer the numinous. The self who addresses it is not transported outside himself; he remains a separated self. The metaphysical relation, the idea of the infinite, ties us to the holy without sacralizing the self through participation in a *numinosum*. It is important to note that Levinas disengages the absolute to whom we relate from the God of positive religions, for no particular positive religion is yet disengaged from mythic participation. For Levinas the idea of the infinite *is* "the dawn of a humanity without myths" (TeI 50/TI 77). Indeed, the atheism with which the metaphysician begins signifies that his relation to metaphysics is an "ethical behavior" rather than a theological construction.

The only access we can have to God, an access that remains direct but nonparticipatory, is the face-to-face relationship with other persons. Such a relationship is justice. Ethics, as we have seen, is an "optics," a direct unmediated relationship. The direct relation with the Other whom we cannot kill is justice. Justice is the sine qua non for the rupture with totality:

The work of justice—the uprightness of the face-to-face—is necessary in order that the breach that leads to God be produced [se produise]—and "vision" here coincides with this work of justice. Hence metaphysics is enacted where the social relation is enacted—in our relations with men. There can be no "knowledge" of God separated from the relationship with men. The other person is the very locus of metaphysical truth, and is indispensable for my relation with God. He does not play the role of a mediator. The other person is not the incarnation of God, but precisely by his face, in which he is disincarnate, is the manifestation of the height in which God is revealed. (TeI 51/TI 78–79)

It is important to note that for Levinas the face is not incarnation but its very opposite. The face carries spiritual weight, is the bearer of values and of human personality. It is thus possible for Levinas to use the term "face" as nearly synonymous with such terms as "meaning," or "teaching," or "justice."

Having established the primacy of the interpersonal realm where the face of the Other speaks in the imperative mode as the realm where the divine appears, I believe we must ask: Is God for Levinas more than the excess of goodness that emerges in ethical relations? Is God identical with the alterity of other persons? The answer to these questions leads directly to an investigation of the problem of justice in Levinas's thought and to an excursus of some length before we can return to the original question. In "The Ego and Totality," an essay that appears somewhat earlier than Totality and Infinity, Levinas develops a phenomenology of guilt, innocence, and pardon (EN 30–34/CPP 29–33). We can only be guilty or innocent with respect to another, either a person or a principle that transcends the self. Guilt or innocence presupposes a free being who can suffer the consequences for an injury that he has inflicted upon another. The possibility of retributive justice, the fact that we can suffer as the result of a wrong inflicted upon another, makes our separation from the totality incomplete. But when we relate to a transcendent God we overcome the incompleteness of our separation from the totality because we are guilty or innocent not in the eyes of an aggrieved party but in God's eyes alone; that is, we maintain our character as separated being, for guilt is not then conferred retributively by the Other within the totality. We remain in relation to both God and the Other as separated being.

Levinas asks if it might not be argued that we do not need God's forgiveness at all, that we can simply be forgiven by the Other. Would not this position in fact be closer to his own? This question is critical, for Levinas's negative answer provides the foundation for his critique of theologies of love rather than justice and his separation from such thinkers as Martin Buber, to whose work he is clearly indebted.[14] Levinas concedes that when the injured party has suffered the full weight of an infraction committed against him, forgiveness of the wrongdoer remains at the disposal of the injured party. But, Levinas maintains, the conditions of pardon can be legitimately realized only in a society of intimates where the injured party, and he alone, has suffered. This is a society in which the third person is excluded. A third person troubles the intimacy of the society in which genuine pardon is possible. Our transgression against another is thrown out of kilter—falsified, as it were—by the Other's relation with a third, a relation that may well be unknown to us. Since we cannot calculate the Other's relation to the third, that third may be injured by our receiving pardon. It is not difficult to design a simple hypothetical case: suppose that we steal bread from someone in time of famine, thereby inflicting a serious loss upon the victim of the theft. We may seek the victim's pardon, which he may be willing to grant. In addition we may even make restitution. But suppose the victim in turn has stolen the bread from a third party. No amends that we make with regard to the victim from whom we have stolen can compensate the original owner. Moreover we have immensely complicated the network of guilt, for example, by facilitating further theft. While the example may be trivial, it establishes a point of some importance. Human society is not a society of two. It is a complex network of persons and relations so that the consequences of the acts of any individual always to some extent go beyond what he has intended. In the intimate society we can receive absolution in dialogue. Pardon is still possible: the will can be freed from the weight of its acts. In a true society this is no longer possible. The act means something that we do not mean. We bear the guilt for initiating a chain of circumstances that no longer reflect our intentions. Our guilt has transcended the order where pardon is possible (EN 32/CPP 30–31).[15] A society that attempts to found itself on love has simply transferred a form appropriate to the intimate society to one in which intimacy has been superseded.

The meaning of love lies in the existence of lover and beloved as though they were alone in the world. The relation of love is therefore not the beginning but the end of society. It is a relation in which an "I" is satisfied by a "thou." Each justifies his being in the other. The presence of the Other, Levinas contends, "exhausts the content" of the intimate society. The relation of lovers cannot be universalized. Any attempt to include others, to universalize, is experienced as an infidelity to the primary relation. That relation, Levinas claims, is "the love of one to the detriment of the other." Contemporary religious thought that founds social relations upon love misunderstands the nature of social reality. With regard to the third, the society of love itself is wrong. The central crisis of religion, man's relation to God, is not exempt from this critique. One cannot, for Levinas, forget those who remain outside the loving relationship, even when one relates to God.

It now becomes possible to return to the initial question that instigated this inquiry into Levinas's view of justice. Is God more than what is present when others are present? How is the presence of God related to the problem of justice in society? Our analyses lead us to see that God is for Levinas the fixed point outside of society from which justice comes, that God is not a mere personification of moral consciousness. Rather, God is the necessary condition for justice, the interlocutor of the totality and all the relations that subsist within it. The mode of being of the being who puts the totality into question is being as a face. That is why the Absolute is a person. God is (EN 34/CPP 33) the "mediator between man and man." The morality that God sustains moves on a different plane from that of supernatural salvation. God is thus not identical with the conditions of his upsurge, the realm of intersubjectivity. Levinas's position is difficult, for neither does God stand apart from the upsurge of the Other, nor is He identical with what transpires in social relations.

But the existence of the third man, which we have just seen inaugurates the very principle of justice, is itself dialectical; it makes possible divine justice and the being of totality. The second possibility arises because the relationship with the third man compromises the irreplaceable singularity of the individual in the society of intimacy, for fault can no longer be examined by the scrutiny of conscience. We can no longer measure the injury we have inflicted upon the Other by measuring our own intentions precisely because once they are released into a pluralized world, a world of more than two, the consequence of our actions may exceed these intentions. Thus when justice is born through the presence of the third man interiority loses all importance. We are forced to play roles in a drama authored by others; no one is any longer equal to himself, coincides with himself in a relation of identity. The face is no longer interiority; it has become a mask. The "I" has been demolished. Once the "I" is lost, thought does not begin anywhere, for the *cogito* has lost its value as a foundation. Since there is now no person whom we address, discourse takes place without an interlocutor. The realm of impersonal reason now governs all relations. Man is in the process of making history (EN 38/CPP 35); he is his works. This is the meaning of totality. The society of intimacy that is structured as injustice is broken with the appearance of the third man, but at the same time the appearance of the third has given birth to totality. This totality must be transcended. How do we recover the self again as singularity? The consciousness of justice arises when the discourse of totality is broken by the intervention of the face as interlocutor, which must appear outside of totality, outside of history. In totality, which is constituted by violence and corruption, the human task becomes a quest for justice, an acceding to the command of the face. The difficulty of simultaneously attesting the upsurge of the divine in social relations while maintaining that the divine is a fixed point of reference making possible the judgment of totality gives rise, in my view, to Levinas's subsequent development of the notion of trace, a way of attesting divine presence within the totality as coming from beyond totality and as that which gives to the face its power and quality. Levinas's later thought moves further and further from the autonomy of Kantian ethics.

NOTES

1. For Levinas it is not capitalism that alienates. In a departure from classical Marxism, he attributes the tyranny that Marx reserves for capitalist economy to *all* economic life.

2. At DEHH 188/TrO 346 Levinas writes: "The God of the philosophers, from Aristotle to Leibniz, by way of the God of the scholastics, is a god adequate to reason, a comprehended god who could not trouble the autonomy of consciousness, which finds itself again in all of its adventures, returning home to itself like Ulysses, who through all his peregrinations is only on the way to his native island." In an even more radical statement at HAH 40/BPW 47, Levinas maintains that the loss of unitary meaning in our time is proclaimed as the death of God. The God thus dethroned, he claims, intervened in human history by force, thus placing himself in a series of economic exchanges and thereby uniting a presumably transcendent being to the world through economy.

3. In the early writings (e.g. TA/TO) Levinas prefers the term "alterity" to "exteriority," but TI is subtitled "An Essay in Exteriority." According to Derrida ("Violence et métaphysique: Essai sur la pensée d'Emmanuel Levinas," in L'écriture et la différence (Paris: Seuil, 1967), 65; translated by Alan Bass in "Violence and Metaphysics: An Essay on the Thought of Emmanuel Levinas," in Writing and Difference [Chicago: University of Chicago Press, 1978], 112), Levinas is compelled to accede to the demands of the only language we have, that of totality, and therefore uses the spatial metaphor interdicted in the earlier work.

4. In "Transcendance et hauteur," Bulletin de la Société Française de Philosophie 56 (1962), Levinas maintains that the putting into question of the self coincides with the nonallergic presence of the Other. To be "allergic" is to make oneself impervious to, to resist, to repel the Other as one would an irritant. Not only are the natural foundations and assurance of the self undermined, but consciousness becomes inadequate to what it wishes to contain. This essay has been translated as "Transcendence and Height" in BPW 11–31.

5. Jean Martin, "Une philosophie nouvelle devant l'athéisme contemporain," Revue Diocésaine de Tournai 19 (1964): 227, writes that to enter into relation is to renounce one's own hegemony, "to fulfill a genuine transcendence (in the etymological sense of the word, scandere trans, to go 'across,' leave oneself, go towards the other)."

6. In a discussion following the reading of "Transcendence et hauteur" (BPW 24), M. Filliozat remarks that Levinas's principle of nonviolence is reminiscent of the political nonviolence of Gandhi, but that for Levinas the nonviolence originates through affirming the reality of the other and negating the egoity of the self. For Gandhi, who derives the principle from traditional Indian sources, both self and other are equally fictitious.

7. Martin, "Une philosophie nouvelle," 228, writes that the ultimate meaning of the relation between the self and the other is not an allergy

in the etymological sense: an exercise of power (*ergon*) by the other (*allos*). It is a nonallergic relation in which the Other does not affect us as the one whom we must overcome, must encompass, but as the one who wells up absolutely.

8. According to Derrida ("Violence et métaphysique," 224; "Violence and Metaphysics," 151), Levinas's insistence upon radical heteronomy, the attempt to maintain alterity at all costs, denotes, despite Levinas's disclaimers, an underlying empiricism. Derrida writes: "The profundity of the empiricist intention must be recognized beneath the naïveté of certain of its historical expressions. It is the *dream* of a purely *heterological* thought at its source."

9. This recurrent theme in Levinas's work can be traced to Franz Rosenzweig's insistence that the history of philosophy is identical with the history of philosophical idealism, that the philosopher reduces God, the world and man to a single principle, identifies all things with one thing. For Rosenzweig's view, see an essay by Alexander Altmann in *Judaism Despite Christianity: The "Letters on Christianity and Judaism" Between Eugen Rosenstock-Huessy and Franz Rosenzweig*, ed. Eugen Rosenstock-Huessy, trans. Dorothy Emmet (Birmingham: University of Alabama Press, 1969), 26–48.

10. Levinas writes in DEHH 177/CPP 58–59 that the idea of the infinite is not a proof of the other's existence because it precedes the possibility of proof. He claims that "proof already presupposes the movement and adherence of a free will, a certainty." The face-to-face relation in which freedom is put into question as injustice precedes all certainty or uncertainty.

11. Levinas speaks of the production of the infinite. At TeI xiv–xv/TI 26, he points out that the verb *se produire* is used to speak of the coming-to-pass of an event and the development of an argument. This ambiguity is reflected in the following: "The idea of the infinite is not an incidental notion forged by a subjectivity to reflect the case of an entity encountering on the outside nothing that limits it, overflowing every limit, and thereby infinite. The coming-to-be [*la production*] of the infinite entity is inseparable from the idea of the infinite, for it is precisely in the disproportion between the idea of the infinite and the infinite of which it is the idea that this exceeding of limits comes to be [*se produit*]. The idea of the infinite is the mode of being, the *infinition*, of the infinite. The infinite does not first exist, and *then* reveal itself. Its infinition comes to be [*se produit*] as revelation, as a positing of its idea in *me*" (translation slightly modified).

12. Derrida, "Violence et métaphysique," 138 ("Violence and Metaphysics," 93), writes that the movement of desire is paradoxical, for de-

sire is what it is only in renouncing its object. The notion is parallel to that of faith in Kierkegaard's *Fear and Trembling*.

13. J. Plat, in "De mens en de oneindige ander bij Emmanuel Levinas," *Tijdschrift voor Filosophie* 26 (1964): 457–99, points out that since for Levinas transcendence does not overwhelm us but rather solicits and entreats, the usual relation as it is understood between man and the transcendent is reversed. Man is powerful and transcendence is now weak. Man is necessarily moral and responsible in the light of this appeal. Plat writes: "At bottom, according to M. Levinas, creation amounts to a kind of election: the transcendent in its poverty and suffering is revealed to individual man in calling him forth, in invoking his goodness. By means of this call he is created as responsible and moral."

14. For Levinas, Buber's I-Thou relation is one in which selfhood derives from the saying of the Thou. Selfhood depends upon the other. Thus the relation to the Thou does not differ from that to any other entity in the world, for the absolute alterity of the Thou has been lost. The formal meeting is achieved in the framework of an intersubjective symmetry. Levinas contends that if he criticizes Buber for extending the I-Thou relation to things, then it is not because Buber is an animist with respect to relations with the physical universe, but "because he is too much the artist in his relations with men" ("Martin Buber et la théorie de la connaissance," in *Noms propres* [Montpellier: Fata Morgana, 1976], 41; translated by Michael B. Smith as "Martin Buber and the Theory of Knowledge," in *Proper Names* [Stanford: Stanford University Press, 1997], 33).

15. Levinas follows Rosenzweig's view that every human deed is liable to become sinful after it enters history, for once trapped in historical existence, every act is caught up in the nexus of cause and effect and is removed from the control of the doer. For Rosenzweig's view, see *Judaism Despite Christianity*, 29.

V

Beyond Temporality

THE BREAK with the time of totality is experienced in the encounter with phenomena impervious to cognitive modes of apprehension, blind spots beyond the field of cognition. In these phenomena something remains extrinsic to self; an alterity persists that cannot be reduced to the same. The self-evidence of these phenomena is unimpeachable, yet they cannot be incorporated into an established frame of reference or interiorized through subsumption under universal categories. The break with cognitive experience that the upsurge of these realities represents is apparent not only in positive moral experience but also in the darker ranges of existence. Levinas, while deviating from Heidegger's analysis of these darker areas, remains faithful to Heidegger in emphasizing their importance. Being-toward-death for Levinas, as for Heidegger, is a fundamental mode of existence and absolutely resistant to cognitive modes of apprehension. In this chapter I shall try to bring to light two species of phenomena that infiltrate and undercut the temporal structure of totality. One is negative: being-toward-death, war, economy. The other is positive: patience, love, finality, fraternity. The latter not only breaks with the time of totality but also introduces an eschatological dimension into the historical order.

The intervention of eschatological processes in history not only wrests man from the depersonalizing effects of totality, but also puts into question the ultimacy of the dark forces that break in upon the comparative security of totality. In uncovering these phenomena, Levinas makes plain the antimoral alternatives to genuine alterity, for while the Other founds morality, he can also be a hostile will. In these phenomena, Levinas shows the Janus face of the face, for while it stays the hand from murder, the domain of primordially destructive possibilities is opened when we resist it. Let us first direct our attention to the negative phenomena that transcend totalization.

VIOLENCE AND TIME

Totality as such can never be the object of reflection, because there is no point of view that we can take with regard to totality. This is true not because the reflecting subject is finite, but because a "surplus," an excess, is implied in intersubjective relations. Social relations are not one among many types of relations that are brought into being but, in Levinas's terms, the ultimate event of being: "Multiplicity therefore implies an objectivity posited in the impossibility of total reflection, in the impossibility of conjoining the I and not-I in a whole. This impossibility is not negative—which would be still to posit it by reference to the idea of truth contemplated. It results from the surplus of the epiphany of the other who rises above me from his height" (TeI 196/TI 221). The social derives its authentic multiplicity from the imperviousness of the Other to conceptualization.

Pluralism established in this way does not leave its terms isolated or out of touch with one another. They are engaged in the negative activities of exchange and war. Levinas emphasizes that these activities already presuppose the face and the possibility of transcending ontology. This means that the phenomenon of war does not arise out of the sheer multiplicity of beings who live side by side and thus inevitably constitute limitations for one another, like the collision of atoms that maintain their identity and reciprocally define one another. For if a limit serves to define a term, it serves as a common term for that which it defines and that which it excludes. A limit therefore unites what it has separated. Fragmented reality in which the parts reciprocally limit one another form a totality because each part implies the part that it excludes. War is, however, the refusal of individuals to belong to a totality; it is a refusal of limit. Each one affirms his transcendence of totality by identifying himself through himself and not via his position in the totality. War is not the outcome of a play of forces, for such an outcome is calculable. Supreme self-confidence and absolute risk rather than logistic science characterize war. Nor is war a refusal of separated beings to relate to one another, for in war we seek out our opponents. Violence is possible only against a being who simultaneously can be grasped yet who eludes all grasp (TeI 199/TI 223).

A being who can oppose others is both independent of them and engaged in relation. Indeed, to be at one and the same time independent of the Other and yet vulnerable to seizure is, for Levinas, what it means to be a temporal being. Against the inevitable violence of death we insert a time that is our time. This personal dimension of time, our time, is a postponement of the violence of death. All life is a "not yet" balanced against death. In war this "not yet" that is impending becomes a present reality: "Time is precisely the fact that the whole existence of the mortal being—exposed to violence—is not being for death, but the 'not yet' which is a way of being against death, a retreat before death at the very heart of its inexorable approach. In war death is brought to what is moving back, to what *for the moment* exists completely" (TeI 199/TI 224). We have seen that freedom is the willingness to begin; now we can understand the assumption of beginning as a postponement of death. It is necessity detained and held back as finite freedom (TeI 200/TI 224).

War cannot be understood as force alone. It requires the delivery of a death blow against an adroit adversary, skillful in marshaling strategies to parry the blow, and who, in turn, seeks us out. Skill in war postpones the inevitable, keeps death at bay. The arsenal deployed in this task includes trickery and ambush; the expertise of war is expressed in the way in which the body itself lives as dexterity. War can only occur where language has appeared, for it already intends a human presence, which, as we have seen, is infinite despite its appearance within the phenomenal realm. In Levinas's view, war always intends a face.

The outcome of war cannot be foreseen precisely because the subjectivity of the Other cannot be calculated. This incalculability is the meaning of his transcendence. Once we recognize that violence is directed at that which is exterior to totality, at transcendence, a very important inference regarding the nature of freedom can be made: freedom itself is manifest only outside totality. If we conceive of freedom as belonging within totality, we reduce it to a mere indeterminacy in being. In that case, we see freedom as " 'holes' of indetermination" (TeI 201/TI 225) that can be enclosed by the totality.

In economy, the world in which exchange is effected, as well as in war, separated being both loses and regains the freedom of its separation. While Levinas assumes that work establishes the feeling of being at home with oneself, nevertheless, in accordance with his Marxist frame of reference, the worker's subjectivity disappears while the commodity or the wage persists.[1] Yet we are exposed through work to the Other.

The understanding of the transposability of human effort into things is first lived as corporeality, for the body is itself the first step in a process of successive alienations. This step is experienced as separation from the elemental. The same will that decreed the original separation from the elemental is nevertheless the will that delivers man to the power of others through work. The will that is the guarantor of interiority is also the means through which we are delivered to the other. Work itself transcends its intention; it rises up against its producer as fate, as an alien will. We are unable to predict the consequences of what we do, for work becomes an independent entity in the world. This transcendence of intention by work in the production of entities whose meaning is no longer defined by the producer establishes the original way in which interiority is traduced. We now can define the unknown as the meaning that will be ascribed to our work by another and that we cannot predict (TeI 202/TI226–27). Our powers may exceed or fall short of their initial thrust (*élan*); this will depend on the consequences of that power in the world of things. Unlike the face that is its expression, that attests presence in its very upsurge, work is a sign of presence in absence. We are exposed through work to misunderstanding.

The only way in which individuals can take on historical significance is through the cumulative effect of their works. While we are alive the meaning bestowed upon our works can be corrected, but this revision is the most that can be hoped for in the domain of history.[2] This task is undertaken by an interiority of which, as we have seen, there can be no history. "Wills without works will constitute no history" (TeI 203/TI 227), writes Levinas. The interesting consequence that flows from this point of view, a standpoint that regards history as appearing only in the concrete productions of individual wills, is that all history is necessarily economic history. The will that produces a work is frozen, congealed in the work itself, a work that obscures the intentional structure that produced it. The living voice that can defend itself against the alienation of history is missing in history itself. History is a world of completed works, a legacy of "dead wills" (TeI 203/TI 228). The survivor can even bestow upon our work a meaning directly contrary to our intentions. For Levinas, this is what is meant by destiny: the use to which works are put by the will of the survivor. Levinas calls this historical process "historiography," a recounting of the way in which survivors appropriate the works of dead wills. In his view, historiography is a profound amnesia with regard to the lives that gave birth to these works and that attempt to protect them from misinterpretation by alien wills.

There is a more primordial possibility through which the other seizes the result of one's will. The way in which will finds itself in the world is not as disembodied but as incarnate will. The body is thus the first betrayal of will, for will is inseparable from incarnation. Body is more than an object, more than what is deployed in our voluntary acts. Subjectivity itself can be injured through the mistreatment of body. Violence not only offends subjectivity, but bends the will, forces us to do what we do not wish to do. To live as body is to maintain simultaneously two distinct points of view with regard to ourselves, an awareness of body as an object in the world of objects and of ourselves as existents who delay the moment of death (TeI 205/TI 229). Thus, the phenomenality of will for Levinas remains incomplete if its vulnerability is understood as merely the possible usurpation of its products; it must also and primarily be understood as incarnate will, will subject to force.

Hegel had considered the vulnerability of incarnate will in his analysis of the trial by death and had foreclosed the possibility of completely independent self-consciousness. The trial by death fails to achieve such independence because the struggle obliterates the consciousness of the loser and leaves the sovereignty of the surviving will unacknowledged. Even if both wills survive the struggle, the victor fails to achieve independence since sovereign consciousness requires recognition by the vanquished. For Hegel, the vanquished also fails to achieve independent self-consciousness because he depends on the master for his freedom.[3] Levinas, in an interesting analysis, raises a new possibility by undercutting the notion that the trial by death is necessarily a conflict of unalterably opposed wills. Levinas argues that it may be true that we are willing to die in the trial by death, but that this willingness may coincide with the Other's deepest wish. Thus, to stake one's life on a point of view in no way guarantees the defeat of the Other's aims. The incalculability of the Other's subjectivity can defeat what we consider to be the expression of our own freedom. Levinas deviates from a strictly Hegelian analysis in his insistence that the aims of the Other cannot be understood in the same way as the givens of a problem, which can then be translated into our own thoughts. The aims of the Other are inherently unthinkable. He is infinite and must be recognized as such; this recognition is not produced as thought but as morality (TeI 207/TI 230). It is at this point that Levinas's analysis transcends the framework of Hegelian dialectic, for he insists that the Other cannot be swallowed up by reason.

This inextinguishable alterity founds the faithfulness of will to itself. We have seen that will betrays itself in war and in economy, that it is ensnared in totality through its very nature as incarnate will. But will can also distance itself from its productions, from its history as inscribed in its work. This act of self-scrutiny cannot itself be made the subject of historical investigation, since the interiority of will remains nonphenomenal. The function of the interiority of will is never to inscribe itself as history but to judge history. It would therefore seem that after careful phenomenological analysis of the will's appearance as work and as war that Levinas reverts to a classical Kantian position with all its attendant difficulties. Moral man belongs to two worlds, to both the natural and the moral order. The will of man as a natural being is the ground of human action within the phenomenal realm. But the will of man as a moral being is the altogether different foundation upon which moral life is built and that remains impervious to investigation.[4] In Levinas's view, the function of the interiority of will is to submit its own activities to judgment, to make what it wants coincide with the judgment of what it wants. This is, in fact, the subjugation of inclination to will, the attempt to make what the will wants coincide with the judgment of what it wants, and lies well within the Kantian frame of reference. Kant writes: "Natural inclinations, *considered in themselves*, are *good*, that is, not a matter of reproach, and it is not only futile to want to extirpate them but to do so would also be harmful and blameworthy. Rather let them be tamed and instead of clashing with one an-

other let them be brought into harmony."[5] For Levinas as for
Kant the will can be faithful to itself: "The interiority [*intériorité*]
of the will posits itself subject to a jurisdiction [*juridiction*] which
scrutinizes its intentions, before which the meaning of its being
coincides totally with its inner will. The volitions of the will do not
weigh on it, and from the jurisdiction to which it opens comes
pardon, the power to efface, to absolve, to undo history. The will
thus moves between its betrayal and its fidelity which simultaneously describe the very originality of its power" (TeI 207/TI 231).
The judgment to which the will submits enables it to undo its
history, to request pardon, but the power to pardon comes not
from the will itself but from the other person. Thus, for Levinas
the faithfulness of the will must be legitimated by the Other. This
fidelity of the will is identified by Levinas as religious consciousness.

BEING-TOWARD-DEATH

Levinas's analysis of death is directed against Heidegger's view
that death is Dasein's "possibility, which is one's ownmost, which
is nonrelational, and which is not to be outstripped."[6] Dasein can
only die for itself: "No one can take the other's dying away from
him."[7] Dasein dies in isolation. There is no surpassing death for
Dasein, since beyond death Dasein is no more (*nicht mehr Dasein*).
Death "is the possibility of the absolute impossibility of Dasein."[8]
Death is Dasein's potential negation of itself; it belongs to Dasein
as its ownmost possibility. The nonbeing of its own finitude gives
rise to Dasein's anxiety. Knowing that it will die, Dasein never
knows when death will come. The end of Dasein threatens its
existence as it is anxious before the "possible impossibility of its
existence."[9] Dasein's major concern is its own finitude. Heidegger writes: "Anticipation reveals to Dasein its lostness in the they-
self, and brings it face-to-face with the possibility of being itself,
primarily unsupported by concernful solicitude, but of being itself, rather, in an impassioned freedom toward death—a freedom
which has been released from the illusions of the 'they,' and
which is factical, certain of itself, and anxious."[10]
Levinas's analysis of death is a rejection of the Heideggerian

view in its very foundations. For Levinas the profound isolation of death is a misunderstanding of its true nature. Levinas places death itself in the sphere of intersubjectivity. The traditional view of death, according to Levinas, understands death as a passing into a novel realm of existence. But for Levinas death can be understood only in the light of the primordial phenomenon of murder. Murder intends the becoming nothing, the annihilation, of its victim. The Other as face is, as we have seen, the one we cannot kill. Levinas's analysis can be envisaged as showing that murder is the negation of the negation: the face itself is the command "thou shall not commit murder" and murder itself the negation of that negative commandment. Death in his view is not a mere passing into nothing, for the passing into nothing is derived from our experience of the death of the Other as his disappearance from the empirical realm.

But the relation to our own death places us outside of the alternatives of being and nothing. Nor can we deduce the meaning of our own death from our experience of the death of others. The sense that we have of our own death derives from the terror that we feel for our very being, for our existence as such. We experience death as a threat when we acknowledge its imminence, its ineluctable approach (TeI 209/TI 233). Terror before death comes not from any specific moment of the future but from the very unpredictability of the final moment.[11] We cannot foresee our own death, not because there are certain facts that at present are unavailable to us to which we theoretically have access, but because death as such cannot be grasped by intelligence. In death we are seized without the possibility of retaliating against our attackers. We are in Levinas's terms exposed to "absolute violence, to murder in the night" (TeI 210/TI 233). What is crucial to Levinas's point of view is that the hour of death seems fixed by "alien powers" who are hostile and malevolent as well as wiser than we. This attitude is amply attested in the traditional Jewish sources that Levinas always bears in mind in his phenomenological analyses.[12]

Levinas does not deny the solitude of death in the sense that no other can die for us, yet the Other affirms his presence as a hostile consciousness, as an inimical presence.[13] Death never presents itself as something natural but always seems to come, as it does for primitive consciousness, from elsewhere. In Levinas's view we do not die in isolation as Heidegger maintains, but vis-à-vis an enemy, a powerful other who remains invisible but of whose enmity we are constantly aware and who intends us as its victims:

> Death threatens me from beyond. This unknown that frightens, the silence of the infinite spaces which terrify, comes from the other and this alterity, precisely as absolute, strikes me in an evil design or in a judgment of justice. The solitude of death does not make the other person vanish, but remains in a consciousness of hostility, and consequently still renders possible an appeal to the other person, to his friendship and to his healing. The physician is an a priori principle of human mortality. Death approaches in the fear of someone, and hopes in someone. "The Eternal brings death and brings life." (TeI 210/TI 234)

In our being-toward-death we stand not before nothingness but over and against an opponent. The onslaught of death is experienced as the relation to another. We feel as though our own will is alienated by another. Death for Levinas does not subvert the interpersonal order. The analysis of death cannot therefore be an analysis of the deprivation of meaning. An alien will at the heart of our own, an experience of the Other, belongs to the most fundamental experience of the personal order in our anticipation of death.

Death signifies not the end of will, since it is an event over which will has no control, but the ultimate violence, the final alienation of will. The will whose sovereignty death puts into question by subjecting the works that it leaves behind to historical judgment itself seeks judgment; it seeks the truth about itself in order to free itself from its alienation. But judgment means to be placed in relation to the infinite. The will therefore cannot judge itself but must submit itself to the judgment of the Other.

The will as freedom, that is, the will that must be submitted to judgment, belongs not merely to consciousness. Indeed, Hegel's analysis of freedom has shown that freedom that belongs to consciousness is empty freedom only. For Levinas, as for Hegel, a good will in and of itself is not a genuine will. In this sense the Kantian analysis of will does not suffice, for the will cannot remain paralyzed, empty subjectivity, in Levinas's thought. The will subject to judgment (the will judged) is an active will that deploys specific means for its concrete realization. We dare not, according to Levinas, mistake the pronouncement of God's universality in consciousness for the completed work of history while society tears itself apart: "Interiority cannot replace universality. Freedom is not realized outside of social and political institutions, which open to it the access to fresh air required for its expansion, its respiration, and even, perhaps, its spontaneous generation" (TeI 218/TI 241).

Only institutionalization can provide the guarantees of freedom; Levinas points out that the Ten Commandments were engraved upon tablets of stone. Institutions may hover perilously between destruction and continuity, but they represent the only authentic mode for the preservation of human freedom. History, Levinas claims, is not eschatology. Will must become objective, find its truth through what it builds, that is, through political institutions and technology. In the interstitial time between birth and death freedom is entrusted to institutions (TeI 219/TI 242). Levinas disavows the Kantian split that I have suggested exists between the noumenality of the practical reason and the phenomenality of life. But does this disclaimer suffice? For Hegel, who does not place history under any judgment save the judgment that it carries out upon itself, the rupture with Kant is believable, for the concrete reality of the historical moment is its meaning. For Levinas, however, as I tried to show in the preceding analysis, a will that submits itself to an ultimate alterity that cannot be incorporated into reason or into history, a judgment that tries to bring the activities of will into correlation with a law not governed by causal principles, remains something nonphenomenal. It would seem that the defense of institutions must ultimately rest upon the moral principles upon which they are founded, and that these moral principles belong to a realm quite apart from the institutions themselves. We are left, in my view, with a puzzle: how can the moral self to which all of our activities are referred for judgment remain available as a separate realm of phenomenological investigation if it is exhausted by the lived realities of acts and institutions?

Levinas acknowledges that the universal order that judges us, the order of institutions, fails to take into account the uniqueness of that individual. We are present to institutions only in the third person. Our first-person singularity lies outside the totality: we are absent from our own trial. How can the voice of interiority be heard? The "I" that is absent from institutions appears phenomenologically as "apology" (TeI 220/TI 242). This situation is complicated by the fact that the "I" that apologizes is in an inherently weak position. It is a guilty "I." It therefore lays itself open to death, by which Levinas does not mean the physical demise of the person but the death of itself as will.[14] In order to maintain itself as will, the "I" must transcend itself as apology; it can do so only by willing its own judgment. It is not physical death but passivity that threatens the active will.

How can subjectivity be preserved in this critical situation? In order that subjectivity not disappear, judgment must be executed against a will that can defend itself, that can be present at its own trial, that despite its existence as apology cannot be swallowed up by the totality. Subjectivity must overcome the world as totality, that is, the world of the visible, of the evident, where history is enacted. What Levinas has attempted to show in constructing this carefully detailed phenomenology of judgment is not that history ought to be judged, but that it in fact is judged by that which lies outside of it. He has attempted to establish through a descriptive analysis of will the necessity before which history finds itself, a necessity arising from the being of will and the being of history as such. It might be objected that the sphere of history and the sphere of will cannot both constitute licit objects of phenomenological investigation: the former is suitable for such inquiry, but the latter is somehow subjective, somehow illusory. Levinas rejects this point of view. He maintains throughout his work that subjectivity is not something distinct from an event: "In raising this question we are not implying the existence of a real sphere opposed to inner life, which would eventually [*éventuellement*] be inconsistent and illusory. We seek to present inner life not as an epiphenomenon and an appearance, but as the *event* of being. . . . The power for illusion is not a simple aberration of thought but a game [*jeu*] in being itself" (TeI 217/TI 240).

Despite the fact that it is contradictory to say that the invisible "appears," Levinas maintains that, paradoxically, the invisible does indeed do so. It appears as that which remains impervious to vision, not as a temporary aberration in being or something unexpressed that will later come to light. The invisible is for Levinas an "offense" (TeI 225/TI 247). It is the necessary consequence of the judgment of history; for no matter how reasonable, the judgment of history is inevitably cruel. Even when inserted into totality, the invisible wounds subjectivity, for anything whatever that is incorporated into totality offends subjectivity. Apology can appear in totality only as rational discourse. There must be a judgment that originates beyond history, a divine judgment that cannot be totalized. We have already seen how the necessity of divine judgment arises from an examination of differing types of societies, that is, of the intimate society and of existent societies. Now Levinas arrives at the principle of divine judgment beginning from an analysis of subjectivity itself, an analysis of will. Subjectivity depends upon its invisibility, yet that which is invisible within totality is visible to God, who sees without being seen (TeI 225/TI 247).

The offense that subjectivity experiences is its "cry," its protest against being engulfed by history. But subjectivity becomes more than a cry, it becomes judgment itself. Levinas overturns the Kierkegaardian dictum that the subject can never be incorporated into history by maintaining that it is the subjectivity of the Other that never is systematized in history. Judgment has become the accusation that is reflected through the Other's subjectivity. The upsurge of human weakness in the world expressed in the face means the interdiction of murder. The will is under the judgment of God, according to Levinas, when its fear of death is inverted into fear of committing murder (TeI 222/TI 244). This aspect of Levinas's work makes clear that not only is a phenomenology of divine judgment possible, but that it is already well founded, for it consists in bringing to light the phenomenon of willing and the necessity for breaking the egoistic structures of will through the intervention of the Other.

Now the singularity suppressed by the judgment of history can be expressed but not as apology, as the defense of self. For subjectivity under divine judgment is subjectivity transfigured. The judgment itself creates the will's infinite sense of responsibility. Divine judgment is not lax; it does not permit the will to speak as egoity. The voice of subjectivity is now subjectivity's awareness of itself as responsible subjectivity. The self that speaks is a responsible self; it acknowledges itself as guilty. With the accretion of responsibility the affirmation of rights diminishes. In one of the crucial passages of *Totality and Infinity* Levinas writes:

> The exaltation of singularity in judgment comes to pass [*se produit*] precisely in the infinite responsibility of the will to which the judgment gives rise. Judgment is pronounced upon me in the measure that it summons me to respond. Truth occurs [*se fait*] in this response to a summons. The summons exalts singularity precisely because it is addressed to an infinite responsibility. *The infinity of responsibility denotes not its actual immensity, but a responsibility increasing in the measured that it is assumed;* duties become greater exactly in the measure that they are accomplished. The better I accomplish my duty the fewer rights I have; the more I am just the more guilty I am. (TeI 222/TI 244; translation modified)

Personality becomes, in Levinas's view, a point in being where responsibility is concentrated. The separated self of enjoyment, as we have seen, is a self that lives with itself as center. The uniqueness that makes a moral self to be a self under the judgment of God is an emptying of power exerted on its own behalf. The "I" understood in this radically new way cannot coincide with the self of history. The "bad faith"[15] of the self would consist in various attempts to sublate moral personality in the interest of the enjoying self. The true nature of justice is revealed when subjectivity understands itself as responsibility, for only now can we understand that justice transcends the universal, that justice in order to be what it is must go beyond the letter of the law insofar as the law represents universality. The letter of the law alone is seen to be inadequate and the intervention of subjectivity necessary in order for there to be justice. We find that we are indispensable to the work of justice. To be a self is, according to Levinas, "a privilege or an election"; it is to find a place outside of the universal, to be simultaneously a moral personality and beyond the law. Truth is neither in the tyranny of history nor in the subjective. Truth *is* only if a subjectivity is "called to speak it." The "call to infinite responsibility" attests subjectivity not as "merely subjective" in a pejorative sense (which in any case has ontological weight) but as belonging to being itself. To say "I" in this connection means to affirm one's own irreducibility as a self, as a privileged center of responsibility: "The accomplishment of the I qua I and morality constitute one sole and same process of being; morality comes to birth not in equality, but in the fact that infinite exigencies—those of serving the poor, the stranger, the widow and the orphan—converge at one point of the universe" (TeI 223/TI 245).

History can neither vindicate nor undercut the inner life delivered to risk. There is a disparity between events in the world and their underlying meaning. History itself must be judged. The danger of supposing a meaning beyond history underlying the apparent flow of events that could be designated as their "substance" lies in supposing that there is more to events than meets the eye. With deep roots in the phenomenological tradition of Husserl, Levinas insists that to place oneself beyond the verdict of history, "to submit to the judgment of truth," is not to presume that there is a second history underlying the first. To live under the judgment of God is to remain in the world of history, for there is no other. But while remaining in history, we must "exalt subjectivity" (TeI 224/TI 246).

THE PHENOMENOLOGY OF LOVE

We have seen that the metaphysical event of transcendence is fulfilled in the encounter with the Other who cannot be reduced to the same, that is, in language and in desire. Can there still be a significant place reserved for the erotic in a metaphysical framework where the Other is the foundation of our resistance to violence, where hospitality is the appropriate response in a life world shared by self and other? Levinas reserves a special role for love, which goes further than language yet cannot go as far. The transcendence of discourse (the *logos* of the world that appears) is linked to love. Love has a definite advantage over knowledge insofar as the object of love is usually a person, yet its intentional structure is in one crucial respect the same as that of knowledge. In love we seek to be reunited with an object to which we have already been bound prior to love itself. Levinas writes: "The adventure par excellence is also a predestination, a choice of what has not been chosen." Love, when it relates to persons, is in its very nature incestuous; it seeks what is kindred to it, a sister soul. The myth of Aristophanes in Plato's *Symposium* 189d–191d reflects a profound understanding of this aspect of the erotic, for love is the power that reunites two separate halves of a single being. Levinas situates the phenomenon of love at a border, at the furthest edge of immanence between the immanent and the transcendent. The phenomenology of enjoyment has prepared the way for an understanding of love. It may be recalled that in enjoyment the self is satisfied when its needs are filled; the enjoying self lives an endless cycle of want and replenishment, emptiness and satiety. Love, insofar as it is a relationship with other persons, is a desire; nevertheless, it finds its satiety as need. Yet this need is aimed at what is unincorporable, at that which can never become part of the same, the other person, the beloved (TeI 232/TI 254). Love is the unique phenomenon in which the Other appears as the object of need while still remaining fully other. In love, one is both within and beyond the limits of discourse; it offers not the disjunction of opposing phenomena desire and need, but their coexistence. It is at one and the same time "lust and transcendence," and the utterable and the unutterable. It is as phenomenon "the equivocal par excellence" (TeI 233/TI 255).

If love is need in its quest for satiety it is also desire in the care and concern it brings for the well-being of the Other. The intentionality of love seeks the Other in the Other's weakness; the lover fears for the Other, brings aid to the beloved, assumes the weakness of the Other. Weakness appears as the feminine, which is the way that vulnerability is lived. The helplessness of the beloved is not a quality superimposed upon an asexual being: it is what makes the beloved to be what she is. To be the beloved is to be fragile and vulnerable. The world is always too gross and too cruel for the beloved (TeI 233/TI 256).

Yet the fragility of the beloved is belied by the crudity of the world of love, its outrageous grossness and materiality. The materiality of the amorous belongs not to the nonhuman realm, the world of inanimate nature, but to body itself, to the materiality of human flesh. What is essentially hidden emerges into the light. But what comes forward fails to become signification. Love belongs to a nocturnal realm that is not interiority since it is shared by another. It is immodesty par excellence, yet it always reserves something clandestine that is not revealed to the world beyond the loving pair. What it keeps hidden belongs to love as such and is not something that can be revealed in the world of appearance at some future time. The phenomenon of love is an appearing of the equivocal (TeI 234/TI 257).

The ambiguity of love is grounded in the phenomenon of profanation, the violation of that which is secret. The pathos of love lies in the impossibility of surmounting what ought to remain secret, of overcoming the nudity of the body; it is immodesty against a background of modesty. The body always presents itself as an illicit revelation. Levinas refrains from psychoanalytic explanations of modesty that would reduce modesty to repression, to the consequence of coercive inhibitions imposed by civilization upon a suffering libido.[16] Instead he interprets modesty as an absolutely primordial expression of corporeality in the erotic.

Femininity itself is the simultaneous presentation of the Other as weighed down in materiality, that is, as belonging to the world of appearance yet at the same time as fully other. This double role constitutes the ambiguity of the feminine; both human and infrahuman, the feminine is poised between the immanential sphere of need and the sphere of genuine transcendence (DL61/ DF37). For Levinas, the lovers' comportment toward the feminine will reveal itself, now as a stance toward the exteriority of woman, now as a stance toward one who dwells in the world as belonging to the natural order. The ambiguity of love is also expressed in the secondary phenomena that derive from it. The caress, for example, both is and is not sensibility. The transcendence of the caress consists not in the seizure of what lies beyond sense experience as though it were possible to grasp transcendence while retaining the intentionality of sense experience. The caress is, rather, the attempt to seize that which in its very nature eludes all form: the subjectivity of the Other. The caress seeks something with which the lover can never coincide, for what is sought slips from his hand. It is as though the object of the caress had not yet come into being (*"comme s'il n'était pas encore"*; TeI 235/TI 257–58).

The intentionality of the caress is not that of sense experience, for it does not seek to uncover what is hidden. On the contrary, it is a quest for the invisible in its very invisibility. The caress fails to bring into the open what it really intends to reveal: "In a certain sense it *expresses* love but suffers from an inability to tell it. It is hungry for this very expression, in an unremitting increase of hunger. It thus goes further than to its end [*terme*], it aims beyond an existent however future, which, precisely as an *existent,* knocks already at the gates of being" (TeI 235/TI 258). Levinas rejects the notion that the caress is a struggle, for in that case the attempt to dominate would be the foundation of the caress. It would derive from the world of freedom, which, as we have seen, is a structure of the self as egoity. But the caress seeks something beyond the future; it does not seek the possible in the sense that we might seek for something whose existence can be predicted. The caress seeks what is inherently not subject to grasp, the flesh. The flesh is for Levinas not to be confused with the body, which is the proper object for physiological investigation or to be used by its owner as a source of power. Nor is it the body as expression. While the body "loses its status as existent" in the caress the form of the body slips away to become erotic nudity, something quite different from expression (TeI 236/TI 258).

The beloved is neither thing nor face; she is essentially virginal. The eternal feminine is for Levinas an eternal return to virginity. The feminine as an object can be violated but as subjectivity remains inviolate. The encounter with femininity must be distinguished from the struggle of lordship and bondage; it represents an ever renewed assault upon a bastion that cannot be scaled. The feminine is easily bruised, fragile, belongs phenomenologically beyond ontology. The virgin transcends erotic anticipation, for she retreats into a future where she cannot be followed. She is both known and unknown, the incarnation of mystery. In an early essay Levinas had written: "Eros in all its ontological purity . . . does not require participation in a third term (tastes, common interests, a connaturality of souls)—but direct relationship with what gives itself in withholding itself, with the other *qua* other, with mystery."[17] The phenomenon of the feminine reintroduces and completes the phenomenology of night that begins in the anonymity of the *il y a* and terminates with the mystery of the feminine, for beyond the night of insomnia as we saw it developed in the early work, beyond hiddenness, the erotic belongs in its very nature to the same order of human existence (TeI 236/TI 258–59).

The body as flesh belongs to the world of power, of being able, of manipulation and productivity. It is no longer related to a future. In love there is no fulfillment in achieving, for the love temporalizes itself as a not yet that lies outside the range of the possible. The secret that love elicits is never illumined as in the case of sense experience. The caress moves not toward clarity and revelation of the beloved, but toward compassion for the suffering, for the fleeting nature of love. Love suffers, yet its suffering becomes happiness through the sensual pleasure that is voluptuosity. Levinas views sensual pleasure not as the fulfillment of desire, but as desire itself. Pleasure is not impatient to be fulfilled, as though impatience were one of its accidental attributes; pleasure lives as impatience. Pleasure is astonished at its terminus, for as impatience it expects never to come to an end (TeI 237/TI 259).

Insofar as it is rooted in the world of being, pleasure makes the hidden appear, but the hidden appears as hidden. It does not step forth into clarity; the mode of its appearing is profanation, for it violates the hidden. Its discoveries are made at the expense of body, which wishes to remain hidden, at the price of exposing the body as flesh. The mode of revelation of body is modesty. Thus, contrary to the intentionality of sense experience, love does not scrutinize what it brings to light; it averts its gaze, lowers its eyelids in shame: "Erotic nudity says the inexpressible, but the inexpressible is not separated from this saying in the way a mysterious object foreign to expression is separated from a clear speech that seeks to circumscribe it. The mode of 'saying' [*dire*] or of 'manifesting' itself hides while uncovering, says and silences the inexpressible, harasses and provokes. The 'saying,' and not only the said [*le dit*], is equivocal" (TeI 237/TI 260). The equivocacy of pleasure hovers between speech and its abandonment. What is expressed in the face of the feminine is the refusal to express. Expression is transformed into immodesty.

It is important to point out that for Levinas the eroticism of the face is not anterior to its upsurge as expression. The sense of violation, of reproach that the erotic evokes, is possible only because the phenomenon of the face precedes it. The face does not disappear in the erotic, it becomes nonsignifying, and this is so only because of a prior signification. The notion of violation pre-supposes the face.

The very equivocacy of the feminine face gives rise to feminine beauty, for ethical significance maintains itself at the edge of its erotic promise. The feminine abandons its status as person, relin-quishes responsibility, becomes a child again. The relation with the Other as person is no longer characterized by the asymmetry in which the Other is elevated by weakness, helplessness, and suf-fering so that we are commanded by the Other. On the contrary, an asymmetry persists but is reversed. The Other becomes a play-thing: "one plays with the other as with a young animal" (TeI 241/TI 263).

Levinas's intention is not to divide humanity so that one sex retains human status while the other fades into the infrahuman, which is neither expression nor reason. His effort is directed not to reducing the human status of women, but to separating the feminine element from the pure humanity of women in order to bring to light the meaning of the erotic. Woman can be "interloc-utor" and teacher; but in her feminine role she is disingenuous, elusive, seductive, and dangerous. The failure is not hers but be-longs to the infraethical status of the erotic itself. Levinas is not interested in the subtle interplay between subjectivities as it is elaborately developed in the work of Sartre with its rich possibili-ties for suffering and bad faith. Although it is clear that the nature of the feminine as such bears the seed for the destruction of the relation to the Other as language, the metapsychological analysis that characterizes Sartre's pessimistic view of human relations is absent. The reason for this lack lies in the *telos* of the erotic itself, which for Levinas is directly related to the eschatological possibil-ity of history. Eros is not a hopeless impasse of subjectivities trapped in one another's gaze but a redemptive engagement in history. We have already seen that this redemptive work cannot arise within the limited sphere of the loving pair, for intimacy, the society of two, inhibits the possibility of justice. Indeed, all erotic love becomes self-love for Levinas, since it is loving the other's love of oneself. But in Levinas's view there is a transcendence possible in erotic love, a transformation of self through love in the birth of a child.

THE PHENOMENON OF TRANSCENDENCE

How can we be said to transcend ourselves in the birth of a child? What is the foundation of human transcendence as such? Levinas maintains that if a subject persists through its transcending, it has failed to transcend itself; it has merely changed one or several of its essential properties. If transcendence effects a genuine change in the subject the latter is no longer identifiable as such and has been demolished as subject. For Levinas a genuine understanding of the problem of transcendence must begin with the problem set for Western thought at its inception, the problem of the unity of being and the one; from the time of its inception, being as being has been understood as the one (TeI 252/TI 275). While a plurality of subjects is acknowledged, genuine multiplicity vanishes before thought, which lends a synthetic unity to multiple appearances in the world. No scissiparity lurks at the heart of the being of the existent; it gives itself to a subject who thinks it yet who remains safely ensconced in being outside the domain of subjectivity itself. Whereas quantity is considered an unimportant metaphysical category, transcendence can be understood only as "a 'simple relation' . . . outside the event of being" (TeI 251/TI 274). The multiple is before consciousness, an event that is merely subjective.

The philosophy of becoming is an attempt to break with the view that being is monadic. It does so by representing existence as temporal; that which truly is is no longer the permanent, the stable, underlying any given succession of appearances. The future is not homogeneous with past and present but is projected not only as thought or knowledge but as the very mode in which the existent is. He is openness to the future or being-toward-death. It is through a novel conception of possibility that the separation of being and the one becomes apparent. Possibility is no longer seen as that which appears in thought as preceding the completed act, as an afterthought, lifeless and overshadowed by the final act itself. Rather, possibility is seen as belonging to the dynamics of the act itself. But for Levinas this conception does not go far enough; possibility is merely projected by the subject and cannot serve as the foundation for genuine multiplicity. Thus, understood, it turns into power, into domination without providing a sound basis for genuine novelty. Our possibles are our projects, the organization of exteriority in terms of our private ends, always reverting to ourselves as the ones who bestow upon exteriority its ultimate meaning.

The major problem in founding transcendence lies in maintaining the integrity of the self while allowing the self to surpass itself. Sheer egoity cannot go beyond power and knowledge while remaining itself. Is it possible to understand the subject in some other way? The erotic subject fulfills these conditions. It could of course be argued that erotic relations could be subsumed under social relations. Such reduction is to misunderstand the uniqueness of the erotic. Those who consider sexual relations as belonging properly to the biological sphere fail to understand that the biological urge operates between persons, that it presupposes a specific duality of persons in its fulfillment. Nor is the Freudian account satisfactory, for it seeks to explain the phenomenon of Eros in terms of the quest for pleasure. Freud's misunderstanding lies in his failure to perceive that sexuality does not begin with the self but with the Other (TeI 253/TI 276). In a brief postwar essay Levinas writes: "The categories of separated sexuality, of psychology and biology where they have been lodged until now are the categories of a pluralistic ontology, of a plurality which does not merely count beings, but which constitutes it as event. The elaboration of these categories irreducible to those of light appear to us a philosophy of transcendence."[18] Sexuality, neither pleasure nor power, founds the multiplicity of human existence.

FECUNDITY

There is a transcendence that is, in Levinas's terms, a "transubstantiation" of the erotic, a transformation of self through love in the birth of the child whose being derives from the union of the loving pair. The self becomes other through the child. In the son the father finds both himself and another. The son is the father and yet remains estranged from him. The child is not one's own in the sense that work is one's own, for the child is not an effect of which one's own power is the cause. Nor is the child a project of the self as the imaginative creations of an artist who projects the limits of his work in toto into a future directed by his own creative powers. One's project is a transformation of the world through a new conception of it. But the advent of the child is an encounter with the Other. The future that we try to grasp in erotic love, the "not yet" that lies outside the world of possibles, is the future of the child. Levinas calls "fecundity" the relation with the future inaugurated in erotic love and consummated in the birth of the child (TeI 245/TI 267). One does not remain within the child as a substance underlying changes in form that would remain residually beneath each transformation. Yet the future of the son is one's own future despite the fact that father and son are not the same persons.

For Levinas erotic love, itself an epiphenomenon neither fully transcendent nor fully immanent, opens a new dimension of temporality. The relation with the child puts one into relation with an "absolute future" or "infinite time." The child is not a mere repetition of the self. The possibility of repetition cancels the alterity of the Other, whereas in fecundity the Other's alterity is fully maintained. The infinite time opened through progeny is not a promise of eternal life. History is, instead, punctuated with the reappearance of the very young, with an upsurge of infinite time (TeI 246/TI 268).

The world of history is transcended not by being thrown back into anonymity, the world of the *il y a,* but by being hurtled forward beyond knowledge, history, and egoity. For Levinas the transcendence of ontology is inherent in the self's function as origin. We have seen that to be the self as egoity is to be able to begin. Through fecundity one becomes the origin of the son who belongs to the world of being and history. We thus persist in the world within ontology yet not as substance, for progeny is also totally other. The modus vivendi of our persistence in being through progeny is as origin, as the commencement of a self who is the self and yet not the self (TeI 246/TI 268–69).

The phenomenon of fecundity is critical for Levinas's thought. In fecundity a phenomenon is brought to light in which the natural and historical orders converge so that human continuity is guaranteed through a fully human relationship with the Other, which is nevertheless brought to fruition as a natural process. It provides a basis for questioning the sacrality of the mystical power of chaos. In procreation we guarantee the continuity of the world, not merely as world but as our own world against the terror of the elemental. Moreover, fecundity is the phenomenon whose upsurge guarantees alterity, for it remains impossible without a self and another. It is in its very foundation antimonistic; it undercuts the philosophical tradition from Parmenides to Hegel, which understands being as one. For Levinas being is produced as "multiple" through the scissiparity of the Other. Being is already social, for it is not one but many. For Levinas, to be many is for being to temporalize itself, for only the one dwells in eternity. Philosophy is merely a moment of this temporalization. But the Other to whom discourse is addressed can never be seized, reduced to the same. Something exceeds our grasp and remains recalcitrant to discursive structure:

> Transcendence is time and goes unto the other person. But the other person is not an end [*terme*]: he does not stop the movement of Desire. The other that Desire desires is still desire; transcendence transcends towards him who transcends—this is the true adventure of paternity, of the transubstantiation which permits going beyond the simple renewal of the possible in the inevitable senescence of the subject. . . . Fecundity engendering fecundity accomplishes goodness: above and beyond the sacrifice which imposes a gift, the gift of the power of the gift [*du don*], the conception of the child. (TeI 247/TI 269)

In the relation between father and son, being is both infinite and discontinuous. The past is not lost, for it is reassumed by every new generation. The son reverts to the past, depends on it, for as a child he is sustained by it through the protective person of the father. Yet the child's relation to the past is not undialectical, for he attests not just continuity with the past but, through his ipseity, a revolt from it. Every son is united to the father while remaining outside of him. Every son is unique, not in the sense of being one in number, but in the sense that the father bestows upon the son the son's ipseity. The selfhood of the son begins not in enjoyment but in election. Paternal love means to love the Other as unique: "The paternal Eros first invests the unicity of the son—his I qua filial commences not in enjoyment but in election. He is unique for himself because he is unique for his father.

That is precisely why, as a child, he cannot exist 'on his own.' "
(TeI 256/TI 279). The son exists as unique in the world but as
one among his peers. He is elect in a society of equals. In fraternity both election and equality are fulfilled, for election is interpreted not as the right of mastery over another but as a
subservience to the Other, as a demand for responsibility. The
Other appears as "solidary" with all the others, as constituting
the social order.

TEMPORALITY AND INFINITY

It is through the consummation of erotic life within the structure
of the family that the self of power and domination is called to
responsibility. The self does not disappear; rather it is promised,
called forth to goodness, to the infinite that lies beyond the self
and without which goodness would be merely subjective. To be
for the infinite means to be "without limits." The existence of the
il y a is the very reverse of an existence without limits, for it is a
being that is as infinite limitation. The subject arises as other, as
beginning, against the *il y a*, which is the absolutely undetermined. According to Levinas, such absolute indetermination is an
incessant negation, for it is to be such that its being negates the
possibility of the coming into being of any specific existent; indeed, it is prior to possibility itself (TeI 257/TI 281). Being for
infinity is produced by a being who can distance himself from
being while still remaining within its confines. This act of distancing is, as we have seen, produced as time and consciousness. The
upsurge of time and consciousness arises through an "elementary
gesture of being which refuses totalization." This refusal to total-
ize is lived as the recognition of the face of the Other, the face
that resists totalization and as such conditions the life of consciousness. Being for infinity is limited not by death, which as the
not yet is posited as a simple diminution of the life remaining to
the subject, as a closing in on the subject by shortening the distance that he must still traverse. Being for infinity is threatened
instead by the very nature of egoity, of the self as power, for in the
exercise of power the self always returns to itself. Its actualization
is the senescence of the self. Thus, it is clear that for Levinas being

for infinity is not the infinite drawing out of the thread of life so that the "not yet," which is one's life over and against the death that awaits it, becomes a postponement to infinity. Rather, a new dimension of temporality is introduced that cuts into the world of totality, resists its mode of temporalization while the self remains within that mode.

This mode of temporality is not lived as a recovery of possibles. The work of Levinas is not a work *à la recherche du temps perdu* since the quest for the past can only recover lost worlds of fantasy but can never restore lost possibles. Such an attempt is a mere evasion of responsible existence. The self is confronted with a genuine future, a future beyond his own destiny, a destiny other than his own. This is the meaning of fecundity. Despite the inevitability of death, existence can be extended through the existence of progeny.

Absolute youth is an absolutely new beginning made possible by the temporality of fecundity. This possibility of beginning again is a victory over the time of totality, becoming and senescence. It consummates the work of time. It is lived as pardon. What first comes to mind in the phenomenon of pardon is its connection to moral failure, to transgression. Levinas's analysis brings to light not merely what is instantly apparent in pardon but its underlying process of temporalization. Pardon inverts the natural order of time. Through pardon time is no longer irreversible, for pardon functions retroactively. It refers to a moment in the past as though that moment had not occurred. It is not a simple forgetting that cannot touch the actuality of past events; pardon "acts on the past." It repeats and purifies a past event, does not cut the subject off from his past as does forgetfulness, but carries the past into the present as the purified past. The one who is pardoned is not innocent. But in pardon there is an excess of goodness that makes reconciliation possible. The phenomenon of pardon enables us to recover the genuine meaning of time, not as a flowing of homogeneous moments indifferent to one another, but as "spreading" from Other to self. According to Levinas time is not simply the unfolding of that which already lies dormant in the first cause of a series. Time adds an absolutely new dimension to being. It is no longer merely "the intelligible dispersion of being." It is the perennial repetition of new beginnings. It is the possibility of breaking with the ultimacy of continuous time and in breaking, maintaining what has been broken (TeI 259/TI 282–83).

The phenomenon of fecundity has been shown to liberate the future from egoity. The future is no longer a time swarming with possibilities that merely emanate from ourselves as our own projects. Beyond all horizons the future now harbors a new birth of the Other, one's own being for the infinite. The past has been freed from its burden of irrevocability through the phenomenon of pardon. The past, says Levinas, is like a drama in which succeeding acts undo the earlier. Fecundity and pardon together are inseparable phenomena, since it is only through unborn generations that the past time can find its redemption. We have seen that death itself is for Levinas not the end of being but an unknown, alien, and hostile presence. But lived time is for Levinas time that dies and is born again. Time is noncontinuous; it is full of breaks. In the production of the interval, a dead time when the old moment dies and the new moment is not yet born, the individual is freed from his egoity (TeI 260/TI 284). It is only through fecundity that time is possible as a new birth. Levinas does not reject the notion of fulfilled time, which is the messianic dimension of temporality. Yet he distinguishes between the perpetuity of renewal and messianic time or eternity. This notion of eternity differs from infinite time in that evil cannot reenter the temporal sphere. But this notion is merely suggested rather than developed in Levinas's philosophical work. He writes at the end of *Totality and Infinity:* "Is this eternity a new structure of time, or an extreme vigilance of messianic consciousness? The problem exceeds the bounds of this book" (TeI 261/TI 285).

NOTES

1. In relation to the division of labor, Karl Marx, *German Ideology* (Moscow: Progress Publishers, 1964), 82, writes: "The productive forces appear as a world for themselves, and divorced from the individuals, alongside the individuals: the reason for this is that the individuals, whose forces they are, exist, split up and are in opposition to one another." These productive forces are indifferent to the relations of indi-

viduals as individuals. In his earlier work, Marx, in an essay collected in *Marx's Concept of Man,* ed. Erich Fromm (New York: Ungar, 1961), 131, writes that "private property is only the sensuous expression of the fact that man is at the same time an objective fact for himself and becomes an alien and non-human object for himself; just as his manifestation of life is also his alienation of life and his self-realization a loss of reality, the emergence of an alien reality." For Levinas, the conditions of alienation described do not result from a special set of historical factors (e.g., the division of labor) but belong to work as such.

2. An analysis of Sartre's view of intersubjective relations lies beyond the scope of this book. It is nevertheless instructive to note that for Sartre other persons deprive us of our field of possibles, of our world, by looking at us. The Other's look makes our world bleed away by orienting itself as world around him as its center. For Levinas, the ontologically primordial revelation of the theft of our world arises from the theft of the meaning of our work by those who come after us. The primordial experience of the Other in his thought is the foundation of our values and proscribes rather than constitutes an original act of violence.

3. Hegel, *Phenomenology of Spirit,* trans. A. V. Miller (Oxford: Oxford University Press, 1977), 114ff.

4. John R. Silber, "The Ethical Significance of Kant's Religion," in Immanuel Kant, *Religion within the Limits of Reason Alone* (New York: Harper & Row, 1960), xcvi.

5. Kant, *Religion within the Limits,* 51.

6. Heidegger, *Being and Time,* trans. John Macquarrie and Edward Robinson (New York: Harper and Row, 1962), 294.

7. Ibid., 284.

8. Ibid., 294.

9. Ibid., 310.

10. Ibid., 311.

11. Levinas notes that in Rosenzweig's view every moment can be the last; thus every moment is eternal. See "Franz Rosenzweig: Une pensée juive moderne," in *Hors sujet* (Montpellier: Fata Morgana, 1987), 79; translated by Michael B. Smith as "Franz Rosenzweig: A Modern Jewish Thinker," in *Outside the Subject* (Stanford: Stanford University Press, 1993), 54.

12. Levinas almost certainly has in mind the malign Angel of Death (*malakh ha-moves*) of Jewish tradition, who is not a somber hypostasis remote from human existence but a hostile presence who intervenes in human affairs. In *Berakot* 51a, the Angel of Death claims: "I go leaping in front of them [women when returning from the presence of the dead] with my sword in my hand and I have permission to harm." See also *Ketubot* 77b.

13. The notion of death as an enemy is not foreign to twentieth-century Protestant theological thought. Karl Barth, *Church Dogmatics,* trans. G. W. Bromiley (Edinburgh: T. & T. Clark, 1960), 3, part 2, 607, writes: "What is the basis of the profound necessity of human fear in the face of death? It is obviously to be found in the fact that death is an enemy with its own destructive purpose and power. This means, of course, that we are threatened on this frontier of our being by the negation which corresponds to the power and purpose of this enemy."

14. Levinas would certainly reject the specifically Christian context but seems to have in mind the idea of Romans 6:6: "We know that our old self was crucified with him so that the sinful body might be destroyed and we might no longer be enslaved to sin. For he who has died is freed from sin. But if we have died with Christ we shall also live with him."

15. Levinas has not yet worked out human typologies that would illustrate strategies indicative of "bad faith." Nor has he elaborated life stages as in Kierkegaard and Nietzsche. Rather, his enterprise is to bring to light what being-in-the-world must be to be moral being. Since it is my purpose to show that it is possible to fall away from the moral demand made by the Other and expressed in the face, I use Sartre's term "bad faith," which, despite its overuse, conveys this falling away for which Levinas has not devised an equivalent.

16. In Freud's work it is society that imposes repression and would thus be responsible for the phenomenon that, in Levinas's thought, is absolutely original. For the early Freud repression is due to economic necessity. The later Freud moves toward the position that "man is the animal which represses himself and which creates culture and society in order to repress himself." See N. O. Brown, *Life against Death* (New York: Random House, 1959).

17. Levinas, "L'autre dans Proust," in *Noms propres* (Montpellier: Fata Morgana, 1976), 122; translated by Michael B. Smith as "The Other in Proust," in *Proper Names* (Stanford: Stanford University Press, 1996), 103.

18. Levinas, "Pluralisme et transcendance," in *Proceedings of the Tenth International Congress of Philosophy* (Amsterdam: North Amsterdam, 1949), 1:381–83.

VI

What Is Language?

LEVINAS'S ESSAYS on language show an extraordinary thematic unity[1] in their attempt to ground phenomenologically the view that the advent of the other person is a primordial upsurge of language. Thus, in the work of this period he attacks one of the most vexing and fundamental concerns of contemporary phenomenological research: What is language? What makes language mean? The novelty of his investigation lies in its assumption that a common ontological basis can be found for language and morality. Moreover he argues that language and morality rest upon nonrational foundations. Together with the question of language, Levinas develops an account of the responsible self, a phenomenology of responsibility as a primordial structure, and brings to light its character as the infrastructure of all decision-making processes anterior to its activation in the world of freedom. The recovery of the moral self for phenomenological inquiry in no way vitiates Levinas's previous investigations that shed light upon such diverse phenomena as the separated self of need, of knowledge, and of productivity. Ultimately these analyses do not presuppose sequentiality in the temporal order in the sense that their appearance in the life of an individual can be supposed to follow a prearranged pattern. Nor need they be considered as surpassed: it is an advantage of phenomenological research that the focus upon one region of being need not invalidate an analysis that arises from a quite different type of existence. The investigation of the moral self provides a reply to a query haunting all of Levinas's reflections concerning the other person. This question is raised in passing in a relatively early work (EN 13–24/BPW 1–10): how can one appear to oneself as face? Let us direct our attention first to the problem of language and then to the question of the moral self.

LANGUAGE AND DISCOURSE

We have already seen that Levinas founds moral life as teaching upon discourse in the intersubjective realm. We are thus forced to ask whether Levinas merely recasts phenomenologically insights already well formulated in the more aphoristic and poetic idiom of such thinkers as Martin Buber. The novelty of Levinas's approach to language lies neither in distinguishing authentic from inauthentic speech nor in positing a language behind discursive language, anterior to it, founding it, making possible its upsurge. Heidegger has already grasped the difference between authentic speech and its degradation in "idle talk" (*Gerede*) and accorded to genuine language the possibility for self-recovery.[2] It can also be shown without difficulty that Buber perceives a primordial language anterior to discursive language. Has Buber not already elaborated the twofold attitude of man without thereby proposing a doubling of our given world in the activation of these attitudes? Has he not also shown that within the everyday world language could sacralize or degrade, relate to and address genuine alterity, or perceive, feel, use, experience the other as the given?[3] Is not Buber's elucidation of the sphere I-It a transformation into poetic metaphor of thematizing consciousness as Husserl, in his more scholastic way, had developed it?

No doubt Levinas is much indebted to Heidegger and Buber, an indebtedness that he is the first to acknowledge. But what is remarkable and innovative in Levinas's thought stems from the strategies he is forced to develop in order to bypass ontology, so that he may situate the meaning of the upsurge of the Other who looms over and against us, not as the figure that emerges from its ground in the fullness of sensory intuiting, nor even in the axiological meaning of the Other already given in his appearance, but in the "something more" guaranteed by another's presence. It is true that for Buber the appearance of the Other, if received as an address, demands a response, bespeaks more than his appearing, is the whole world.[4] Yet alterity in Buber's thought merely absorbs the background and is lodged within the framework of phenomenological givenness so that there is nothing, no one but the Thou. For Levinas this interpretation of the Other is simply a restructuring of world and not the total transcendence of it. What Levinas demands is the recognition that what is world can never become other. So long as the Thou of Buber's reflections is merely a new perception of what remains immanent to the world and not a breakthrough into transcendence, Buber's approach to alterity still remains within the enclosed sphere of the world fully accessible to phenomenological discovery.

Levinas's theory of language confronts the problem of transcendent meaning given within the world while at the same time admitting that the world is recalcitrant to transcendence precisely because there is no phenomenon that can garner, consolidate within itself, that which by its very nature cannot appear. When what appears is the world concentrated in a Thou, Buber recognizes the need for alterity but dilutes its meaning; the need for alterity has been given expression, but the insight has not come to fruition. If further justification were needed to show that the Thou is still well within the limits of the world, amenable to phenomenological inquiry, one would only have to pinpoint Buber's insistence that the I-Thou relationship need not presuppose persons. According to Buber, genuine relation can subsist between man and nature, between man and intelligible forms, as well as between man and man.[5] Between man and nature, "the relation sways in gloom, beneath the level of speech. Creatures live and move over and against us, but cannot come to us, and when we address them as Thou our world clings to the threshold of speech."[6] In the sphere of intelligible essences (*geistige Wesenheiten*), man is also accosted, although not by any form, and man replies. His response comes from a realm beyond speech.[7] But, against the value of all other encounters, Levinas maintains the sui generis quality of the human face that alone can found the sphere of human values. Buber's inclusion of what lies outside human dialogue, outside the meeting between man and man, as authentic revelations of alterity establishes for Levinas, unquestionably I believe, the point of divergence between his own view of language and that of Martin Buber.

Despite Buber's remarkable acumen in establishing the relationships that obtain in the world of I-Thou and its transformation into the world of I-It, these relationships are alluded to, elicited metaphorically, but remain inexplicit to the consternation of those who would wish to honor Buber by arriving at a more exact understanding of his intent. These spheres are half-hidden and half-revealed within the elliptical style of the thinker. It can be argued that this ambiguity is the result of deliberation rather than of inadvertence; it places upon subsequent thinkers the onus of precise exegesis. Levinas's philosophy of religious language, while insisting upon the intersubjective foundations of language, does not suffer from the same elusiveness: in addition to carefully developing the infrastructure of discursive language, Levinas shows, through a radically innovative approach to the sensible world, how the break with thematizing consciousness is possible.

How, from Levinas's point of view, does discourse arise in the sphere of activity and knowledge (what Buber would call the realm of I-It)? What gives to events spread out in time, indifferent to one another, the remarkable unity that extends through their sequentiality? How do linguistic signs "mean" within the unity of a system, or rather, what makes a sign to be a sign at all? Through the most disparate events, a process of narration constitutes their unity, a process that underlies even nonthematic, nontheoretical manifestations. Just as long as being manifests itself, it does so starting from a theme (DEHH 217/CPP 109). Levinas insists upon this point. It is crucial to recognize that, for Levinas, words do not result from an intention to substitute signs for things or for other signs, but that the reverse obtains: the establishment and use of verbal signs is borne by a thematizing (narrative) intentionality that leads directly to the uncovering of being. What Levinas argues is simply this: the notion of language is not rendered intelligible by viewing its upsurge as essentially passive, as arising from the impact of objects striking an inert mental apparatus waiting to be awakened. Language produces, elicits, brings forth into full presence that which manifests itself, just as for Husserl meaning is already present in sense perception through the intentionality of sensation.

To put the matter somewhat differently, the language of activity and knowledge can be interpreted as a "bodying forth" of being, as the "way being takes to show itself" (DEHH 217/CPP 109). The logos of discourse (what Buber calls the language of the relational event) is overwhelmed by the "logos as rationality." Communication becomes an accidental feature of language, a means

to guarantee the distribution of messages, as one guarantees the
distribution of goods within an economy. The word thus understood is communicable only insofar as it is carried by a thought
(DEHH 218/CPP 110). Such an allegation makes sense when one
understands that Levinas means that a fundamental relation between the word that is carried and the carrier of the word has
been severed. Communication becomes subject to an end other
than itself. The word has acquired a purpose foreign to itself: it
proceeds teleologically from truth as its end.

For Buber the return to the world of I-It is the bleak but necessary sequel to every genuine relational act.[8] The powerful afflatus
of the Thou is degraded, but the movement to the world of "It"
is unavoidable. The realm of "It" cannot be circumvented because "It" is the licit if unredeemed sphere of human doing and
knowing. In this respect Levinas follows Buber's view. Levinas too
concedes that rational discourse is the necessary vehicle for the
conduct of human affairs within the totality, the sphere of human
work and activity. Narrative intentionality for Levinas does not
exist in this world but is its modus vivendi. It is a structure essential to thought as thought, for all thought is thematization.

But Buber does not analyze the structure of thought, while for
Levinas the process itself holds considerable interest. For Levinas
thematization does not consist in *perceiving* a "this" or a "that"; it
consists in *understanding* something by the given (by the given
such and such is meant). Although thematization means something by the given, it in no sense prejudges the content of what is
given. The act of meaning a "this" insofar as it is a "this" does
not distance one from the object, from "being in the original"; it
simply means that in understanding a "this" insofar as it is "this,"
not the object but its meaning is understood. There is no mere
object; there is only an object meant. The understanding of this
as that does not understand the object, but its meaning. Being
has neither to fulfill nor to disappoint meaning. The meaning,
neither given nor non-given, is understood. But a being is manifest as a being on the basis of its meaning" (DEHH 218/CPP
110).

Levinas does not deny that for Husserl the world is immediately
present to consciousness, a presence guaranteed by its being. But
this being is not subject to subsequent recreation or reconstitu-

tion by consciousness. The presence of being cannot be interpreted as a weighing down upon the subject of the being of the world, nor of the impact of the manifold sensible upon a passive consciousness. If any lesson has been learned from Husserl it is that to be present to consciousness is not equivalent to the filling of an empty container, that the notion of a "this" unwinding before a passive gaze is happily defunct. Every "this" that is experienced is already a "this" that is intended. Once it is thought, it is thought as "this" or as "that," and *as* present. Levinas argues that the authority of Husserlian intuition belongs to it as meaning bestowal rather than to its primary content (DEHH 218/CPP 110).

What Levinas derives from Husserl's understanding of intentionality is that it functions as designating something as one, "the proclaiming of something as something." In Levinas's view "the understanding as . . ." lies at the foundation of consciousness; it functions in Levinas's thought as an a priori of consciousness without which consciousness would not be what it is. Every designation of truth or falsity already presupposes it. Levinas is careful to insist that the apriority to which he refers is neither "temporal anticipation" nor "logical antecedence." In his view, to proclaim meaning is first and foremost to name, to proclaim that the object intended is "this" or "that." Levinas writes that the a priority of the a priori "is a *kerygma*" (DEHH 219/CPP 111). What Levinas means is that the "a priority of the a priori" is that by virtue of which a simple proclamation that the object is what it is becomes possible because of the intention that animates it. The intention bestows upon it its unity. The object maintains an identity, an ideality through its multiform and vanishing appearances. Levinas adds: "Everything is, one might say, imaged in experience, except the identity of individuals, which holds sway over the instants of the image. This identity is possible only as *claimed*" (DEHH 220/CPP 111). Again in a later essay he says:

> Subjectivity as consciousness is thus interpreted as an ontological event, namely, the rediscovery of being on the basis of an ideal principle or *arche* in its thematic exposition. The detour of ideality leads to a coinciding with oneself, that is, to the certainty that remains the guide and guarantee of the whole spiritual adventure of Being. That is why the "adventure" is not exactly an adventure. It

is never dangerous. It is always a self-possession, sovereignty, *arche.* (S 487–88/BPW 80/AE 125–26/OBBE 99)

Experience presupposes identity through multiplicity, "understanding as the same," or "taking to be the same." Thus, for Levinas, Husserlian phenomenology, which reinstates the primacy of being so that the object is interpreted as fully present, as being, also and primarily understands thought as conferring an ideal meaning. Being could not show itself without this ideal meaning. To put it otherwise, bestowing a meaning upon being is neither more nor less than letting being be. There is no appearing beyond meaning or outside of it. All meaning in turn reverts to the "kerygmatic" structure of thinking. The consequences of this approach to phenomena is extremely significant, for now every phenomenon is discourse or a fragment of discourse (DEHH 221/CPP 112).

To avow that a thing is a "this" or a "that" is for Levinas a function of judgment. Thus, not only are all phenomena "language," even if only in a rudimentary way, but all saying is already judgment. It is not a subsidiary or accidental feature of language but belongs to speech as predicative. It is as proclamation that language is signifying. The contiguity of linguistic signs is not an arbitrary event. Language signifies because it is as kerygma, the avowal of an identity.

We have already seen that Levinas's interpretation of Husserlian intentionality enables him to show that every phenomenon does not merely bear a freight of language but is already a fragment of discourse, that to appear is quite literally to have been spoken for. Levinas arrives at a second equally critical conclusion: the individual can only be attained in discourse through the "detour of the universal" (DEHH 222/CPP 113). The universal is a priori and precedes the individual. Strangely enough, in my view, we see again that Levinas has been led from Husserlian presuppositions to a Hegelian conclusion: when thought thinks itself to be most concrete, to have achieved the truth of sense certainty, to have attained the particular, it reaches only a "this" or a "that" that is universal.[9]

The last conclusion (that thought thinks the universal) sheds new light upon what has already been uncovered in the phenomenological analysis of totality and its modes of operation. We have seen in *Totality and Infinity* that thought proceeds from self to same. Now, by continuing to investigate the nature of language, Levinas shows, in my view, not only that the self of totality intends the same, but also that the same that is intended is an empty universal. Nor will the problem of uncovering alterity, without impairing it as alterity, remain unaffected by the new dimension that the analysis of language adds to the understanding of thought. At this new juncture, must one ask not only how to find the Other, but also if thought cannot intend the individual, how can singularity be attained? Alterity has been linked to the problem of singularity, to the problem of the unique individual. Now one must inquire how, if language is the work of thematization and identification, can singularity without universality be understood? From this point of view, nothing real, no individual, can appear outside universality.

It might be contended that this very universality means that the truth that appears is a truth for all. It could then be argued that universality as the truth for all opens the possibility of communication. Does not the truth *qua* universal, equally true for all, mean that the content of truth can be shared? But singularity cannot be found by pursuing universality as the truth for everyone; the "everyone" that is evoked is merely formal. "True for everyone" means that what is true is available as *theoria* to everyone: it is available through the bestowal of meaning, through thematizing consciousness. The truth for all can never attain unique subjectivity, for it does not found the logical work of discourse but is rather the consequence of that work (DEHH 224/CPP 115).

The relation with a subjectivity, an interlocutor, is in no way presupposed by the universal essence of truth. What is wrong with the universal essence of truth is that it presupposes that everything can be known. When the interlocutor is himself an object of knowledge, discourse belongs to the impersonal level of thought. But, Levinas contends, what is kerygmatic in thought carries more than universality, more than the proclamation that a "this" is a "this." It is "*proximity* between me and the interlocutor" (DEHH 224/CPP 115). Whatever the content of discourse, genuine speech is contact presupposing a relation with a particularity that lies outside the message that it transmits. The bearer of the message is impervious to thematization; he can only be approached. Discourse is not subsidiary to knowledge for Levinas because the interlocutor can, as such, never be known. Discourse arises from an already anterior proximity. The imperviousness to thematization arises because there is a being such that its being is too rudimentary, too insignificant to be brought into plenary presence. The being that cannot be thematized, that is incommensurable with being, must be understood as a meaning coming from beyond being.

The notion of proximity that Levinas develops is not a diminution of the distance between beings, as in the case of Buber where the world shrinks and the Thou swells to immense proportions; it has nothing to do with spatial contiguity. Proximity is rather the immediacy of human presence. It "means" in and of itself: "Proximity is *by itself* a signification" (DEHH 225/CPP 116). Levinas writes: "Proximity is a relationship with a singularity, without the mediation of any principle or ideality. In the concrete, it describes my relationship with the neighbor, a relationship whose signifyingness is prior to the celebrated 'sense bestowing'" (S 488/BPW 81/AE 127/OBBE 100). Proximity is a new ethical intentionality: "We call ethical a relationship between terms such as are united neither by a synthesis of the understanding nor by a relationship between subject and object, and yet where the one weighs or concerns or is meaningful to the other, where they are bound by a plot which knowing can neither exhaust nor unravel" (DEHH 225n/CPP 116n, reading "united" for Lingis's "untied").

Since the particularity in any relation is sublated in a synthesis of the understanding, Levinas is compelled to reject any notion that attempts to integrate the one and the other into a universal order. Thus, he dissociates his view of the ethical from the Kantian kingdom of ends (DEHH 225/CPP 116). The ethical relation is a welling up of subjectivity in which the particularity of each term remains intact. The Other is approached; he cannot be posited or thematized. The singularity of the ethical excludes mediation through universals, an exclusion that Levinas claims belongs to language in its original upsurge, to the primordiality of its original entry into human existence. Language as the foundation of alterity sublates all positing: "The precise point at which this mutation of the intentional into the ethical occurs, and occurs continually, at which the approach *breaks through* consciousness, is the human skin and face. Contact is tenderness and responsibility" (DEHH 225/CPP 116).

We have seen that universality belongs to knowledge as its infrastructure. Is the idealizing intentionality of cognition the only access to reality? It may be recalled that in Levinas's early investigations of being in the elemental, feeling or sentience, an affectivity that puts one into relation with the pure quality of the elemental, is the mode in which the elemental is lived. This affectivity is neither a thought lacking clarity and distinctness nor a representation not brought into sharp focus. Feeling does not subvert the credibility of intelligence: it is an altogether novel mode of relating, sufficient unto itself and satisfied with the felt.

In Levinas's writings from 1968 onward, the deficiencies of intentionality and its requirements are reconsidered, and sentience is again introduced as an affectivity that circumvents the universalizing intentionality of thought. In the present context, Levinas is not interested in the lambent world of the elemental, a life world midway between thought and blind participation in being, so strikingly illumined in *Totality and Infinity*. His current interest is directed to rescuing language from the sphere of logical discourse. So long as thought is the functional model governing all uses of language, it must remain hopelessly embedded in the ideality it acquires from the basic intentional structures of thought. It is for this reason that Levinas again discusses the nature of the sensible. The immediacy of the sensible is an event of nearness. The sensible is not known; it is approached. The sensible does not bring before consciousness elements refractory to consciousness, nor does it offer what cannot be integrated into the structure of the world. But the sensible establishes a unique access to the real (DEHH 226/CPP 117).

The error of assuming that sensible intuition is a thought thinking itself stems from the primacy of vision among the senses. Yet vision itself signifies in ways not immediately apparent. It is common to say that one eats something up with one's eyes. Such an expression is more than rhetorical exaggeration, for it shows the primacy of consuming, of devouring, incorporating into oneself. The sense of taste clearly transcends the cognitive model, for the object is pierced and demolished. The real meaning of the sensation of taste lies not in the information received but in its penetration into the intimacy of things. If sensation is read as the fulfillment of an intention by the given, it is misunderstood, for it is then modeled on an aspect of vision cognitive in its intentionality and false to the sensuous itself. In sensation something *happens* between the feeling and the felt in the strongest sense (DEHH 227/CPP117–18). To feel the world is to consume it.

The primacy of touch has also been subverted by the cognitive aspect of the visual. In touch, what has been primordially revealed is not the quiddity of the existent, although touch can turn into doxic positing by transforming the palpable into information, into knowledge of the surface of things. Touch is "pure approach and a proximity" irreducible to experience before it eventuates in information or understanding. The act itself is not an experience of the act; the caress, for example, is contact, not a metalevel experience of it. Proximity in the caress remains what it is, although it may express something in addition to contact and nearness. The way in which these things are given in their *Leibhaftigkeit*, in "flesh and bone" reality, is through proximity (DEHH 227/CPP 118). The felt is defined by this relation; it is tenderness. The concreteness of the sensible is language. Intentionality fails to take account of the nearness of being. From the point of view of understanding, what the sensible contributes to understanding seems superficial. But the ethical relation to the real is rooted in the lived reality of the sensible. It is an engagement in life. Even vision, insofar as vision belongs to the sensible, retains something of the primordiality of contact with the real, for one speaks of the visible as "caress[ing] the eye." In Levinas's thought one sees in the way that one touches rather than touching in the way that one sees (DEHH 228/CPP 118).

Moral relations bypass intentionality; they are relations of nearness. The moral relation is the relation with the next one touching rather than intending the next one in his nonideal unity. There is an absence of horizon against which the identity of the Other is revealed. He is the Other who means prior to all *Sinngebung*, prior to all intentionality. To have a meaning before all meaning is bestowed is to be other (DEHH 228/CPP 119).

The temporalization of nearness, of proximity, reflects its difference from consciousness as a mode of access to the real. Proximity is an anachronism to consciousness: it has vanished before consciousness can take cognizance of it. Consciousness is always "late for the rendezvous with" human presence, arrives too late upon the scene, and is therefore from Levinas's point of view already bad conscience (DEHH 229/CPP 119–20).

For Levinas the notion of proximity is not merely an exception to intentionality so that consciousness still retains a privileged standpoint with regard to axiology and *praxis;* it undercuts the importance of consciousness as a privileged mode of entry into the real. It is through approach that the face emerges and the manifestation of being is transfigured into ethical relation. "Consciousness," writes Levinas (DEHH 229/CPP 120), "reverts to obsession." Similarly,

> It is the summoning of myself by the other (*autrui*), it is a responsibility toward those whom we do not even know. The relation of proximity . . . is *already* a summons of extreme exigency, an obligation that is *anachronistically* prior to every engagement. An anteriority that is older than the a priori. This formulation expresses a way of being affected that can in no way be invested by spontaneity: the subject is affected without the source of the affection becoming a theme of re-presentation. The term *obsession* designates this relation which is irreducible to consciousness. (S 489/BPW 81/AE 127/OBBE 100–101)

The term "obsession" has been overlaid with psychological meaning so that it is generally taken to mean pathological exaggeration, but its original import implies a nearness of being. The near one allows no choice, summons and commands, places upon one the onus of a responsibility without choice. Levinas writes:

> The extreme urgency of the assignation, which is the modality of obsession, breaks up the equality, or serenity, of consciousness, its equality with the object it understands intentionally. The neighbor's presence summons me with an urgency so extreme that we must not seek its measure in the way this presence is presented to me, that is, manifests itself and becomes a representation. For this still, or already, belongs to the order of images and cognition, which the assignation overwhelms. Here urgency is not a simple lack of time, but an anachronism: in representation presence is already past. (DEHH 230/CPP 120)

Proximity is not simple coexistence of two existents. In the presence of the near one an absence wells up that is the very reverse of serenity, a hunger that Levinas designates in so much of his work as desire, a proximity that could not be nearer and an appetite that remains insatiable. That which is absent is the presence of the infinite, which cannot be put into words. Elusive and ineluctable, it "contests its own presence." It is absence "on the verge of nothingness," always in flight but leaving behind it a trace as the face of the near one.

An Alternative View of Language

We have seen that for Levinas the failure of representation to attain the other lies in its emphasis upon vision as the model for the understanding of language.[10] Is a new understanding of language possible in which language does not merely identify the things represented but already refers to a horizon that transcends them? The structure of correlation in classical phenomenology, as Levinas understands it, distinguishes intelligence from the intelligible. But language can, from this new perspective, be seen as linking intelligence to the intelligible on the plane of the world. Intellect can be subordinated to expression.[11]

The notion that to perceive is to understand has characterized such divergent thinkers as Plato, Hume, and Husserl, according to Levinas, for in their views meaning is reduced to contents given to consciousness. The meaning borne by language must be justified by a reflection upon the consciousness that intends it. All metaphor that language makes possible must be brought back to the given, all figurative meaning justified by the literal meanings given in intuition. The hallmark of Husserlian philosophy is a return to the given to the things themselves (*zu die Sache selbst*). By claiming that categorial intuitions are possible, Husserl has merely extended the scope of what can be considered as given (viz., relations and essences are included), but intuition remains the source of all intelligibility. Indeed, Levinas remarks, Husserl's transcendental philosophy is nothing but a species of positivism in this regard, for even if what is given is not brought into clarity, it is by reference to the given that deficiency or absence is understood: "Every absence has the given as its *terminus a quo* and *terminus ad quem*" (HAH 19/BPW 36). Language only serves to communicate what has already been fixed in intuition. Expression plays no role in constituting these meanings.

But metaphor (the referring to absence) belongs to an entirely different order than pure receptivity. The absence to which it leads is not that of missing content but belongs to the past or to the future. It is against a horizon or world, that is, against a language or culture, that meaning is situated; meaning is always contextual. Words do not have isolated meanings but already refer to other words rather than to givens. Language itself already refers to the one who hears and the one who speaks, to the contingency of his history. One can never summarize all the contexts of language and all the positions in which interlocutors could find themselves. Like language itself, experience is no longer made of bits and pieces locked into Euclidean space. The elements of experience "signify" starting from a world, from the position of one who looks. Customary definitions of words cannot be trusted, for, as Dufrenne has shown, certain experiences "mean" outside of their presumably univocal contexts; for example, spring has a meaning beyond the season: it can refer to childhood and so on with equal primordiality.[12] Significations are not limited to any special realm of objects, are not the privilege of any content. The meanings refer to one another, can arise within the totality of being all around the one who speaks and perceives.

It is in this connection that for Levinas Heideggerian etymologies are important, for they start with the ordinary meaning of a term but lead to the illumination of concatenated experiences. Experience can be a reading of meaning, an exegesis, a hermeneutic and not an intuition (HAH 22/BPW 38). A "this" insofar as it is a "this" is not a modification brought to a content apart from language but lives in a world, the structure of which resembles the order of language. The "this" is not given outside of that order; signification does not emerge from a being that lacked signification. Objects become meaningful starting with language and not the reverse; the figurative sense takes priority over the literal (HAH 23/BPW 38).

The essence of language now belongs to the illumination of what is found beyond the given, of being as a whole. The given itself takes on its meaning from this totality. The totality itself is not composed of isolable elements but is chameleon-like in its fluidity and instability: it is the product of a "creative gesture of subjectivity." Signification thus understood is a free and creative arrangement (HAH 24/BPW 38). The eye itself is embodied, that is, it is ensconced in a body that is also hand-sound-emitting, and so on. The one who looks does not introduce relativity into a congealed totality from a fixed vantage point, for the look itself "is" already as belonging to a body relative to a position.[13] The fact that the totality inundates the sensible given and that vision is embodied is not, for Levinas, an accidental feature of receptivity. Nothing is given according to this view, apart from the ensemble of being that illumines it. The one who is receptive to this illumining totality is not a passive spectator but helps bring the ensemble into being. The subject is not one who is vis-à-vis that which is; he is within and alongside it. He participates in its assemblage. This "ubiquity" is what it means to be body.

This assemblage is one of nonnatural entities, that is, of cultural objects: paintings, poems, and the like. But it is also the less studied effect of all activities and linguistic gestures.[14] These cultural objects gather up otherwise dispersed entities into meaningful configurations that are themselves totalities. They express a period, a historical era; they make meaning possible. Expression is not organized in terms of a thought anterior to its exteriorization but is the expressive gesture itself. Meaning moves into a preexisting cultural world.[15] Corporeity itself means that one is plunged into that world, that one expresses it as soon as it is thought. The corporeal gesture is itself a kind of poetry, a celebration of the world. One becomes subject and object at the same time, imitating the visible and coinciding with the perceived movement kinesthetically. Levinas writes: "It is visible that throughout this conception, expression defines culture; culture is art, and art or the celebration of being constitutes the original essence of incarnation" (HAH 28/BPW 41). Art is not a project to make something beautiful but part of the ontological order.

To accept such a modification of standard phenomenological thought as offering a possibility of attaining genuine alterity would run counter to the very presuppositions upon which Levinas's own thought is based. For we have seen that in his view art represents a greater evil than rational discourse; the latter, while it is not the foundation of the ethical, protects man from being overwhelmed by the sacrality of the pagan, by the *il y a*. Clearly a point of view that exalts all gesture, all language as art, cannot provide the basis for the apprehension of genuine alterity. To express is for Levinas the very opposite of celebration. His critique of the present view of language rests upon the assumption that this philosophy shares with Hegelian thought the notion that truth is inseparable from its historical manifestations. Levinas concedes that this notion of language provides rich and novel insights for understanding the conditions that language fulfills when it is the language of activity and event, when it is metaphor. It explicates and makes panoramic the role of the creative self. In that sense it is important and valuable.

But Levinas attacks this view of language as a foundation for ethics strangely enough upon Platonic principles. The reason for this rests on the assumption that such a view of language is essentially a theory of becoming and therefore subject to Platonic correctives. Intelligibility is lodged in becoming itself, in the historical process. For Plato the world of genuine meaning is prior to the language and culture in which it is expressed; indeed, there is a privileged vantage point from which all historical cultures can be judged (HAH 31/BPW 42). This transhistorical angle of vision that judges all cultures expels the mimetic poets from the realm of being that it legitimates. Their language leads not to "meanings preexisting their expression" but to the imitation of existing cultures. For contemporary philosophies of language, as for the unfortunate poets of Plato's *Republic,* meaning cannot be separated from what bears it: "*The access is part of the meaning itself.* The scaffolding is never taken down; the ladder is never pulled up" (HAH 33/BPW 44).

It might be argued that there is an entry into the real apart from changing cultures through the permanence of human need and the technology that has evolved in order to satisfy it. Need remains constant so that the mode of achieving satiety remains limited. Does not the technical and scientific enterprise confer meaning upon being through work? Indeed, Levinas shows a marked preference for the scientific and technological enterprises, not because they are in themselves valuable or because they confer value, but simply because they are opposed to the false sacrality of language and culture: "Everywhere we should find the sense beneath the meaning, beneath the metaphor, the sublimation, the literature." Levinas also acknowledges that technology itself is a modality of culture already imposing an interpretation upon reality, a reduction of the real to an "Object in general." Science as a worldview impinges upon human need modifying its expression and its fulfillment. Human need can never be univocal in the same sense as animal need, for in its very upsurge it appears as culturally interpreted (HAH 36/BPW 45).

Levinas also points out that contemporary philosophies of signification claim that being is properly revealed only through a multiplicity of meanings, not as a congealed substance, as a single totality; there are numerous totalities. A loose unity is conferred upon being by the mutual permeability of cultures, not by means of a metalanguage into which all languages can be translated. Indeed, no such metalanguage exists. Levinas claims that languages penetrate one another "laterally" (HAH 39/BPW 46).

Since Levinas remains phenomenological and since he therefore addresses himself to the problem of meaning within the nexus of history, he must develop a category of meaning that will reveal transhistoricity, an eschatological dimension, within history itself. This category must run counter to signification and expression, which themselves provide a new hermeneutics only for what Buber would call the world of I-It but which fail as a viable ground for axiology. Such a category is work. We have seen that there is a kind of work that liberates man from the elemental, that allows him to take account of his needs and to provide for them. Such work is a protection against possible adversity in an unknown future. But work in the authentic sense is the very opposite: rather than providing against the eventualities that may strike at the security of existence, it expects no realization of its ends in one's own time. Such work is not an expenditure of energy that eventuates in commodities. Work thought through radically is a movement of the same to the Other that never returns to the same. It demands that the Other be ungrateful, for gratitude would reverse the movement of self to other by returning what was given to the self from which it derives. Nor is work the accumulation of merit, for merit is always acquired on one's own behalf. Authentic work is possible only as patience; the one who works does not seek a personal soteriological goal. He renounces all hope of being contemporary with the successful outcome of his labors. To intend a work whose victory lies outside of one's own time is to establish an eschatology without hope. It is being in the mode of being for what comes after oneself. This is the sacrifice of personality demanded of personality within the framework of history and cannot be understood as an expression of cultural multiplicity (HAH 46/BPW 50). Levinas does not deny that meaning begins in a cultural context, but the scaffolding falls away, and what is left is the transhistorical dimension of work.

THE TRACE

How is an authentic philosophy of language possible apart from cultural multiplicity?[16] Is there a being such that its being is the same for all cultures? Levinas claims that the being of the Other revealed within the totality signifies transhistorically and transculturally. This being is seen as a human face, a category elaborately developed in his thought to function as the corporeality of spiritual existence, just as the hand is the corporeality of effort or the eye of vision.

Where does the face come from? If its origin lies beyond being, beyond the very possibility of appearing within the limits of a horizon, then the beyond is not a simple background against which the face appears, from which it emerges as things emerge in the world. Levinas is careful to disclaim a world behind the visible world. The face is not a symbol that through its very upsurge brings what is symbolized into the discursive realm. The face is "abstract." This does not mean that its appearance leads from the particular to the general, nor does it mean that eternity has entered into time. The face that enters into the world disturbs the order of the world and is reflected in the destruction of immanence; the face cannot be placed against a horizon within the world. It comes from elsewhere without the intention of conveying more than itself. It is indicative of itself alone, not a mask that hides the truth of its existence, nor does it point to anything. Its abstractness refers only to the fact that it comes from elsewhere (DEHH 197/TrO 354–55).

In one of his infrequent references to Sartre, Levinas cites Sartre's observation that the other person is a pure hole in the world.[17] For Levinas this is so, not because one's own world drains away through the Other, but because the other bears a relationship to the absolutely Absent. This is the "beyond" from which the Other comes. Yet the Other does not reveal his origin as the sign reveals what is signified; that which is absent is not unveiled as being through the appearance of the face, for the absent is beyond both being and revelation. It is a mistake to assume that the elsewhere that is evoked by the face can yield a meaning for investigation; to assume that is to assume that the elsewhere is world. It is also to ignore the fundamental lesson of phenomenology: there is no world behind the world that appears.

Nevertheless the face belongs to the world of immanence as a thing in the world while it retains its alterity and its origin beyond appearance. It is experienced as a disruption of the correctness of the world, as though no impropriety belonged to the world as such but only emerged with the entrance of human categories. The beyond from which the face comes appears as a "trace." The face is as an absolutely completed past, a heretofore that is completely irrecoverable. Through the face alone transcendence appears without being destroyed as transcendence. In Levinas's thought transcendence disturbs the surface of the world as a stone thrown into a pool ruffles its deceptive serenity: "For a face is the unique openness in which the signifyingness of the transcendent does not nullify the transcendence and make it enter into an immanent *order;* here on the contrary transcendence refuses immanence precisely as the ever bygone transcendence of the transcendent" (DEHH 198/TrO 355). The meaning of the trace issues from an immemorial past, a past impervious to memory. This past is also, according to Levinas, "eternity." Eternity belongs to the past as its irreversibility; this eternity is the "refuge of the past." When Levinas speaks of eternity he means a dimension that cannot be converted into the present as beginning, commencement, origin, which are the lived modes of egoity. Levinas is careful to preserve certain modalities of the past and the future as impervious to cognition and to historical knowledge so that the temporal dimension of the beyond of being, of the elsewhere, is not eroded by the historical process.

The beyond of being opened by the face is a personal order irreducible to rational discourse or to the world of need, the *il y a,* the elemental, etc. It is a third person, He who cannot be defined: "Through a trace the irreversible past takes on the profile of the 'He'" (DEHH 199/TrO 356).[18] The third person is the beyond. He is as absolutely unavailable, withdrawn into an irreversible past. This irreversibility is designated by Levinas as his "illeity." Levinas maintains that the trace means, that is, it puts one in touch with illeity, establishes a relation with the third person (DEHH 199/TrO 356).[19] Since the trace is not a bringing forth into light, an unveiling or "appearing" is recalcitrant to phenomenological analysis because it cannot be integrated into the order of what can appear, what approach can properly be taken to it? One can locate the meaning of the trace in the phenomenal world that it interrupts.

Levinas insists that the trace is not a sign. Yet he also claims that it can play the role of a sign, just as the track of the prey that leads the hunter to his quarry and the work of the criminal that serves as a trail leading to his apprehension are characteristic marks that point to the one who has left them behind. But the trace differs from other signs; the track or trail is emblazoned in the order of being and becomes part of that order, but the trace "means" while retaining its transcendence. It means without intending to be a sign, without meaning to mean.[20] It means beyond any project that has the trace for its intention. Unlike those activities that are planned to leave tracks, or that leave tracks inadvertently but that can be integrated into the order of being, can be made to appear, the authentic trace disturbs the order of the world. It is like the trail of the criminal in this respect: it is the imprint of one who wishes to erase his tracks, as though a master of crime who wished to commit the perfect crime attempted to extirpate all marks of his presence.[21] One cannot make these tracks the object of an intention as the traces that are integrated into the order of the world can be apprehended, brought to light through the proper methods of inquiry. The one who had left his tracks had no wish in effacing his presence, to leave behind his work or his word. The tracks neither say nor do anything: "Disturbance is a movement that does not propose any stable order in conflict or in accord with a given order; it is movement that already carries away the signification it brought: disturbance disturbs order without troubling it seriously. It enters in so subtle a way that unless we retain it, it has already withdrawn. It insinuates itself, withdraws before entering" (DEHH 208/BPW 70). The order of the world has been upset in the absoluteness of his passing: "*To be* qua *leaving a trace* is to pass, to depart, to absolve oneself" (DEHH 200/TrO 357).

It can be argued that every sign is a trace in that it delivers not merely the signified but also the one who bears the sign. In this sense the trace can be said to have doubled the meaning of the sign. Levinas cites the example of the letter in which handwriting and style bespeak a human presence, in addition to the message and its content, that we apprehend directly. The trace itself can be interpreted such that, for example, the psychoanalyst might try to read unconscious intention into these extraneous features and come to certain conclusions about the author. Yet Levinas maintains that something of the handwriting and style of the letter remains impervious to analysis, remains simply "trace." Nothing is revealed; nothing is hidden. What Levinas means is that all access to the subjectivity of the writer at the time of his writing remains closed. The trace is merely what it is. In the trace an absolutely completed past has been sealed. No world can be recovered through the trace in the manner in which the original meaning of a world in all its richness and abundance can be recovered through a sign.

The trace is the weight of being behind "its acts and its language." Levinas speaks of the weight of being because being is irreversible, cumulative, cannot be limited or encompassed by a self: "A trace would seem to be the very indelibility of being, its omnipotence before all negativity, its immensity incapable of being self-enclosed, somehow too great for discretion, inwardness, or a self. . . . A trace does not effect a relationship with what would be less than being, but obliges with regard to the infinite, the absolutely other" (DEHH 200/TrO 357). But the superiority of which Levinas speaks cannot be deduced from the being of the existent. It takes its significance from the immemorial past. Levinas speaks of the trace as "the insertion of space in time," as a point where the world turns toward the past (DEHH 201/TrO 358). It is difficult to understand precisely what Levinas means by the spatiality of the trace since he has been careful to insist that the trace cannot be brought to light, cannot be unveiled, be brought into the order of the world, or be understood as phenomenon. It is possible, of course, that he is thinking of the other person, of the face that appears in space but is beyond all appearing, that it "means" beyond what can be the object of cognitive intentionality, the face as "incarnate" not in a specifically Christian sense but in a broad etymological sense. The time into which it intrudes is the temporal modality of remembrance from which the Other has retreated, a temporality that makes present that which has been. The immemorial past of which Levinas speaks as having left its trace can never be remembered, for to remember it would be to bring it into the present and thereby make it subject to origination, to commencement, the mode of temporalization of the subject as egoity. The transcendence of the trace is not present in the world. It is, according to Levinas, the presence of what in effect has never been there, for in order to have been there, the transcendent would have had to belong to the order of being. The transcendent is that which is perpetually past.[22]

Things, Levinas maintains, do not leave traces; they leave only effects. Cause and effect in the visual sense do not belong to the same order of existence as the trace. Things are exposed to cause and effect without any awareness of this fact. It is always possible that the intervention of human consciousness may attribute trace to mere effect. The history of things is without a past, that is, events in the world are contemporary insofar as the world of cause and effect is concerned, but the order of causal efficacy can be reinstated through human agency. A cause can be brought into the present through memory or through inference. The trace as trace, however, does not lead to a past that can be elicited, but is the past of an extremely ancient past impervious to all effort to bring it into the light of the present (DEHH 201/TrO 358).[23] The other is *in* the trace of "illeity"; this is the origin of its alterity. All other seeming alterity betrays the true origin of alterity, the trace (DEHH 201/TrO 359).

What comes to mind at once as a result of Levinas's discussion of the trace is the classical conception of the *imago dei*. This is indeed Levinas's point of view: the face is in the image of God. But what does it mean to be in the image of God? It is not to be an "icon" of God but to "find oneself in his trace." The God of Judaeo-Christian tradition retains "all the infinity of his absence." He shows himself only through his trace, as is written in Exodus 33 (DEHH 202/TrO 359).

The approach to God cannot be effected by following the trace. Levinas means that to do so is to make a trace stand for a world. To approach the divine is to turn to others who "stand in the trace of illeity" (DEHH 202/TrO 359). To follow the trace is not to be guided as by a map to an outlying region but to be commanded by a unique language. In diplomacy what is said by one diplomat to another can be taken to mean some entirely new proposal that could change the course of world affairs, or, Levinas maintains, it could signify absolutely nothing. Words themselves are always open to interpretation: language, as we have seen, is by its very nature equivocal, oracular, manifesting at the outset all the ambiguity of delphic utterance. A god was revealed upon a mountain, Levinas tells us, or in a bush that was not consumed. These biblical events are attested to in sacred literature, yet what is attested to can still properly be interpreted as a natural phenomenon or as a projective human fantasy. Other persons solicit recognition in the same way as events recounted in the biblical text: they retain their hiddenness. This mode of self-manifestation is the reverse of phenomenon; Levinas calls it "enigma" (DEHH 208/BPW 70).

The crucial question for Levinas remains: How is it possible for a meaning beyond meaning to slip into the meaning structure of the phenomenal? Is the trace really amenable to two interpretations, both equally satisfactory? The situation is peculiar since the primary meaning is already erased as soon as the trace appears. The phenomenon itself refutes the very meaning it conveys, for phenomenality contradicts the nonphenomenal character of "illeity." The God who is revealed as persecuted and misunderstood is revealed in this way, because to be dominated, to be beyond understanding, are the very characteristics of nonphenomenality.[24] For Levinas the truth of Christianity, persecuted truth, is possible only in a world where atheism has proffered the best imaginable reasons to reject Christianity.

Levinas is careful to distinguish the disarray or disorder into which the phenomenal is thrown by the entrance of the transcendent from ordinary nonrationality. The nonrational is always judged to be what it is against a background of prior intelligibility in terms of which it can be defined. Once it is brought to reflective self-awareness, the nonrational loses its irrationality. Levinas does not attribute the equivocacy of the trace to a single phenomenon. The work of art, for example, might incorporate two such orders. The life of the artist might appear together with the political and social order within the work of art. The two orders converge at some point. The trace, however, presents an order that cannot be accommodated within the order in which it appears.

RESPONSIBILITY

If Levinas's thought were to be translated into the schematic framework of Martin Buber, we could say that our investigation of language as metaphor has yielded the phenomenology of the world of It, and our investigation of trace has yielded the world of Thou. The task that now remains is to illuminate the meaning of the "I" in Levinas's work, which is developed in his recent thought as a phenomenology of the responsible self.[25] According to Levinas, "language . . . is the obsession of an I 'beset' by the others" (DEHH 233/CPP 123). This obsession is a responsibility anterior to all choice. In Levinas's view, choice belongs to Husserlian intentionality as "consciousness-of": it belongs to the thinker who broods in splendid isolation, to the solitary *cogito*. Genuine language is, however, responsibility, not only in the ordinary sense of the word, but beyond it, because one is responsible not only for what one has done, but also for what one has not done. One is responsible for the Other's suffering, for that for which no responsibility in the ordinary sense of the word accrues. Responsibility arises from proximity and not from freedom: "It is the state of a creature in a world without play, in the *gravity* that is perhaps the first coming of meaning to being *beyond* its stupid 'that's the way it is.' It is the state of being a hostage" (DEHH 233/CPP 123).

Genuine subjectivity arises at precisely the point where the full weight of the world is experienced. The individual as absolute interiority is not born in self-reflection, for the self that is being reflected upon is precisely what must be explained. The reflexive pronoun (the French *se*) provides a clue to the meaning of self. It cannot be interpreted as a distance-making maneuver. It is rather totally passive. Levinas notes that the "*se*" is not merely the gram-matical accusative but already qualifies the self as guilty. The own-most self is indeed the very fact of being weighed down in being.[26]

The authentic self cannot get rid of itself. Driven into itself, it becomes the nonbeing of being. It is important to distinguish Levinas's understanding of the self as the nonbeing of being from Sartre's view of *pour-soi*, which at first glance it might seem to resemble.[27] Sartre's for-itself is a nonbeing at the heart of being, an emptiness of in-itself; it exists for the object. It seeks endlessly to found itself through relations of identity with being. These op-erations are doomed to failure, for the for-itself can never be any-thing nor coincide with itself. It is what it is not and it is not what it is.[28] It posits itself as not being the in-itself, as being lack, desire.

Levinas's philosophical anthropology begins with man's satiety. The drama of need and replenishment that fully commensurates with it is enacted against a background of the elemental that pro-vides the subject with its requirements. Want does not go beyond the possibility of its fulfillment. The sphere of ontology is pre-cisely the sphere in which world and the structures that intend it are sufficient to one another. For Levinas desire, genuine lack, intends what is beyond ontology; it does not intend a coincidence with ontology, does not seek the fullness of *en-soi*. Desire cannot want to be what it is not, as in the case of Sartre's *pour-soi*, for genuine alterity, which is the object of desire in Levinas, thought cannot even be sought. In order to seek it, one would have to know in advance what one seeks. Since the Other cannot be known, this quest is impossible. The lived modalities of the for-itself inventoried by Sartre belong to the realm of ontology. What then is the meaning of the nonbeing of being as the structure of the ownmost self in Levinas's work? "The ethical event of 'expia-tion for another' is the concrete situation which the verb *not to be* designates." The nonbeing of subjectivity is the emptying of an already preexistent fullness for the sake of another. One substi-tutes for the Other, becomes what Levinas designates as his hostage (DEHH 234/CPP 124). The notion of substitution is central in Levinas's later thought.[29]

Substitution is possible only for a moral consciousness obsessed with the other person, with what is strange, unbalanced, what escapes all principle, origins, and will. Levinas designates obsession, the nonbeing of subjectivity, as an an-archy, an absence of principle anterior to sheer disorder that always appears upon a background of order and is explicable in terms of a fundamental coherence of being. It arrests ontology in this sense: insofar as consciousness is the arena in being that loses itself and finds itself again, it remains beyond recovery. It is always irrevocably past and therefore irrecoverable. It does not belong to the ordinary past that can always be regained through memory, but to an eternal past. Its irrecoverability can, however, become language: "An inability which is *said* all the same. An-archy does not *reign*, and so remains ambiguous and enigmatic. It leaves a trace which discourse, in the pain of expression, tries to say. Yet it leaves only a trace" (S 489n. 5/BPW 180n. 10/AE 128n. 4/OBBE 144n. 4).

The Other interrupts the smooth flow of the same, leaving it speechless. One is "obsessed" with the Other; the Other disrupts the web of conscious life as responsibility that cannot be justified, for which no ground exists. Levinas is not afraid to say that the Other "persecutes," not in the sense in which the Other devises strategies antagonistic to one's own interest, but because the moral life itself is persecution (S 490/BPW 81/AE 128/OBBE 101). Nor can this obsessive interiority be attributed to a pathological delusive system. It is the self's way of abnegating itself as egoity. The an-archy of which Levinas speaks belongs in this context.

In his earlier work such terms as "subjectivity" or "self" or "consciousness" have been used interchangeably. It now becomes Levinas's task to develop more fully the implication of the moral self (*le soi-même*), which I shall designate as the ownmost self. Throughout Levinas's work it can be argued that there is a highly inflected phenomenology of conscious life, of the self as need, of the cognitive processes, but that since response is based on none of these, the moral act is without foundation. The thread that bears conscious life, narrative intentionality, has been explicitly rejected as the source of moral values, as we have seen. Are the recesses of the moral self buried beyond all possibility of recovery? How can the continuity of moral life be developed without reinstating such substructures as the Kantian good will, or the transcendental ego? Levinas now directs his attention to these pressing questions.

For Levinas there is an ipseity underlying moral consciousness that accounts for "the *living* recurrence of subjectivity," the unity of self that does not stem from temporal flux. It is a living unity that, unlike consciousness, never slackens. It is not a movement of loss and recovery that characterizes consciousness, nor does it enter into appearances. The selfhood of the ownmost self is not the consequence of an intention to maintain itself as unitary; rather, it belongs to the self as not needing justification (S 493–94/BPW 84/AE 132/OBBE 104).

The moral self is in itself "as one is in one's skin." It is the very opposite of the personal pronoun "I," which masks singularity. It is the reflexive pronoun that, as we have seen, is in the accusative voice, the very opposite of power and domination and that belongs to the anteriority of the ownmost self. Genuine ipseity is a retreat into the ownmost self, without foundation elsewhere. It is always previously identified and so does not bear the onus of having to identify itself; it is always already older than consciousness. The identity of singularity is not the essence of the existent or a result of the synthetic operation of the intellect. Singularity is an identity that cannot even be asserted and therefore certainly cannot be vindicated. Furthermore Levinas writes: "These negative qualifications of subjectivity pertaining to the *oneself* do not hallow some ineffable mystery. They confirm a unity of the self which is presynthetic, prelogical, and (in some way) atomic, precluding the splitting up or separation of the self from itself, preventing it from showing itself (since no longer under a mask) and from being named otherwise than by a pro-noun. This prevention is the positivity of the One" (S 494/BPW 85/AE 136/OBBE 107). It is, in my view, not difficult to perceive the model of negative theology underlying Levinas's description of the self that transcends egoity.[30] Having already shown that thematizing consciousness guarantees that a being be what it is by bestowing a meaning upon that which is profiled in its numerous appearances, Levinas is compelled to insist that the ownmost self lie beyond the conferring of identity, beyond the function of intending the quiddity of a thing through manifold appearances. What appears to be a denial is, as William James puts it, "a denial made on behalf of a deeper yes."

Indeed, it is Levinas's purpose not to diminish the self by defining it, which is precisely the point of the *via negativa* in theology. As William James has pointed out: "Whoso calls the Absolute anything in particular, or says that it is *this,* seems implicitly to shut it off from being *that*—it is as if he lessened it. So we deny the 'this' negating the negation which it seems to us to imply, in the interest of the higher affirmative attitude by which we are possessed . . . qualifications are denied . . . not because the truth falls short of them, but because it so infinitely excels them. It is super-lucent, super-splendent, super-essential, super-sublime, super everything that can be named."[31] For Levinas the unity of the self precedes all process; it is the "very content of the self" and prior to all possible distinction. The self, as Levinas puts it, is always in a skin that is already too tight for it, that is, it exceeds its own enclosure. It may be recalled that the infinite always exceeds any idea one could have of it. Similarly the self exceeds the self that it is. What prevents the self from immediate coincidence with itself is its vulnerability to injury, which marks it as pure passivity. But this passivity is not to be confused with inert receptivity or with an effect that is passive in relation to the cause from which it proceeds. This "falling short" of identity does not revert to egoity, which perceives difference but adjudicates difference by reducing alterity to the same. The anguish of the self is an anxiety, a stifling, experienced as contraction. It is the feeling of being pursued into oneself (S 495/BPW 86/AE 137/OBBE 108). Coincidence with oneself results in serenity, the at-homeness of a being for whom satiety is possible.

Levinas seizes upon the metaphors of everyday language to express the reality of being in oneself. Living in one's own skin, or the dead time between heartbeats, or the time between inhalation and exhalation convey the sense of contraction Levinas has in mind, metaphors that are not arbitrary, for the body is not incidental to the ownmost self but its lived modality. Body is the in-itself of the deepest level of the self; it is the self's vulnerability.

It might be argued that the radical passivity that Levinas claims belongs to genuine subjectivity destroys all possibility of a subject. He concedes that this is true if the self is understood as thematizing consciousness, as the cognizing self, as pure egoity, for all of these functions originate activities of one sort or another. But prior to the upsurge of the world of freedom Levinas posits a primordial (*preoriginaire*) self. The paradox of the interiority described lies in the fact that there is a being such that its being precedes beginning: "*Interiority is the fact that in being the beginning is preceded.* But what precedes does not present itself to the free gaze that would assume it, does not become present or a representation. Something has already come to pass 'over the head' of the present, has not crossed the cordon of consciousness and does not let itself be recuperated, something that precedes the beginning and the principle, that is an-archically *despite* being, reverses or precedes being" (HAH 82/CPP 133). The something that lies outside the logos structure of reality precedes axiology, is a "susceptibility" through which the subject is responsible. This responsibility makes the subject accountable for responsibility itself. It is anterior to all intentional structure (HAH 83/CPP 134).

If there is a responsibility anterior to the world of freedom, Levinas must show that there is a responsibility that cannot be avoided. But if there is a responsibility that cannot be avoided, is one not enslaved to responsibility? In the case of slavery, Levinas argues, what is determined remains other than what determined it. For the determined to be other than what determined it, the determined must be free, that is, it must remember the moment when that which determined it did in fact determine it, when they both existed in a common present. However infinitesimal, freedom is conferred by the power of recollection. That is precisely why slavery can never be pure determination. But in the case of absolute passivity the term that does the determining is never present even in memory to the one who is determined by it (HAH 84ff./CPP 134ff.). Such radical determinism transcends the disjunction freedom or slavery. An object beyond choice that can never be presented to the determined is the Good itself. To be seized by the Good is for Levinas total submission. It is inescapable; it is an election. The good precedes all choice, for it is somehow present to the subject as the prediscursive foundation of his values. It commands obedience prior to specific commands. This responsibility prior to obedience is designated by Levinas as the an-archic; it transcends all principles that can be universalized. To be elect is to be invested with noninterchangeability, to have a unique meaning. Language only serves to obscure the meaning of the Good since language can bring to light only that which is. The closer one comes to a proper conceptualization of the notion of the Good, the closer one is to God's invisibility as it is presented biblically. That to which one is responsible is a nonthematizable value, unique and inescapable without a corresponding disvalue. Levinas does not hesitate to name this value: it is God (HAH 87/ CPP 136).

If this conception of the moral self is justified, how can the de facto condition of the world, the radical evil that meets the eye everywhere within the totality, be accounted for? Levinas suggests that the very nature of responsibility makes one vulnerable to what lies outside of the self; one is vulnerable to exteriority by virtue of being in the world as body. Being as body is what it means to be present in being. Levinas sees the *telos* of body itself as necessary for maintaining the duality structure required by a world of self and Other. Responsibility is always prior to the realm of choice, which is therefore a secondary phenomenon. Levinas is profoundly anti-Manichean in his insistence that evil is a falling away from an anterior realm of responsibility rather than being an independent phenomenon. It derives from a being's very need to persevere in his being that belongs to all beings. Indeed, it is this very fact that undercuts the sui generis quality of man; in the realm of ontology man is like all other beings. It is only when the self is brought back to itself that it undercuts the right to persist in being and introduces meaning into being.

NOTES

1. Many of Levinas's views on language are contained in a half dozen strategic essays: "La trace de l'autre," DEHH 187–202 ("The Trace of the Other," TrO 345–59); "Enigme et phenomène," DEHH 203–17 ("Enigma and Phenomenon," BPW 65–77); "Langage et proximité," DEHH 218–36 ("Language and Proximity," CPP 109–26); "La signification et le sens," HAH 17–70 ("Meaning and Sense," BPW 33–64);

"Humanisme et anarchie," HAH 73–91 ("Humanism and An-archy," CPP 127–39); and "La substitution," S 487–508 ("Substitution," BPW 79–95). "La substitution" was later expanded by Levinas and appeared in 1974 in AE 125–66 (OBBE 99–129).

2. Martin Heidegger, *Being and Time*, trans. John Macquarrie and Edward Robinson (New York: Harper and Row, 1962), 211ff.

3. Martin Buber, *I and Thou*, trans. Ronald Gregor Smith (2d ed.; New York: Scribner's Sons, 1958), 2–6.

4. "With no neighbors, and whole in himself, he is Thou and fills the heavens. This does not mean that nothing else exists except himself, but all else lives in his light" (ibid., 8).

5. "The spheres in which the world of relation arises are three. First, our life with nature. . . . Second, our life with men. . . . Third, our life with spiritual beings" (ibid., 66).

6. Ibid.

7. "There the relationship is clouded, yet it discloses itself; it does not use speech yet begets it" (ibid.).

8. Ibid., 33–34.

9. The remarkable proximity of Levinas's view to that of Hegel is evident in the following passage: "It is as a universal too that we *utter* what the sensuous [content] is. What we say is: 'This,' i.e. the *universal* This; or, 'it is,' i.e. *Being in general.* Of course, we do not *envisage* the universal This or Being in general, but we *utter* the universal; in other words, we do not strictly say what in this sense-certainty we *mean* to say. But language, as we see, is the more truthful; in it, we ourselves directly refute what we *mean* to say, and since the universal is the true [content] of sense-certainty and language expresses this true [content] alone, it is just not possible for us ever to say, or express in words, a sensuous being that we *mean*" (Hegel, *Phenomenology of Spirit*, trans. A. V. Miller [Oxford: Oxford University Press, 1977], 60).

10. The alternative discussed by Levinas refers mainly to Merleau-Ponty.

11. The term "expression" in this connection is broadly used. In the technical sense in which it usually appears in Levinas's work it means to "mean" in an unmediated way. Only the face in this latter sense truly expresses.

12. Mikel Dufrenne, *The Notion of the A Priori*, trans. Edward S. Casey (Evanston, Ill.: Northwestern University Press, 1966), 82, writes: "General meaning is given both as the meaning of the object and as vastly surpassing the objects, i.e., as true of other very different objects. Yet this generality is not obtained at the price of an abstraction forcefully separating it from these objects. Thus a playing child expresses youth, but youth is also expressed by one of Mozart's melodies or by spring."

13. Levinas has in mind Merleau-Ponty's view of body's existence as motility prior to all representation. Merleau-Ponty, *Phenomenology of Perception,* trans. Colin Smith (London: Routledge and Kegan Paul, 1962), 138–39, writes: "In the action of the hand which is raised towards an object is contained a reference to the object, not as an object represented, but as that highly specific thing towards which we project ourselves, near which we are in anticipation, and which we haunt. Consciousness is being towards the thing through the intermediary of the body. A movement is learned when the body has understood it, that is, when it has incorporated it into its 'world,' and to move one's body is to aim at things through it. . . . Motility is not . . . a handmaid of consciousness, transporting the body to that point in space of which we have formed a representation beforehand. . . . We must therefore avoid saying that our body is *in* space or *in* time. It inhabits space and time."

14. "Feelings and passional conduct are invented like words. Even those which like paternity, seem to be part and parcel of the human makeup are, in reality, institutions. It is impossible to superimpose on man a lower layer of behavior which one chooses to call 'natural,' followed by a manufactured cultural or spiritual world" (ibid., 189).

15. "I begin to understand the meaning of words through their place in a context of action, and by taking part in a communal life—in the same way an as yet imperfectly understood piece of philosophical writing discloses to me at least a certain 'style' " (ibid., 179).

16. I have chosen to translate "la trace" by its English cognate "trace" rather than by track, trail, spoor, footprint, and so on, so as to allow the widest possible meaning. The English "trace" not only conveys the evidence of a passing presence but can also mean the "residue" of a once fuller presence (a trace of blood, etc.). Moreover, anything may leave a trace or residue of itself, whereas tracks refer more specifically to an imprint left by creatures. In an early use of the term, Levinas indicates that one's acts leave tracks. He writes (EN 15/BPW 4): "like the prey that flees the noise of the hunter across a field covered in snow, thereby leaving the very trace that will be its ruin." This early use of the term places it in the context of being responsible for one's acts.

17. Jean-Paul Sartre, *Being and Nothingness,* trans. Hazel E. Barnes (New York: Philosophical Library, 1956), 256.

18. Levinas's third is a presence in absentia. His view is perhaps best expressed in the following lines from T. S. Eliot's "Waste Land," in *Collected Poems, 1909–1935* (New York: Harcourt, Brace, 1936), 87:

> Who is the third who walks always beside you?
> When I count there are only you and I together

But when I look ahead up the white road
There is always another one walking beside you . . .

According to Eliot, an account of a "party of explorers at the extremity of their strength" who sensed the presence of "one more member than could be counted" provided the occasion for these lines (97).

19. See also "A Man-God?" EN 73–74/ENT 57.

20. Nowhere else in Levinas's work does the problem of avoiding a world behind the scenes appear more pressing. In the attempt to bypass Kantian noumenality on the one hand, and the Hegelian reduction of being to reason on the other, Levinas seeks to solve the dilemma by reading a double meaning into already present instantiations, into what already exists phenomenally. What is present is all that *is*. What lies beyond being intrudes into the world of phenomena, but its meaning wells up from the phenomenon itself and eliminates the need for intermediate idealization. Meanings lie hidden yet are available to immediate moral awareness rather than to thematizing consciousness. It is not difficult to see that Levinas has given ethical weight and import to Heidegger's notion of forest trails. To those who understand forest lore, these trails are meaningful. Similarly, there are signs for those who seek a retrieval of being. Martin Heidegger, *Holzwege* (Frankfurt am Main: Vittorio Klostermann, 1957), 3, writes:

Holz lautet ein alter Name für Wald. Im Holz sind
Wege, die meist verwachsen jäh im Umbegangenen aufhören.
Sie heissen Holzwege. Jeder verläuft gesondert, aber im selben
Wald. Oft
scheint es, als gleiche einer dem anderen. Doch es
scheint nur so.
Holzmacher und Waldhüter kennen die Wege, Sie
wissen, was es heisst, auf einem Holzweg zu sein.

("Woods" is an old word for forest. In the woods there are/Paths that are mostly overgrown/And end in the untrodden./They are called woodpaths. Each runs separately but in the same forest. Often/It seems as if one was the same as the other. But/It only seems so.Woodcutters and forest rangers know these paths. They/Know what it means to be on a woodpath. [my translation]). Heidegger's idea becomes *religio* in Levinas's thought since there is no interrogation of being guided by traces, but an instant upsurge of transcendence in the field of the other's presence.

21. The English reader may be struck by the resemblance that

Levinas's view of the trace bears to John Wisdom's view of the ambiguity of divine presence in his essay "Gods" in *Proceedings of the Aristotelian Society* (1944–45). In Wisdom's parable two observers return to a long neglected garden where some plants are still seen to be thriving among the weeds. Investigation yields no positive evidence that anyone has been working in the garden, yet one of the observers perceives the trace of purposeful activity, of beauty and arrangement, while the other sees nothing but the work of chance.

22. In "Franz Rosenzweig: Une pensée juive moderne," in *Hors sujet* (Montpellier: Fata Morgana, 1987), 83; translated by Michael B. Smith as "Franz Rosenzweig: A Modern Jewish Thinker," in *Outside the Subject* (Stanford: Stanford University Press, 1993), 57, Levinas writes that for Rosenzweig the relation between God and the world is completed as always past.

23. It is impossible to clarify the meaning of a past that is admittedly beyond discourse. Levinas's view of the past is perhaps best captured by reference to poetic expression of a similar idea. T. S. Eliot, "The Dry Salvages," in *Four Quartets* (New York: Harcourt, Brace & World, 1943), 36–37, illustrates the point:

> The tolling bell
> Measures not our time, rung by the unhurried
> Ground swell, a time
> Older than the time of chronometers, older
> Than time counted by anxious worried women
> Lying awake calculating the future
> When time stops and time is never ending.

24. "It is without a doubt Kierkegaard who best understood the philosophical notion of transcendence which the biblical idea of the humility of God provides. Persecuted truth is not for him simply a truth poorly approached. Persecution and humiliation to which it exposes are modalities of the truth" (Levinas, "A Man-God?" EN 72/ENT 56).

25. I have translated the term "*soi-même*" of Levinas's later work as "ownmost self" to distinguish it from "*moi, subjectivité, soi,*" and so on, which were used interchangeably in his earlier work.

26. While Levinas explicitly rejects Simone Weil's view of the Old Testament (DL 189–200/DF 133–41), most recent analyses of the responsible self closely resemble her views in *Waiting for God,* trans. Emma Cranford (New York: G. P. Putnam's Sons, 1951), 130. Weil writes: "Christ proposed the docility of matter to us as a model when he told us to consider the lilies of the field that neither toil nor spin. This means that they have not set out to clothe themselves in that color; they

have not exercised their will or made arrangements to bring about their object; they have received all that natural necessity brought them. If they appear to be infinitely more beautiful than the richest stuffs, it is not because they are richer but a result of their docility." It is in connection with extreme affliction ("a marvel of divine technique") that the self experiences God.

27. What Levinas has written of Hegel's for-itself could have been applied with equal felicity to the for-itself of Sartre's *Being and Nothingness*. Levinas writes of Hegel (S 490/BPW 82/AE 129/OBBE 102): "The *for-itself* is thus the power that a being exercises over itself, its will and sovereignty." Similarly, "For Sartre, like Hegel, the [ownmost self] is posited as a *for itself*. The identity of the *I* would thus be reducible to a turning back of *essence* upon itself, a return to itself of essence as both subject and condition of the identification of the Same" (S 492/BPW 84/AE 131/OBBE 103).

28. Sartre, *Being and Nothingness*, 79.

29. In Levinas's thought expiation for others can never be undertaken as a task. The ownmost self is the primordial form of this expiation. The notion of substitution, of atoning for the sins of another, is fundamental to the Judaeo-Christian view of sacrifice. To cite at random one contemporary version of the meaning of full humility as being of others, Karl Barth in a chapter entitled "Jesus the Man for Other Men," in *Church Dogmatics*, vol. 3, part 2 (Edinburgh: T. & T. Clark, 1960), 212, writes: "There is not in Him a kind of deep inner rapture from His fellows. His relationship to His neighbors and sympathy with them are original and proper to Him and therefore belong to His innermost being. They are not a new duty and virtue which can begin and end, but He Himself is human, and it is for this reason that he acts as he does. . . . It means that He interposes Himself for them, that He gives Himself to them, that He puts Himself in their place, that He makes their state and fate His own cause, so that it is no longer theirs but His."

30. See also Jacques Derrida, "Violence et métaphysique: Essai sur la pensée d'Emmanuel Levinas," in *L'écriture et la différence* (Paris: Seuil, 1967), 170–71 (translated by Alan Bass as "Violence and Metaphysics: An Essay on the Thought of Emmanuel Levinas," in *Writing and Difference* [Chicago: University of Chicago Press, 1978], 116).

31. William James, *The Varieties of Religious Experience* (New York: Mentor, 1958), 319.

VII

Philosophy and the Covenant

WE HAVE SEEN how the biological continuity of man remains incomprehensible if an explanation is sought in the perpetuation of the species or in the pursuit of pleasure. Levinas has shown that the erotic as a phenomenon hovers at the brink of relation but sinks back into the biological domain of need. Love is fulfilled in fecundity and inaugurates a new dialectic, attesting continuity with the past while breaking with it through the emergence of an absolutely new self. The past is not a destiny. In the family, the self as egoity is called to responsibility and a distinctive mode of temporalization established, a mode in which existence is extended without denying the inevitability of death. Time is redeemed through the appearance of a new generation that unmakes the work of the past yet develops in fundamental continuity with it.

While Levinas refrains from the use of religious language in his philosophical work, it is not difficult to discern the religious perspectives in which these themes arise. It will be the purpose of this chapter to bring to light the religious sources from which his phenomenological analyses emerge and to which he devotes considerable attention in his nonphilosophical writing. The intrusion of the eschatological dimension into history consigned to the upsurge of the Other in *Totality and Infinity* will be seen in the perspective of traditional rabbinic commentary. It is from Talmudic sources that Levinas derives his emphasis upon the unique relation with the Other, not only as the most immediately given datum of experience, but as a datum that is ethical in its very upsurge.

WHAT JUDAISM MEANS

It is fundamental to Levinas's characterization of himself as thinker to disclaim the role of theologian. Even when asked to comment at a conference of Catholic intellectuals upon so patently theological an issue as the humanity and divinity of Jesus, he takes up the question as a problem for Husserlian phenomenology rather than as a question for theological speculation.[1] His diffidence stems not from lack of familiarity with the ongoing concerns of theologians, but from a more fundamental dissent arising from his view of Jewish religiosity.

For Levinas, authentic Judaism conceptualizes itself in terms of moral interiority; the supernatural is not its primary concern. Indeed, its relation with the divine is determined by the extent to which it is ethical (DL 76/DF 49).[2] Thus, the authentic enterprise of Jewish thought is a bringing to light of the ethical life world as it is understood in traditional Jewish texts. Judaism is "an extreme consciousness" for which Talmudic science provides the programmatics (DL 17/DF 6). Judaism unites men in terrestrial justice; its messianism is the promise and the completion of the work of justice. It is the task of the thinker to bring into the clarity of philosophical reflection the ethical insights found in the teachings of the Talmud and in the paradigmatic activities of the rabbis. These activities do not unfold as the sequentially ordered biographical narrative of sacred lives—that is, as hagiography—but as the recounting of instances of holy activity and conversation. Levinas notes that unrelated episodes, instantiations of divine presence, and biblical commentaries are the life world of the Talmud. Rabbinic religious consciousness can insert itself into contemporary life only as an irreconcilable countercurrent.

What is seductive in contemporary philosophical thought is the certainty men have of being in the presence of calculable powers that affect the being of things, of having insights into the meaning of history. The forces that govern human actions seem amenable to systematization just as the forces that govern nature can be understood and predicted. Through the apparent disorder of history we can discern the operation of laws governing that history and placing it within the purview of scientific analysis. There is no region, even that of interiority, which seems impenetrable to the power of reason (DL 294/DF 210).[3] This peculiarity of contemporary life does not, in Levinas's view, promise wisdom, that is, the conquest of eternity, since it fails to depart from the world of events. It inaugurates no dialogue with God as did Platonic speculation. The real world no longer presents itself in its primordiality but everywhere appears transformed by human agency. Things are now rendered intelligible through the human imprint they bear. Man is dominated by his world. The individual is enmeshed in a historical role often without being able to take a point of view with regard to it. The great vocation of reason is the appeal of a universal society homogeneous in essence (DL 292–93/DF 208–9).

Yet Levinas's understanding of contemporary existence goes beyond the presentation of modern life as the polar antithesis to Jewish values, for he also recognizes that paradoxically Judaism's own values run parallel to those of contemporary consciousness. Has it not been the historical role of Judaism to demythologize the pagan religions of the ancient world as the modern world has been demythologized by science? Is not the notion of a universal society the consequence of prophetic vision? The question must be asked: Is contemporary life the adversary or the double of Jewish consciousness? (DL 295/DF 211).

The primary meaning of Israel, however, belongs not to its demythologizing tendencies or to its vision of a universal society but to the fundamental emphasis it places upon inner life. Contemporary existence puts inner life itself into question by attributing the values that arise from inner life to the social conditions of their origin. Ideas themselves now belong to the world of becoming, are born and die in the societies in which they appear. Prophecy is seen as the consequence of historical forces, as having no inner life except what is lent to it by the socioeconomic factors that eventuated in its appearance. The meaning of Israel has lost its unique quality and has been integrated into the historical process itself. Thus, for Levinas, the Hegelian view of cultures is the most formidable threat to the absolute values presented by the ethics of Judaism.

But even Hegelian philosophy requires the disengagement of the thinker who evaluates the work of history and who stands outside of history. The historical process cannot be invoked to explain away the thinker himself, the one before whom the process in all its richness unfolds. To put the problem in Levinas's terms, someone must be as old as the world to think it. The contemporary world needs this point of fixity, a point of reference in the person rather than in the thought of the thinker. Having disengaged the thinker from the content of his thought, Levinas regards the person as the instantiation of justice, a motionless point in the world from which all truth emanates and to which all truth refers, a foundation of fixity antecedent to any thought that we can have of it or any system into which we can integrate it. Judaism is in its essence a reinstatement of the person as the final source of all values. Thus, Judaism can serve as a corrective to what Levinas understands as the contemporary worldview which attempts to become more and more encompassing while losing sight of the interiority of the individual.

Judaism establishes a vigorous obedience to law that breaks into the sequentiality of the cause-and-effect mode of reasoning by judging it. In addition, the contemporary worldview attempts to conform to its own time in order not to renege on its contemporaneity. It may be recalled that in his analysis of the trace, Levinas refers to the trace as being unable to coincide with the time of its upsurge. It belongs to an immemorial past that can never be made present through an effort of recollection and is therefore an anachronism. This description applies to the role of Judaism in contemporary life. It is and must remain anachronistic in the sense that it represents a noncoincidence with its time (DL 297/ DF 212). Judaism maintains the temporality of interiority against the time of history. To be human, that is, to be the self as responsibility, is to be an anachronism: "Monotheism and its moral revelation constitute the concrete fulfilment, beyond all mythology, of the primordial anachronism of the human" (DL 297/DF 213).

The self cannot be institutionalized. Prophecy, at least from the standpoint of its own self-understanding, is the phenomenon most recalcitrant to integration into social institutions. According to Levinas, only the false prophet is the member of an officialdom. This is expressed most dramatically in the biblical description of Elijah whose self-sufficiency is so complete that he is divorced from economy; he is even fed by ravens (DL 298/DF 213).[4] The point of Levinas's analysis is this: history has provided no new categories for the judgment of man. What is revelatory in revelation is the modus operandi of judgment, which no new data in the historical order can unseat. The Talmud "means" in the sense that it provides all categories necessary for the judgment of novelty. Everything that is required for the moral evaluation of events already preexists in the sacred texts. In his terms, "It is the eternal anteriority of wisdom with respect to science and history" (DL 299/DF 213–14).

While for Levinas the biblical text together with its traditional commentaries provide norms for ethical judgment, his is far from a naive fundamentalism. This claim is true both because he asserts that Israel is an ethical rather than a soteriological community and because he refuses to deny the dramatic quality of historical change. In the former respect he differs little from neo-Kantian rationalist interpretations of Jewish tradition. In the latter respect, despite his view that man, wherever he has arisen, is fully human, that Adam does not await completion through the historical process, Levinas gives full credence to the dimension of the unanticipated, to the genuinely novel elements in history: "History is not simply a diminished and corrupted eternity, nor is it the mobile image of immobile eternity; history and [becoming] have a positive meaning, an unforeseeable fecundity; the future moment is absolutely new, but it requires history and time in order to come about" (DL 101/DF 67).

If Judaism is an ethical community, a community of "hypertrophied" conscience, what meaning can be given to the psychology of divine revelation in which the ethical is grounded? How are we to understand the Jewish notion of the holiness of God? According to Levinas, the rabbis understand divine holiness in a way that undermines its significance as numinosity. Judaism is a disenchantment of the world. The numinous carries man beyond his own powers, but divine transport is an offense to human freedom. The uncontrollable seizure that constitutes the human experience of the numinous annuls the relation between persons that is the foundation for all ethical relations. Thus, the numinosity of pagan religion appears to Jewish consciousness as a transgression of human freedom. But freedom is not for Judaism an end in itself; rather it is the presupposition without which human values cannot be realized. The God of Israel is not the survivor who follows upon the departure of mythical pagan deities but is radically different from them. Jewish monotheism does not consolidate the cosmic powers so that its God represents the sum of all power, nor does it arrange the pagan manifestations of the numinous into hierarchies. Instead it denies the numinous as such (DL 28/ DF 14).

The destruction of the numinous portends not the appearance of monotheism but the risk of atheism. We have already seen how freedom from the *il y a*, the absolutely impersonal sacred, from a formlessness without light encountered in horror could be attained only by a movement of radical severance. The spirituality of Israel is now understood as already presupposing this movement of separated being, lived as atheism, which has freed itself from the numenality of primitive religion to emerge as a free self (DL 29/DF 14–15). Judaism appears only when knowledge and truth have become possible, for it represents an access to truth without ecstatic experience. It presupposes human sovereignty and the value of consciousness. We have seen that consciousness appropriates reality without engulfing it. "Consciousness-of" is the very opposite of possession in the sense that consciousness does not touch the independence of the existent to which it addresses itself. It resists the violence of enthusiasm and the absorption by a reality outside the self that obliterates the distinction between self and world.

The consciousness of justice is inseparable from consciousness as such. According to Levinas, the interpretation of Genesis by the eleventh-century commentator Rashi already presupposes this point of view. Rashi asks: Why does Genesis begin with the creation rather than with the commandments? Because it is important for man who now possesses the earth to know that he has a right to it. It is his as a gift from God and therefore has not been acquired by usurpation. Thus, man has been taught that to possess is always to receive (DL 32/DF 17). While the peasant is attached to the earth without the necessity of vindicating his claim to property, the child of Aram who is a wanderer must legitimate his right of ownership. The moral self appears at the outset to Jewish tradition as its elemental mode of being. For Levinas, the ethical is not an adventitious addition to a vision of God but belongs to it essentially: "The moral relation therefore reunites both self-consciousness and consciousness of God. Ethics is not the collorary of the vision of God, it is that very vision. Ethics is an optics" (DL 33/DF 17).

All morality is grounded in a heteronomous will. To know God is already obedience to another. The face of the Other opens the realm of transcendence. How can Levinas insist upon the freedom of the moral agent in accordance with the principles of Kantian ethics while maintaining at the same time that moral action begins with a heteronomous will? The sense of responsibility belonging to the agent is at the deepest level of the self a sense of unimpeachable moral responsibility, a sense that emerges simultaneously with the separated self. But to maintain that it is intrinsic to human personality is still not to free it from the incursions of heteronomy. For Levinas, heteronomy is not the imposition of a divine will, but a revelation through the appearance of other persons (DL 33/DF 17). The notion that the Other does not compel but solicits is consistent with traditional Jewish thought yet does not impose itself as an alien will destructive to freedom. Levinas's attempt to save human freedom, while maintaining that human action depends upon the recognition of heteronomy, rests upon understanding the term in its authentic sense as nonviolent and therefore noncompelling. He thus avoids the coerciveness attached to the Kantian interpretation of heteronomy while still affirming heteronomy as an absolutely passive principle of alterity that founds moral action. This view of heteronomy belongs for Levinas to the Jewish understanding of the Other as one who is suffering and helpless, who cannot compel but only solicit and appeal. To know God is to obey the will of the Other; God becomes accessible through the appearance of one's neighbor.

Levinas recognizes that doing precedes hearing in Judaism and that the doing in question refers not only to ethical action but also to ritual practice. What is the justification for Jewish ritual if ethical action is founded in the upsurge of the Other and if such action is the way in which Judaism appears in the world? What, in short, accounts for the necessity of Jewish ritual praxis? According to Levinas, the obedience to ritual law constitutes a discipline that tends toward justice (DL 34/DF 18). In obeying ritual law, the demand of the Other is recognized; the Other, in this case God, has a right to suppress the egoity of the separated self. Levinas emphasizes the difference between Jewish ritual and Christian sacrament. In the former, nothing is transformed; what is done is done because it is commanded and one chooses to obey the commandment. In the latter, a transformation occurs as a result of the sacrament. The value of ritual in Levinas's thought lies in its governance of everyday life, as well as in its hallowing of the world. The preeminence of ritual can be seen from the following text:

> Here is a passage in which three opinions are given: the second indicates the way in which the first is true, and the third indicates the practical conditions of the second. Ben Zomma said: "I have a verse which contains the whole of the Torah: '[Hear] O Israel, the Lord is our God, the Lord is One.' " Ben Nanus said: "I have a verse that contains the whole of the Torah: 'You will love your neighbor as yourself.' " Ben Pazi said: "I have a verse that contains the whole of the Torah: 'You will sacrifice a lamb in the morning and another at dusk.' " And Rabbi, their master, stood up and decided: "The law is according to Ben Pazi." (DL 35/DF 18–19)

Levinas does not attempt to transform the commandment or ritual law into ethical teaching. What he stresses is the value of obedience as a discipline. But if ritual is merely a discipline and if the appearance of the Other in and of itself commands obedience, the question must be raised: why, from Levinas's point of view, is ritual law necessary? If transcendence is experienced in the very upsurge of the one who is near, ritual seems superfluous. Indeed, this is the point of view adopted by nineteenth-century liberal theologians for whom moral law alone sufficed to maintain the integrity of Jewish religiosity. Given Levinas's emphasis upon the upsurge of alterity as the prerequisite for religion, both as its necessary and sufficient condition, it is difficult to understand his stress upon the necessity for ritual praxis.

Together with the centrality of ritual, Levinas maintains that Judaism is the acceptance of a biological identity. One is not a Jew because one has certain qualities or lacks others, but rather one is in Judaism, according to Levinas, as one is in oneself. It may be recalled that this modality of being is, for Levinas, a being in one's own skin anterior to the self of thematizing consciousness; it involves the vulnerability of incarnation, of being as body. One is born a Jew; this identity is anterior to all other goals that are the consequence of becoming. It is to be what one is prior to all allegiance, to obey "like a guard who never expects to be relieved" (DL 79/DF 50). The Jew is responsible for all of creation; Jewish identity is "patience, fatigue and . . . responsibility" (DL 79/DF 51). It is the very opposite of Western worldviews that refuse obedience without a prior act of acquiescence so that personal sovereignty is always maintained. The spontaneous acceptance of Jewish life is replaced in Western thought by a distancing of oneself from whatever is accepted.

Jewish praxis, both ritual and ethical, is prior to understanding. The exemplar of this life view is the Pharisee who struggles with questions and obtains answers not through brute violence but through intellectual conflict. On the one hand, his way of entering the divine realm is the very opposite of enthusiasm, and on the other he rejects monolithic truths that lose the concreteness of life, with all of its possibilities, by uniting what is disparate into a concept.[5] To the consciousness of the Pharisee, apparent platitudes conceal subtleties available only to the trained eye of an interpreter. The Pharisee draws from the source of life without mistaking himself for it. In asserting that Pharisaism represents Jewish religiosity, Levinas does not have in view the Jewish-Christian polemic, the defense of the Pharisee against Christian attack. He is, rather, asserting the integrity of legal Judaism against the romantic exponents of Hasidism as the appropriate wellspring of authentic Jewish experience: "In this romantic age when spirit is confused with drama, when Jews understand only the Hassidic tales, what purity this represents in this world [of Talmud] that in giving loses not even what the tip of a brush would take from the sea" (DL 50/DF 29).

The Pharisee as a type grows up in the expectation of justice in an as yet unredeemed world. What is visible to authentic Jewish consciousness is the fearful quality of human existence when God veils his face. When God leaves the world to its own devices men are sacrificed to the philosophy of their instincts. Since these are the instincts that dominate the world, it follows that those who preserve the divine presence in the world will be the first to fall victim to this domination. The veiling of God's face is the hour when the just man finds no refuge (DL 203/DF 143). If God is hidden, how can he be recognized as intimate and present to the world? For Jewish consciousness, divine presence is attested in the "nonincarnate word." The relation between God and man is not for Judaism a communion of feeling in love but a relation between minds, through the teaching of Torah.

HISTORICAL METHOD AND TRADITIONAL TEXTS

Levinas does not restrict his attention to general and abstract conclusions concerning the nature of Jewish religiosity but comments directly upon particular traditional texts. It therefore becomes a matter of some importance to elicit from his specific references to method and from an examination of his interpretations the procedures that he follows in textual exegesis. He wishes to exclude neither the significance derived from a text by the naive believer nor that which is elicited by the sophisticated theologian. Both are licit modes of interpretation. However, he insists that his own approach begin from a philosophical viewpoint. Such a viewpoint, he maintains, affirms that the problems with which a text deals can be transposed into "philosophical language," and, significantly, that sacred texts already refer to "philosophical problems" (DL 101/DF 68). It is the "rational meaning" of the text that forms the object of his quest. The "rational meaning" is not to be confused with an abstract meaning since for Levinas philosophical investigation is directed to questions of human concern. It is to these questions that he expects to find answers in Talmudic study: "The laconic formulae, images, allusions and virtual 'winks' through which thought finds expression in the Talmud can [release] their meaning only if one approaches them from the angle of a concrete problem or social situation, without worrying about the apparent anachronisms committed as a result" (DL 101/DF 68).[6]

Levinas insists that this approach can only displease fanatical adherents of the historical method. He explicitly rejects what he considers to be the chief obstacle in a strictly historical approach, namely, the presupposition that thought unfolds historically, that before certain historical epochs certain thoughts were unthinkable. Levinas assumes on the contrary that intelligence at the outset, from the moment of its appearance, is intrinsically capable of understanding whatever will emerge in the course of time.[7] Thus, for Levinas an ancient text necessarily provides answers to contemporary questions. The new self-understanding yielded by the study of traditional texts means that the text is adequate to contemporary problems, but not that contemporary exegesis must be a mechanical repetition of its historical precedents. Without such an approach guiding investigation, the biblical and Talmudic texts to which Jewish faith refers would be mere compendia of ritual and folkloric material of interest to the historian alone.

Levinas does not contest the value of historical research that opens new and interesting avenues for Jewish self-understanding. But he maintains that such research fails to uncover the inner life of the text since through any given text the absolute structure of thought is given. Levinas concedes that this confidence is, if one wishes to designate it as such, faith: "No one can refuse the insights of history. But we do not think they are sufficient for everything" (QLT 14/NTR 5). It is clear that for Levinas the Talmud is the *viva vox* of teaching. The putting of questions to a text from the perspectives of one's own existence enables the thinker to retain a relation to the sacrality of the text, without disregarding the fruits of historical research.[8] Thus, Levinas feels justified in reading a text to elicit what the text "intends" rather than what it reveals concerning the historical circumstances of its origin. It is then possible to translate what is given into the language of contemporary civilization. The goal of exegesis is to disengage universal views from the particularism of Israel's history as given in its sacred texts (QLT 15/NTR 5).

Levinas distinguishes what he calls "two regions" of the past: the first belongs to historical research proper and requires scholarly interpretation; the second is one to which believing communities are still attached in a living way through the continuity of ongoing textual exegesis (QLT 17/NTR 6). The Bible belongs to the former category, the Talmud to the latter. The life world of the Talmud, because of the unbroken succession of students who addressed themselves to its problems, remains immediately accessible.[9] The existence of an uninterrupted tradition, Levinas finds, makes the Talmud part of modern history. The Talmud is not an adjunct to the Bible, completing it as the New Testament is understood by some to complete the Old (QLT 18/NTR 7). It does not pretend to prolong the narrative sequence begun in the biblical world, for it is not an extension of biblical revelation. Nor does the "literal meaning" in Talmudic thought yield the required meaning. The "literal meaning" is that "which *completely* signifies" while being "not yet the signified" (QLT 19/NTR 7). The signified is precisely the object under investigation. Interpretation does not merely add on conventional elements to an original given, nor does it confer a privileged status on one or another aspect of the symbols of a text. Instead the symbol remains what it is but becomes subject to the enrichment of historical accretions.

In examining material borrowed from other sources in a Talmudic text, what is important is the spirit in which the borrowing is made. The borrower seeks not historical accuracy but to found his own point of view in an ancient tradition. He thus gives to that tradition the meaning that he himself bestows upon what he borrows.

The Talmud begins with life, not merely in order to understand the experience to which it refers, but in order to perceive the meaning of the symbols themselves. The materials of the Talmud are signs, for they never give themselves in their entirety but remain latent, as it were, retaining the power for self-renewal: "Thus, these signs—biblical verses, objects, persons, situations, rites—function as perfect signs: whatever the modifications that the passage of time introduces into their visible texture, they keep their privilege of revealing the same meanings or new aspects of these same meanings. . . . Never does the meaning of these symbols fully dismiss the materiality of the symbols which suggest it. They always preserve some unexpected capacity for renewing this meaning" (QLT 20–21/NTR 8). For Levinas the symbol "means" despite its detachment from its historical origins. He calls this mode of thought "paradigmatic." In this way the possibilities of the symbol are respected yet the ideas to which they give rise are never divorced from the symbols that both suggest and limit them.

Can Levinas's method of inquiry properly be termed phenomenological? Herbert Spiegelberg writes at the conclusion of his history of the phenomenological movement: "On all levels the phenomenological approach is opposed to explanatory hypotheses; it confines itself to the direct level of intuitive seeing. . . . It constitutes a determined attempt to enrich the world of our experience by bringing out hitherto neglected aspects of our ex-

perience. . . . One might describe the underlying unity of phenomenological procedures as the unusually obstinate attempt to
look at the phenomena and to remain faithful to them before
even thinking about them."[10] In this sense Levinas's Talmudic
exegesis falls well within the phenomenological tradition, since
the investigation of phenomena by intuitive and descriptive
means belongs properly to that procedure. Levinas has insisted
that a study of Talmud is the quest for meaning apart from genetic considerations. These meanings are not immediately manifest and must be uncovered. We have also seen that Levinas claims
that Talmudic texts begin with problems of existence, with concrete situations and experiences. He presupposes the transhistorical unity of Jewish consciousness and the permanence and
continuity of Israel. In this sense Levinas interprets the text from
what could more properly be termed an "existential" standpoint.
Thus, his Talmudic interpretations bear witness not only to a deep
indebtedness to Husserlian principles but also to Heidegger's her-
meneutical phenomenology.[11]

THE PHENOMENON OF ATONEMENT

In what is for him a key ethical issue, Levinas cites this text:

> For transgressions between man and the Omnipotent the Day of
> Atonement procures atonement, but for transgressions as between
> man and his fellow the Day of Atonement does not procure any
> atonement until he has pacified his fellow. (Yoma 85a)

The first significant feature that Levinas takes into account is that
our sins with regard to God are forgiven without any dependence
upon God's good will.[12] Despite the fact that God is the Other par
excellence, forgiveness rests with oneself. The means for obtain-
ing pardon are within one's own grasp. Levinas denies that pardon is automatic as soon as the Day of Atonement dawns. A
contrite heart is also required. But if repentance is genuine, God
forgives the sins committed against him, but transgressions
against another must be pardoned by one's fellow man. One is
required to pacify the aggrieved party. The danger in this case is
considerable since one may remain unpardoned (QLT 36–37/

NTR 16). Can one then conclude that the sin committed against the other man is a more grievous fault than the sin committed against God? Levinas uncovers the subtle nature of the process of repentance by showing first that the sin against the Other is also a sin against God, second that sins that require healing through repentance now include sins against the Other, and last that the infractions committed against God are the source of our cruelty toward others.

If *teshuvah* (repentance) takes place at the deepest level of interiority, why then is the Day of Atonement required? The damaged moral consciousness requires redemption. This dialectic of collective worship and interior purification is an essential feature of Jewish repentance. Ritual awakens the vigilance of conscience, conditions it, urges it to repentance:

> [We learned] for transgessions committed by man against his fellow man, the Day of Atonement procures no Atonement, but it is written (I Sam. 2:25): *If one man sins against his fellowman God* [Elohim] *will pacify him.* (Yoma 85a)

This passage cites Scripture in direct opposition to the Mishna we have just examined. The difficulty is resolved in the following way: the word *Elohim* is translated either as God or as judge. The passage can then be read as conforming to the text of the Mishnah. If a man commits a sin against another man, divine intervention need not be sought. An earthly court can institute and maintain justice among men. Thus, several new elements are introduced in the relation between persons: justice, the judge, and sanctions (QLT 41/NTR 18).

It may be recalled that in Levinas's phenomenological analysis of justice the third person is introduced as the one who suffers the repercussions of human activity that might originate in the intimate society of two. Human action is for Levinas always social in its foundations and always bears repercussions beyond the original intention of the action itself. Consistent with this point of view Levinas interprets the Talmudic text to mean that forgiveness itself demands social intervention, which is introduced with the use of the term *Elohim*, which can mean judge. But the Talmud points out that the biblical verse cited, which seemed to resolve the question on this basis, is only one-half of the original verse, which is actually completed in the following way: "But if a man sin against YHVH who shall entreat for him?" Does not the entire verse then refer to YHVH after all? The Gemara refuses to grant the legitimacy of this position and proposes the following resolution of the question:

> If man sins against his fellowman, the judge will judge him, he [his fellow] will forgive him; but if a man sins against the Lord God who shall entreat for him? Only repentance and good deeds. (Yoma 85a)

Levinas perceives in the thesis that proclaims the offense against man to be an offense against the Lord the presentiment of a Hegelian point of view. The Rabbi who expounds it underestimates the gravity of the sin against the individual. But the Gemara insists that the pardon of God himself depends upon respecting the injured party. Levinas adds: "God is perhaps nothing but this permanent refusal of a history which would come to terms with our private tears" (QLT 44/NTR 20).

The paragraph that follows in the text of the Gemara brings to light a new element in the relationship with others, the gravity of breaking one's word to the Other:

> Rabbi Isaac said: Whosoever offends his neighbor and he does it only through words, must pacify him as it is written: *My son if thou art become surety for thy neighbor, if thou hast struck thy hands for a stranger—, thou art snared by the words of thy mouth . . . [D]o this now, my son and deliver thyself, seeing thou art come into the hand of thy neighbor; go humble thyself and urge thy neighbor.* (Proverbs 6:1–3) If he has a claim of money upon you, open the palm of your hand to him, and if not send many friends to him. (Yoma 85a)

The Talmud tries to show here that a verbal offense is as serious as a material offense. The forgiveness of the injured party must in both cases be obtained. Thus, a case concerning money is cited from Scripture to show that the neighbor must be pacified, although the injury in question at the beginning of the passage is a verbal slight. Why? According to Levinas, the Talmud wishes to teach the meaning of one's word. The original meaning of the word is a promise made on behalf of our neighbor in the presence of a third person. This indeed is the founding act of society. Here again Levinas shows the basic significance of language from a philosophical point of view, for language is not the designation of an object that we may bring into the realm of discourse common to ourselves and others, "a game with no consequences," but the assumption of responsibility for one's neighbors in the presence of witnesses.

The Talmud does not hesitate to depict the payment of money as an indication of the seriousness of one's commitment to one's word. This is for Levinas an indication of the Talmud's steadfast refusal to "spiritualize" since spiritualization can become a stratagem for evading responsibility (QLT 47/NTR 21). The text that follows proceeds to the heart of the matter, the real meaning of offense to the Other.

> R. Jose b. Hanina said: One who asks pardon of his neighbor need do so no more than three times, as it is said: *Forgive I Pray thee now . . . and now we pray thee.* (Yoma 87a)

Levinas notes that the biblical quotation refers to the brothers of Joseph, who beg pardon after the death of Jacob. The brothers repeat the apology dictated by Jacob:

> "Forgive I pray you, the transgression of your brothers and their sin because they did evil to you," and now, we pray you, forgive the transgression of the servants of your father. (Gen. 50:17)

For Levinas the choice of the biblical passage in question is significant. Brothers have sold a brother into slavery. "The exploitation of man by man" is for Levinas the prototype of all offense (QLT 49/NTR 22).

Levinas concludes his analysis of pardon by commenting upon two anecdotes in the same chapter, one concerning a matter of forgiveness between the famous Rab and a butcher, the second concerning another similar matter of forgiveness that transpired between Rab and his teacher Rabbi Hanina. Consider the first anecdote:

> Rab once had a complaint against a certain butcher and when on the eve of the Day of Atonement he [the butcher] did not come to him, he said: I shall go to him to pacify him. R. Huna met him and asked: Whither are you going Sir? He said, To pacify so and so. He thought: Abba is about to cause one's death. He went there and remained standing before him [the butcher] who was sitting and chopping an [animal's] head. He raised his eyes and saw him

[Rab], then said: You are Abba, go away, I will have nothing to do with you. Whilst he was chopping the head, a bone flew off, struck his throat, and killed him. (Yoma 87a)

Levinas notes first of all that the commentators vindicate Rab (QLT 50/NTR 22). It was the obligation of the butcher to ask Rab's pardon on the Day of Atonement for an offense committed against Rab. Rab then determines that he is obligated for the sake of the sinner to present himself before the sinner and thus, in a manner of speaking, "demand" pardon. In this case the injured party feels a deeper sense of responsibility than the aggressor. Rab goes out of his way to awaken a sense of moral responsibility in the sinner. The odd episode of the encounter on the road with the student is interpreted by Levinas to mean that the student understands at once that the butcher will remain unmoved. He thus knows that Rab, despite his excellent intention, has signed the butcher's death warrant. For now the sin has grown. The original hardheartedness of the sinner is augmented by his refusal to beg pardon in the presence of the teacher who comes to remind him of his fault. The appearance of Rab elicits the following words from the butcher: "Go away, I will have nothing to do with you." The butcher, according to Levinas, remains locked into his own world refusing reciprocity to the other. He lives in a world of mutual exclusivity. Rab on the other hand has assumed a great responsibility in the confidence that he bestowed upon the other (QLT 51/NTR 23).

The second and longer passage depicts the relation not between a good man and an evildoer but between two sages of great repute:

Once Rab was expounding portions of the Bible before Rabbis, and there entered R. Hiyya, whereupon Rab started again from the beginning; as Bar Kappara entered, he started again from the beginning; as R. Simeon, the son of Rabbi entered he started again from the beginning. But when R. Hanina b. Hama entered he said: So often shall I go back? And he did not go over it again. R. Hanina took that amiss. Rab went to him on thirteen eves of the Day of Atonement, but he would not be pacified. But how could he do so; did not R. Jose b. Hanina say: One who asks pardon of his neighbor need not do so more than three times?—It is different with Rab. But how could R. Hanina act so (unforgivingly)? Had not Rab said that if one passes over his rights, all his transgressions are passed over (forgiven) ?—Rather: R. Hanina had seen in a dream that Rab was being hanged on a palm tree, and since the tradition is that one who in a dream is hanged on a palm tree will become head (of an Academy) he concluded that authority will be given to him, and so he would not be pacified to the end that he departed to teach Torah in Babylon. (Yoma 85b)

Levinas notes that two possible interpretations of the offense can be given, one trivial, the other serious: (1) that an offense between "intellectual" peers is the least reparable of breaches, and (2) that it is better not to have offended in the first place. Despite the oft-cited view that no just man can attain the place reserved for repentant sinners, Levinas is emphatic upon this point: the just man who has not sinned is to be preferred.

But the Talmud raises many questions still unanswered by these interpretations. Why does Rab appeal more than the required three times for pardon? Because Rab is an exceptional man who is not satisfied to fulfill minimum requirements and perhaps because the offended party is his teacher. Levinas shifts the argument to a philosophical framework by suggesting that the Other is always one's teacher and pardon can never be requested a sufficient number of times: "The seeking for forgiveness never comes to an end. Nothing is ever completed" (QLT 53/NTR 24).

Why, however, did Rab's teacher allow his pupil to solicit so many times? Levinas's explanation reverts to these lines: "One forgives all sins to whoever cedes his rights" (QLT 53/NTR 34). The one who passes over his rights is as one who has only obligations. Thus, Hanina in allowing Rab to pass over his rights actually puts him in the position of one whose sins have been forgiven.

The explanation given by the Gemara is at first glance a mechanical and mythological resolution of the question. Through a dream, Hanina has learned that his pupil will be the head of an academy and makes him depart without granting him pardon. What does this story really mean? Levinas proffers a psychoanalytic explanation. An offense can be pardoned when the offender is conscious of his fault. But does the offender know the true extent of his transgression? R. Hanina has learned in a dream more than Rab knows about himself. The dream reveals to the master the extent of the student's secret ambitions. Rab really desires the place of his master. Thus, R. Hanina cannot really pardon him because Rab does not really know what he wants. An offense that cannot be brought to consciousness cannot be pardoned.

Levinas also suggests an interpretation that could be called the reverse of the preceding. It is perhaps possible to pardon someone who is rash and quick-tongued, someone without deep moral self-awareness. But Rab is the very opposite of the quick-tempered man and therefore the transgression is less pardonable than that of the simple man, for his is a heightened moral consciousness (QLT 55–56/NTR 25).

JEWISH MESSIANISM: THE BREAK WITH TOTALITY

Judaism's view of Messianism enables Levinas to establish a link between the world of injustice and a hypothesized just social order. Classical Jewish messianism claims that there is a difference between the future world and the messianic era:

> Rabbi Hiyya b. Abba said in Rabbi Johanan's name: All the prophets prophesied [all the good things] only in respect of the messianic era; but as for the world to come, *the eye hath not seen, O Lord beside thee what he hath prepared for him that waiteth for him* (Is. 64:3). (Sanhedrin 99a)

The thesis that is here sustained posits a difference between an era whose fruition can be expected because prophesied and an order exterior to historical fulfillment. The messianic era is a link between the historical order, whose promises are fulfilled at its advent, and the mysterious world-to-come. In messianic times the injustice and alienation of historical time will be brought to a close. Judaism, Levinas maintains, teaches not only the truth of communal good, of what is proper to the social order. It is a relation of risk, since it provides a model for justice without any guarantee for personal salvation:

> Personal salvation of men, the discreet and intimate relationship between man and God, escapes the indiscretion of the prophets; no one can fix in advance the itinerary of this adventure. (DL 92/ DF 61)

The Gemara that follows announces an opposing opinion:

> Now he disagrees with Samuel who said: This world differs from
> that of the days of the Messiah only in respect of servitude to for-
> eign powers. (Sanhedrin 99a)

At first glance it would seem that Rabbi Samuel is merely nar-
rowing the scope of what will occur in the messianic era: it portends only the end of political violence and may refer as well to
the end of Israel's diasporic existence. This can be taken to mean
that political violence will no longer appear to interfere with the
moral work of man. Does this mean that for Rabbi Samuel social
inequality will persist, although political violence will be brought
to an end? The biblical verse "The poor will not disappear from
the earth" (Deut. 15:11) would appear to sustain this point of
view. Yet Levinas maintains that the verse "that there be no poor
among you" (Deut. 15:41) could not have been unknown to him.
What meaning can then be attributed to his position? For R.
Hayya b. Abba speaking in R. Johanan's name, we have seen that
the messianic era puts an end to both political and social problems to initiate a new type of life, artistic, contemplative, or active.
The position of Rabbi Samuel now becomes clear. Despite the
advent of messianic times economic solidarity with the Other
does not cease; giving cannot be suppressed even by the messianic
era because it is at the heart of the moral life (DL 93–94/DF 62).
If a too literal construction is put upon Samuel's interpretation,
we see the status quo of a repressive economic order remaining
so that the rich might retain the poor in order to feed them. But
Levinas maintains that what is meant is that the Other as Other is
always poor, for this is the way in which alterity is defined. It may
be recalled that in Levinas's philosophical work a fundamental
asymmetry characterizes our relation to the Other. We can only
respond to his elevation with a gift: the offer of self. Thus, for
Samuel the end of history cannot do away with poverty, for it *is*
the alterity of the Other. This thought can be developed further.
Messianic times still belong to the historical order and thus can
only deepen and reveal the moral requirement opened up within
that order while retaining its perspectives. Only the interior life
of the individual, on the other hand, which belongs to the world
to come, inaugurates a transhistorical dimension. Rabbi Samuel

sees in messianic times the requirements of stern moral vigilance. The text continues:

> Rabbi Hiyya ben Abba also said in Rabbi Johanan's name: All the prophets prophesied only for repentant sinners; but as for the perfectly righteous [who had never sinned at all], *the eye hath not seen, O God beside thee, what he hath prepared for him that waiteth for him.* (Sanhedrin 99a)

We learn from R. Johanan that the prophets prophesied for the repentant sinner, but that the future world is reserved for the just who are wrenched from the contradictions of historical life.

A second saying of Rabbi Johanan reads as follows:

> R. Hayya b. Abba also said in R. Johanan's name: All the prophets prophesied only in respect of him who marries his daughter to a scholar, or engages in business on behalf of a scholar, or benefits a scholar with his possessions; but as for scholars themselves, *the eye hath not seen, O God, beside thee, etc.* (Sanhedrin 99a)

The prophet prophesies for those who continue their everyday occupations but remain spiritually detached from them, who dedicate themselves to nonworldly pursuits typified by the study of the law. It they cannot do this, then they dedicate what is most precious to them to mediate between them and the study of Torah. It is also clear from this text that Rabbi Johanan believes that the advent of messianic times depends upon human merit. Samuel, in a text to follow shortly, dissociates himself from this position. Radical intervention of a transhistorical event in the person of the Messiah is required before messianic times can begin.

The next text reads (Sanhedrin 99a): "To the wine that has been kept maturing with its grapes since the six days of creation." According to Levinas the wine that has been maturing since the six days of creation is a promise to reveal what now is hidden, the meaning of Scripture, the true meaning of all language. It may be recalled that in Levinas's philosophical writing, language, the trace, is enigmatic, swathed in ambiguity. The promise of an end to this condition cannot be a making present of the immemorial past for all the reasons previously adduced. It can only be a promise to inaugurate a new dimension of temporality for which, in religious language, the world to come provides the symbol.

Yet another opinion can be found in the same text with regard to the question of "what the eye hath seen":

> To Eden which no eye has ever seen; and should you demur, where then did Adam live? In the Garden. And should you object the Garden and Eden are one: therefore Scripture teaches, *And a river issues from Eden to water the Garden* (Gen. 2:10). (Sanhedrin 99a)

The text points to a difference between Eden and the garden. The garden is watered by a river that does not originate in the garden itself: thus we know that Eden and the garden are not the same, for "that which no eye hath seen" is something beyond the garden itself. The consequences that flow from this conclusion are momentous: history and becoming do not merely lead to a return to the time of origin but are fraught with positive meaning (DL 100ff./DF 66ff.).

We have now seen that messianism differs from the world to come, that the messianic era can be understood as a spiritualization of man or as a retention of the historical conditions which make morality possible, and that the world to come is not a return to the time of origins. The Talmud also considers the crucial question of whether messianic times depend on any set of conditions or are ushered in irrespective of conditions:

> Rab said: All the predestined dates (for redemption) have passed and the matter (now) depends only on repentance and good deeds. But Samuel maintained: It is sufficient for a mourner to keep his period of mourning. (Sanhedrin 97b)

For Rab history is finished; deliverance awaits only the good deeds of men who through extraordinary effort can bring about the new era. Moral action will no longer be the moral work of man alienated from himself and will therefore not need the state (DL 103/DF 69).

Samuel maintains that, on the contrary, deliverance cannot be the fruit of human effort but can occur only when the mourner has kept his period of mourning. Who is the mourner to whom Samuel refers? Jewish tradition conserves four opinions: (1) God himself, the ruler and director of the historical order; (2) suffering Israel distinct from repentant Israel; (3) suffering Israel whose suffering incites to repentance (thus uniting Samuel and Rab);

and (4) the Messiah. The text then cites a Tannaitic discussion of the same problem (DL 104–5/DF 70–71):

> Rabbi Eliezer said, If Israel repent they will be redeemed; if not, they will not be redeemed. Rabbi Joshua said to him, If they do not repent they will not be redeemed. But the Holy One blessed be He, will set up a king over them, whose decrees shall be as cruel as Haman's, whereby Israel shall engage in repentance, and he will thus bring them back to the right path. (Sanhedrin 97b)

In the case of the reply, historical oppression is situated in a messianic perspective. Thus, something still within the political arena but extrinsic to Israel's own volition will bring about salvation.

Sets of Tannaitic sayings of crucial importance to Levinas's account of redemption and repentance develop the problem:

> Another (*Baraitha*) taught:
> 1. Rabbi Elizer said: If Israel repent, they will be redeemed as it is written: Return, *ye backsliding children, and I will heal your backslidings* (Jer. 3:22). Rabbi Joshua said to him, But is it not *written ye have sold yourself for naught; and ye shall be redeemed without money?* (Is. 52:3). *Ye have sold yourselves for naught*, for idolatry; *and ye shall be redeemed without money*—without repentance and good deeds.
> 2. Rabbi Eliezer . . . But is it not written *Return unto me, and I will return unto you?* (Mal. 3:7). Rabbi Joshua . . . But is it not written, *For I am master over you: and I will take one of a city and two of a family, and I will bring you to Zion?* (Jer. 3:14).
> 3. Rabbi Eliezer . . . But it is written, *In returning and rest shall ye be saved* (Is. 30:15). Rabbi Joshua . . . But is it not written . . . *The redeemer of Israel, and his Holy One, to him whom man despiseth, to him whom the nations abhoreth, to a servant of rulers. Kings shall see and arise, Princes also shall worship?* (Is. 49:7).
> 4. Rabbi Eliezer . . . But is it not written, *If thou will return Oh Israel, saith the Lord, return unto me?* (Jer. 4:1). Rabbi Joshua . . . But it is elsewhere written, *And I heard the man clothed in linen, which was upon the waters of the river, when he held up his right hand and his left hand unto heaven, and swore by him that liveth forever that it shall be for a time, times and a half; and when he shall have accomplished to scatter the power of the holy people, all these things shall be finished* (Dan. 12:7). (Sanhedrin 97b–98a)

It is clear that Rabbi Joshua is the partisan of unconditional salvation, whereas Rabbi Eliezer is the advocate of moral requirements for deliverance. In the first set of sayings, Rabbi Eliezer recognizes a radical evil that requires healing. But the healing can only begin with Israel's effort. Levinas maintains that being is so corrupt that it has become impenetrable to external ministrations. Man is lodged within himself and cannot be saved through grace but must make the movement of turning. For Levinas evil is the disease of being itself. We are reminded that the work of totality is the human reduction of being to the same, that authentic existence begins only when ontology is transcended through the advent, within the framework of the phenomenal world itself, of that which had its origin elsewhere. Being as being is always already corrupt. For Rabbi Joshua the sin that "separates and isolates" is the sin of idolatry, a sin that begins with an absence of right teaching (DL 110/DF 75). It is therefore a sin that can be corrected only by right teaching. Human decline is now a doctrinal matter, and the advent of the Messiah can only be anticipated in the light of doctrinal rectitude. Levinas notes at this juncture a curious reversal of the Christian view of grace, for in the positions brought to light, doctrinal error requires help beyond human powers, whereas fault can only be corrected through human initiatives.

In the next set of sayings, Rabbi Eliezer posits a reciprocity of relation between man and God. Rabbi Joshua replies: Is it possible to refuse God? Has one not accepted him prior to all acceptance and refusal? The anteriority of all responsibility before the positing of the alternatives of freedom and necessity may be recalled as a central theme of Levinas's later work, of a demand upon the self prior to the upsurge of thematizing consciousness.

In the third set of sayings, Rabbi Eliezer attests the possibility of suspending one's grasp of things, of letting go, of revoking our distance-making stance with regard to the world. Levinas's view that the abandonment of thematizing consciousness is required for the inauguration of the moral self is reflected in this text. Rabbi Joshua replies: how can those who do not have the requisite conditions, the despised of mankind, the alienated, find peace without external intervention (DL 113/DF 77)?

The denouement of the dialogue is lodged in the last pair of sayings, in which Levinas notes the appearance for the first time of the conditional word "if." Thus, "If thou [O Israel] will return . . ."[13] raises an entirely new question. What will happen if Israel does not return? If morality depends upon human freedom, it is at least as conceivable that man will continue to sin as it is that he will repent and turn toward God. The question, appalling to religious consciousness, arises: is it possible that the Messiah will never come, that the world will be delivered to the control of evil powers? Rabbi Joshua's reply is nothing but a brute insistence upon the salvation of the world at a fixed time irrespective of human conduct. Rabbi Eliezer is silenced, for he does not dare raise the question that flows from a denial of the messianic advent: can there be a world in which God is defeated and the triumph of evil assured? (DL 113/DF 77).

The Talmud is also explicit with regard to the internal contradictions of messianism:

> Ulla said: Let him the Messiah come, but let me not see him. . . . Rabbi Joseph said, Let him come and may I be worthy of sitting in his ass's saddle. Abaye enquired of Rabah: What is your reason for not wishing to see him? Shall we say, because of the birth pangs of the Messiah? But it has been taught, Rabbi Eliezer's disciples asked him: What must a man do to be spared the pangs of the Messiah? [He answered] Let him engage in study and benevolence; and you Master do both. He replied [I fear] lest sin cause it, in accordance with [the teaching of] Rabbi Jacob ben Idi, who opposed [two verses] viz. It is written, *And behold I am with thee, and will guard thee in all places whither thou goest* (Gen. 28:13): but it is written, *Then Jacob was greatly afraid and distressed* (Gen. 32:8). He was afraid that sin might cause [the nullification] of God's promise. Even as it was taught, *Till the people pass over, O Lord* (Ex. 15:16). This refers to the first entry [into Palestine]; *till thy people pass over what was purchased* (ibid.). This refers to their second entry. Hence you may reason: The Israelites were as worthy of a miracle being wrought for them at the second entry as at the first, but that sin caused it to happen. (Sanhedrin 98b)

The coming of the Messiah is fraught with danger; a time of catastrophe portends its advent. Yet it has been said that the upright man could escape the calamities of the coming era. Raba has spent his time in study and good deeds. What has he to fear? But no man, even Raba, can escape all suspicion of sin. Jacob himself received the divine promise yet was guilty before Esau.

It is possible to sin without knowing that one sins. Moreover, a miraculous return was promised by God for the second exile as well as the first, yet the Jews returning from Babylon witnessed no divine intervention. Sin had intervened, nullifying the divine promises (DL 115/DF 78).

Levinas interprets this rabbinic understanding of sin as a perpetual putting into question of egoity. The more righteous one becomes, the more one feels the weight of the demands put upon him. This is a recurring motif of rabbinic thought. The subject does not "have" himself once and for all but is in constant jeopardy. Levinas has insisted that the passivity of the ownmost self is the deepening of the sense of what one owes the Other, an ever increasing feeling of burden, of moral responsiveness to the Other. One becomes increasingly aware of the self as bearing the weight of the Other's need:

> Rabbi Johanan said likewise: Let him come, and let me not see him. Resh Lakish said to him: Why so? Shall we say because it is written, *As if a man did flee a lion, and a bear met him; or went into the house, and leaned his hand on the wall, and a serpent bit him?* (Am. 5:19). But come I will show you what it is like even in this world. When one goes out into the world and meets a bailiff it's as though he met a lion. When he enters the town and is accosted by a tax collector, it is as though he had met a bear. On entering his house and finding his sons and daughters in the throes of hunger, it is as though he were bitten by a serpent. (Sanhedrin 98b)

Resh Lakish raises the question: Is not contemporary existence like the anguish expected before the coming of the Messiah? Could anything be worse than the injustice that now prevails? "Is the return to bestiality that Rabbi Johanan would have been unable to stand more terrible than the inhuman politics and the economy of the world in which we live? Has one something to lose in the horrors of revolution?" (DL 116, my translation).[14]

But Rabbi Johanan has in mind the following verse of Jeremiah, which describes a travail still more anguished and qualitatively different from the iniquity experienced up until now:

> *Ask ye now and see whether a man doth travail with child? Wherefore do I see every man (gever) with his hands on his loins, as women in travail and all faces are turned into paleness* (Jer. 30:6).

Every man (*gever*) is the principle of virility itself, which is now undermined. The reason for this strange precursor lies in the necessity for separating the saved from the condemned, for a verdict to be delivered: condemnation or acquittal. Rabbi Johanan says: "God says these (the gentiles) are my handiwork, and so are these (the Jews); how shall I destroy the former in the count of the latter?" (Sanhedrin 98b). For Levinas the final act of justice entails a final violence. The angels, of whom the Talmud also proclaims their "faces are turned into paleness," are pure reason for whom considerations of compassion have no weight, who fear that God will be merciful and change his mind. This fear is shared by the earthly victims of injustice. Yet Levinas points out that what is significant in this passage is God's hesitation before the demands of strict justice. The following text is a commentary upon who will enjoy messianic times:

> Rabbi Giddal said in Rab's name: The Jews are destined to eat [their fill] in the days of the Messiah. Rabbi Joseph demurred: Is this not obvious; who else then should eat—Hillek and Billek [every Tom, Dick and Harry]?—This was said in opposition to Rabbi Hillel, who maintained that there will be no Messiah for Israel, since they have already enjoyed him during the reign of Hezekiah. (Sanhedrin 98b)

Rabbi Giddal announces what would seem to be obvious: that Israel will enjoy messianic times rather than Hillek and Billek. But to announce that it is Israel who will enjoy messianic times also distinguishes these times as those times enjoyed by Israel at the end of history, that Israel did not yet experience the Messiah. One commentator ascribes to Hillek and Billek the identity of two magistrates from Sodom. The ancient city is taken by Levinas to mean the earthly city par excellence where men live according to the rules of polity and history. But now in the messianic era, they cannot be vindicated by arguing that they were driven by the necessities of their time, for in messianic times, historical relativism is obliterated (DL 118/DF 81). Levinas's philosophical work is directed to showing that a rupture with totality is possible, that history comes under judgment that originates elsewhere and that this judgment is in its very upsurge a condemnation of the political order. Thus, his thought is an attempt to show that messianic consciousness is already at work in the historical order.

There is still another meaning lodged in Rabbi Giddal's text. Levinas claims that it speaks of a future messianic time to be enjoyed by Israel as a rebuke to the message of Rabbi Hillel, which follows it in the text. Hillel's thesis is that messianism as a historical stage has already been transcended during the reign of King Hezekiah. For Levinas this represents an allegation that messianic possibility is dead, that it belongs to an archaic level of thought no longer appropriate to one's own time. This idea, repugnant to Jewish messianic consciousness, has been traditionally treated in the following ways: (1) Israel has seen the Messiah and now God himself will come to aid his people; (2) if the moral order is always being perfected, then a termination of this meliorative process through the advent of the Messiah could only be an end to progress, to an open-ended process and therefore in and of itself an immoral act; and (3) that the Messiah is himself human, one of the kings of Israel, and that messianism is political (DL 119–22/DF 81–84). The last alternative is the least acceptable. A critique of Israel's quest for an earthly sovereign is already well developed in the book of Samuel (1 Sam. 8:4–9). The ideal in which each man enters a direct relation with God as opposed to a mediated relation with God via an earthly sovereign is a perennial motif of Jewish thought.

The difference of opinion with regard to the source of redemption is reflected in the following opinions of the Rabbis:

> Rab said: The world was created only on David's account. Samuel said: On Moses' account; Rabbi Johanan said for the sake of the Messiah. (Sanhedrin 98b)

Each of the Rabbis seeks the meaning of the creation elsewhere except Rabbi Johanan, one in psalm and prayer, one in the law, and one in the advent of that which remains inexplicit, save that it shows that more than prayer and more than the law are required for the redemptive process in man.

The Talmudic passage that immediately follows is an investigation into the names of the Messiah:

> What is his (the Messiah's) name? The school of Rabbi Shila said: His name is Shiloh, for it is written, *until Shiloh come* (Gen. 49:10). The school of Rabbi Yannai said: His name is Yinnon, for it is written, *His name shall endure forever: e'er the sun was his name is Yinnon*

(Ps. 72:17). The school of Rabbi Haninah maintained: His name is Haninah, as it is written, *Where I will not give you Haninah* (Jer. 16:3). Others say his name is Menahem, the son of Hezekiah, for it is written, *Because Menahem* (the comforter) *that would relieve my soul, is far* (Lam. 1:16). The Rabbis said: His name is "the leper scholar" as it is written, *Surely he hath borne our griefs, and carried our sorrows* (Is. 53:4) yet we did esteem him a leper, smitten of God, and afflicted. (Sanhedrin 98b)

It is clear that the first three names of our text result from a play on words in which each school, wishing to honor its founder, names the Messiah after him. The messianic experience according to Levinas is illumined in the relationship of pupil to master, in teaching (DL 124/DF85). The relation of pupil to teacher is not one in which ideas are communicated but one in which messianic times are inaugurated. The names also bear a vague relationship to roots meaning peace, justice, and pity (*pitié*), respectively (DL 126/DF 87).[15] For Levinas, the fourth name, Menahem, brings to light the personal dimension of messianism, which relates to the recognition of the redeemed personality beyond his participation in the political or historical structures of the totality. This name can be taken to revert to one of the interpretations we have seen given to the thesis of Rabbi Hillel: that the Messiah had already appeared in the time of Hezekiah, the interpretation that proclaimed that the salvation of Israel would be effected by God himself. Levinas ties this interpretation to the saying that claims that the day when one tells the truth without falsifying the name of its bearer will be the day when the Messiah will come. Levinas's view of truth as expression, as belonging to the one who speaks rather than to the content of his utterance, is clearly related to this teaching.

The text continues:

Nahman said: If he (the Messiah) is of those living (today), it might be one like myself, as it is written, *And their nobles shall be of themselves, and their governors shall proceed from the midst of them* (Jer. 30:21). Rab said: If he is of the living, it would be our holy master (Rabbi Judah the Nasi); if of the dead, it would have been Daniel the most desirable man. Rab Judah said in Rab's name: The Holy One, blessed be He, will raise up another David for us, as it is written, *But they serve the Lord their God and David their King, whom I will raise up unto them* (Jer. 30:9). Not "I raised up" but "I will raise up" is said. Rabbi Papa said to Abaye: But it is written, And my servant David shall serve, be their prince [*nasi*] forever?, e.g., an emperor and a viceroy. (Sanhedrin 98b)

The Messiah has become the one who suffers; it is equally conceivable that it be Rab in the time contemporary to the issuance of the saying or Daniel in historical times. History has become irrelevant to the upsurge of messianic personality; there is a Messiah in every age. The meaning of the saying of Rabbi Nahman lends itself to the interpretation that Rabbi Nahman could belong to the line of David and could therefore fulfill one of the messianic requirements. But Levinas prefers a far-fetched interpretation that, according to his own admission, taxes historical credulity but that, he claims, belongs to the Talmudic understanding of messianism. The text of Jeremiah 30:21 refers to a time when Israel will regain her sovereignty. The Messiah is the prince of Israel who governs in such a way that "the sovereignty of Israel is no longer alienated." It is a sovereignty that coincides with the passive radical interiority that lies at the foundation of the self. For messianic consciousness is an assumption of the suffering of Others carried to its radical extreme:

> The Messiah is the Prince who governs in a way that no longer alienates the sovereignty of Israel. He is the absolute interiority of government. Is there a more radical interiority than the one in which the self [*Moi*] commands itself? Non-strangeness *par excellence* is ipseity. The Messiah is the King who no longer commands from outside—this idea of Jeremiah's is brought by R. Nahman to its logical conclusion. The Messiah is Myself [*Moi*]; to be Myself is to be the Messiah. (DL 129/DF 89)

We have seen that the acceptance of the burden we bear as a result of human suffering is the very meaning of the ownmost self: "Messianism is no more than this apogee in being a centralizing, concentration or twisting back on itself of the Self [*Moi*]" (DL 130/DF 90). Messianism is thus not the conviction that a historical savior will appear upon the scene but a universal recognition of responsibility. Each one must act as messianic consciousness.

This view, in my opinion, brings Levinas close to the formula of Luke 17:20–21: "The kingdom of God cometh not in visible form.

Neither shall they say, lo here; or lo there! For behold the kingdom of God is within you." I have emphasized that the self of moral responsibility does not, in Levinas's thought, coincide with a Kantian self that adheres to universal laws and that provides maxims for its actions such that these maxims can be taken to legislate universally. Nevertheless, Kant already recognizes as the great virtue in the teaching of Jesus the condemnation of those who evade moral duty by misconstruction of the law. Jesus combines all duties in a universal rule that includes for Kant both "the inner and outer relations of all men."[16] And the unconditioned esteem for duty is nothing other than the love of God himself. For Kant the service to be rendered to God is ultimately a service outside institutional forms because institutions as such cannot provide a basis for the worship of the heart. Thus, the Kantian kingdom of God that is elaborated only in his latest work already prefigures a sovereignty that, to borrow Hegelian language, is not alienated. It is a sovereignty in which the rule of the deepest level of self coincides with the law of God.

The saying of Rabbi Judah in the name of Rab still speaks of the reestablishment of the Davidic kingdom. It speaks in the future tense of a new king whose name will be David and whom the old King David will serve as viceroy. This text suggests, according to Levinas, the view that all historical personages have a double. To rabbinic consciousness a David beyond history makes the David of history meaningful. It is a commanding that directs the work of the historical king. Levinas writes:

> Each historical event transcends itself, taking on a metaphorical meaning that guides its literal significance. The metaphorical meaning commands the literal and local meaning of events and ideas. In this sense, human history is a spiritual work. The historical character is transcended by the suprahistorical character who is his Master. The historical character who founds the State has meaning only when he obeys the as yet unreal character who is yet more real and effective than the real king. (DL 131/DF 91)

The following verses distinguish between those who have a sense of messianic expectation and those to whom this sense is lacking:

Rabbi Simlai expounded: What is meant by, *Woe unto you, that desire the day of the Lord! To what end is it for you? The day of the Lord is darkness, and not light* [i.e., dawn] (Am. 5:18). The cock said to the bat, "I look forward to the light, because I have sight; but of what use is the light to thee?" And thus a *min* said to Rabbi Abbahu: When will the Messiah come? He replied, "When darkness covers those people." "You curse me," he exclaimed. He retorted, "It is but a verse: *For behold the darkness shall cover the earth, and gross darkness the people* (Is. 60:2). But the Lord shall shine upon thee." (Sanhedrin 98b–99a)

Levinas sees the first verse as expressing the stern execution of judgment and a refusal of universal pardon. But the day of the Lord also refers to the darkness of souls who cannot be enlightened. What the cock distinguishes is not day from night, since to do so requires no fine degree of discrimination. Rather he discerns the coming of the light before its actual appearance. The darkness of the bat is damnation, for he would not perceive light even in its presence.[17]

The Judaeo-Christian heretic [*min*] asks: "When will the Messiah come?" The reply is interpreted by Levinas to mean when the darkness covers your people. Salvation is an exclusive matter (DL 134/DF 93). The obscurity will precede the light; the Messiah will come when these people are covered with darkness. Levinas notes that the subsequent verse in Isaiah shows that the world is not left desolate and salvation accomplished for Israel alone, that through Israel the light will be brought to all the nations. This strange denouement comes about in the messianic drama in order to distinguish the messianic kingdom that will appear only after the reign of darkness from a political earthly state. Political terms are required for us to think it, but these terms are removed from its actual expression. This drama of darkness and light enables us to distinguish the order of totality from what lies beyond it. The universality of the political order lies not necessarily in uniting incompatible beliefs by making them compatible but by finding appropriate rhetoric to encompass them and thereby sublating their particularity. This "light" that lies beyond totality can never be thus sublated. This is Israel's apolitical vision of itself. A people whose history has until recent times been lived in diaspora cannot accommodate its morality to politics.

THE TEMPTATION OF MODERNITY

According to Levinas, the difficulty of Western man is rooted in his need to experience everything that can be experienced, to taste all the possibilities that life affords. This is the temptation of temptations. The paradigms of Western man are Ulysses, whose life is filled with novel and perilous adventure, and Don Juan, for whom a multiplicity of seductions provides a heightened sense of existence. It is of great moment to engage one's passions in life and to live dangerously. Innocence seems infantile and merely provisional, awaiting transformation by life itself.

For Levinas, Christianity presupposes this drama, for it antici-pates man's confrontation with the tempter. Christianity is the life of temptation even though these temptations are ultimately overcome. Comtemporary life, which is continuous in this respect with Christian existence, is bored with the serenity of a life lived in accordance with the law. Yet the life of temptation allows one to experience everything without actually undergoing the vicissi-tudes of that experience by envisaging all human possibilities and returning safely to the harbor of the self. This confers a purity upon the life of temptation, which is a temptation not to do or to suffer but to know. Nothing is risked; the self remains untainted before its numerous possibilities. The self is simultaneously out-sider and participant in the game of life. This temptation is, for Levinas, philosophy as opposed to a wisdom that knows without experiencing, a philosophy that is simultaneously committed but disengaged from the game of life:

> The temptation of temptation is thus the temptation of knowledge.
> . . . It is infinite. . . . The temptation of temptation is philosophy,
> in contrast to a wisdom which knows everything without experienc-
> ing it. Its starting point is an ego which, in the midst of engage-
> ment, assurs itself a continual disengagement. The ego is perhaps
> nothing but this. An ego simply and purely engaged is naive. It is a
> temporary situation, an illusory ideal. But the ego and its separa-
> tion from its engaged self so that it may return to its noncomprom-
> ised self may not constitute the ultimate condition of man.
> Overcoming the temptation of temptation would then mean going
> within oneself further than one's self. (QLT 74–75/NTR 34)

It is the task of philosophy to subordinate the act to knowledge of the act. The act appears only after calculation, thus depriving it of its initial generosity and risk. It brings the other within the purview of a horizon and thus misunderstands the irreducibility of the other to an item that can be calculated. We have already seen that Levinas proposes an alternative view of truth. It is now Levinas's intention to show that it is possible to recognize alterity without the spontaneity which evades theoretical exploration, that is, without a naive engagement of faith. What he proposes is no less than a novel view of what is meant by an "act" that is neither opposed to contemplation nor naive and spontaneous engagement. It is his intention to uncover a notion of doing anterior to hearing or understanding, a view of doing that appears in the Talmudic interpretation of their interrelationship. The paradigm of doing prior to hearing is seen in the person of Jacob, who is not a naive child of faith but a shrewd and worldly man absolutely upright and ethical (DL 99–105/DF 45–48).

Western philosophy of religion has been beset by the paradox of a divine revelation whose elements are refractory to integration within a reasonable scheme. Revelation demands of the believer an unquestioning adherence irrespective of its irrational elements, thus forcing the believer to run the risk of falling victim to the demonic.[18] If the recalcitrant elements are reconciled, then the knowledge of the one who compares them and submits them to judgment becomes the decisive factor. Even when reason passes judgment only upon the authority of the message without attempting to evaluate its content, the certainty of revelation depends upon the believer whose reason certifies the source of revelation (QLT 79/NTR 36). Revelation itself pretends to be beyond reason, yet reason judges not only its content but also the authenticity of the vehicle that bears the divine message.

Levinas asserts that the Talmudic view of revelation offers an alternative to the traditional impasse. The crucial text begins as follows:

And they stood under the mount (Ex. 19:17). Abdimi b. Hama b. Hasa said: This teaches that the Holy One, blessed be He, overturned the mountain upon them like an inverted cask and said to them, "If ye accept the Torah, 'tis well; if not, there shall be your burial." (Shabbat 88a)

The Talmud interprets the giving of the Torah as an act that coerces; the mountain literally weighs down upon the people who will be buried there if they reject the Torah (QLT 82/NTR 37). They are already made responsible in choosing responsibility. It is a "choice" between accepting a law which has already been imposed or acquiescing in death. Indeed, this is the "difficult freedom" (*difficile liberté*) that is beyond freedom to which Levinas refers in the title of his book bearing that name. The Torah is already present; there is no freedom anterior to its imposition. Torah is not a source of knowledge like other natural sources of knowledge. What Levinas means is that the first experience of Torah is not an experience of content, of a doctrine, but an experience of the weight of doctrine itself. The Torah is not imposed by violence in the usual sense, for the basis of all education, according to Levinas, is this alternative: truth or death. This is the true meaning of the teacher's stick. Nor is the acceptance of Torah a species of naiveté, for the naive is ignorance of that which reason can teach.

It is possible that the text can be construed to mean that a Judaism outside Torah can lead only to catastrophe and death, and that therefore the choice of Torah is reasonable. But according to Levinas, the free choice of Torah is still a choice without temptation, for there is no dazzling array of multiple options: there is merely truth or death. The text continues (Shabbath 88a): "R. Aha b. Jacob observed: This furnishes a strong protest against the Torah." The meaning of this comment is that man is furnished with an excuse for nonobservance since the Torah was forcibly imposed. But Levinas maintains there is a way of understanding the acceptance of Torah not as the consequence of violence, but as a founding act that becomes subject to the subsequent scrutiny of reason: "If temptation defines the philosophical reason of the West, does this definition exhaust the notion of reason? The answer: the refusal of temptation, the trust granted from the start, should not be defined negatively. The order thus founded extends, after the fact, to the act of foundation. Reason, *once it comes into being,* includes its pre-history" (QLT 84/NTR 38).

What happened at Sinai is assumed after the fact by the Jewish people; the de facto situation is given conscious sanction. Lived history is willingly shouldered:

Said Raba: Yet even so they reaccepted it in the days of Ahaseurus, for it is written, (the Jews) *confirmed and took upon them* . . . (Est. 9:27). They confirmed what they had accepted long before. (Shabbat 88a)

To receive the Torah is to carry it out even before it is freely accepted.

Is there still another reason for accepting the Torah long after the events at Sinai? Levinas asserts that there is. Israel, in accepting its lived history, affirms the value of Torah itself. Exposed to the perils of violence that belong to ontology as such, only Torah has the power to resist this violence. It is a potent no-saying to the domination of totality. For Levinas, Torah provides a way beyond ontology.

Yet being too must have a meaning. The text continues:

Hezekiah said: What is meant by, *Thou didst cause sentence to be heard from heaven; The earth feared and was tranquil* (Ps. 76:9): if it feared why was it tranquil, and if it was tranquil, why did it fear? But at first it feared and subsequently it was tranquil. And why did it fear? Even in accordance with Resh Lakish. For Resh Lakish said: Why is it written, *And there was evening and there was morning, the sixth day?* (Gen. 1:31). This teaches that the Holy One, blessed be He, stipulated with the works of creation and said thereto, "If Israel accepts the Torah, ye shall exist; but if not, I will turn you back into emptiness and formlessness." (Shabbat 88a)

The text establishes that the earth both feared and was tranquil. These emotions were not experienced simultaneously but successively. Why did the earth fear? Because on the sixth day (Levinas notes that this is a reference to the sixth day of Sivan when the Torah was received) the universe is confronted with the possibility of total destruction should Israel refuse the Torah. The creation has a meaning that lies beyond sheer brute presence; it is intended to fulfill an ethical purpose. The divine creation is undertaken for the sake of Israel's acceptance and obedience to the precepts of Torah: "God, therefore, did not create without concerning himself with the meaning of creation. Being has a meaning. The meaning of being, the meaning of creation, is to realize the Torah. The world is here so that the ethical order has the possibility of being fulfilled. The act by which the Israelites accept the Torah is the act which gives meaning to being. To refuse the Torah is to bring being back to nothingness" (QLT 90/NTR 41). According to Levinas, the way in which Israel accepted the Torah was to reject precisely that thesis that underlies the inauthenticity of contemporary existence. It avoided succumbing to the temptation of temptations, to experience; it thus eluded radical evil.

The mode of Israel's acceptance is contained in this text, which stresses primordial obedience:

> R. Simlai lectured: When the Israelites gave precedence to *we will do* over *we will hearken* (Ex. 24:7) six hundred thousand ministering angels came and set two crowns upon each man of Israel, one as a reward for *we will do* and the other as a reward for *we will hearken*. (Shabbat 88a)

Israel has confidence in the one who speaks and promises to do. Its entire history will then be a hearkening after its allegiance is already given. This inversion of the logical order, to act before hearkening, is what is rewarded by the angelic crowns:

> But as soon as Israel sinned, one million two hundred thousand destroying angels descended and removed them, as it is said, *And the children of Israel stripped themselves of their ornaments from Mount Horeb* (Ex. 33:6). R. Hama son of R. Hanina said: At Horeb they put them on and at Horeb they put them off. At Horeb they put them off as we have stated. At Horeb they put them off, for it is written, *And* (the children of Israel) *stripped themselves,* etc. (Shabbat 88a)

The elevation of Sinai is now joined to the fall; the text joins them as being almost simultaneous. From the preceding texts we have learned what the sin of Israel is. It consists in a reversal of the proper order of doing and hearing. It is a submission to the temptation of temptations. Ordinary sin that is committed within the framework of the proper order, that is, within a framework that accepts the anteriority of doing, is not the equivalent of a total lapse. Thus, Israel loses its crowns, but so long as the priorities are recognized the way to repentance is open.

We have already seen that the doing to which the text refers is not merely praxis opposed to theory, but it is a "way of *actualizing without beginning with the possible*" (QLT 95/NTR 43). It may be recalled that to begin is already to dominate, to reassume oneself each instant, to break with what has gone before, to live as freedom, and so on. Thus, the doing to which the Talmud refers precedes the choice between good and evil by assuming a relation anterior to the Good. The perennial temptation of Israel to be like the other nations is a temptation to reverse the order that the original acceptance of the Torah implies.

But the hope for redemption is not lost. The text continues:

> R. Johanan observed: And Moses was privileged and received them all, for in proximity thereto it is stated, *And Moses took the tent* (Ex. 33:7). Resh Lakish said: [Yet] the Holy One blessed be He, will return them to us in the future, for it is said. *And the ransomed of the Lord shall return, and come with singing unto Zion; and everlasting joy shall be upon their heads* (Is. 35:10): the joy from of old shall be upon their heads. (Shabbath 88a)

Moses retains his crown. Although Torah is lost to the multitude, the tradition is retained by the few who are willing to bear its weight. But ultimately all Israel will regain its crowns.

The next text takes up again the order of doing and hearing:

> R. Eliezer said: When the Israelites gave precedence to *we will do* over *we will hearken,* a heavenly voice went forth and exclaimed to them: Who revealed to my children this secret, which is employed by the ministering angels, as it is written, *Bless the Lord ye angels of his: Ye mighty in strength, that fulfill his word. That hearken* (Ps. 103:20) unto the voice of his word: first they fulfill then they hearken? (Shabbat 88a)

This order is a mystery that Israel has managed to wrest as a Promethean feast from the angels.

A second passage emphasizes and extends the meaning of the preceding text:

> R. Hama son of R. Hanina said: What is meant by, *As the apple tree among the trees of the wood?* (S. of S. 2:3) [So is my beloved among the sons]. Why were the Israelites compared to an apple tree? To teach you: just as the fruit of the apple tree precedes its leaves, so did the Israelites give precedence to *we will do* over *we will hearken.* (Shabbat 88a)

The tree to which the passage refers was assumed by the Tosafists to be a pomegranate (citron) tree on which the fruit rests for two years and thus seems to precede the leaves. We are in the presence of a miraculous reversal of precedence. The fruit is present from the outset. For Levinas, the Torah is received before it is subjected to scrutiny: "The truth of the Torah is given without precursor, without first announcing itself in its idea" (QLT 100/NTR 46).

The final text reads as follows:

> There was a certain Sadducee who saw Raba engrossed in his studies while the fingers of his hand were under his feet, and he ground them down, so that his fingers spurted blood. "Ye rash people," he exclaimed, "who gave precedence to your mouth over your ears: Ye still persist in your rashness. First ye should have listened, if within your powers, accept; if not, ye should not have accepted." Said he to him, "We who walked in integrity, of us it is written: *The integrity of the upright shall guide them* (Pr. 11:3); but of others it is written, *but the perverseness of the treacherous shall destroy them.* (Shabbat 88a–88b)

The strange posture of Raba bespeaks the extraordinary effort exerted by the sage in his study. The Sadduccee objects to the precipitious haste with which Israel rushed to accept the Torah. Raba's reply refers to the integrity of the upright. Levinas interprets this integrity to mean the proper subordination of hearing to doing. This order implies a direct relation to truth that, for Levinas, is a relation to alterity, to the other person. To hear a voice that addresses is already to be under obligation to the one who speaks. Although the dialectical implications are not lost on Levinas, the primacy of obedience before reflection is clear.

THE MEANING OF SOCIETY

Levinas interprets a text from the treatise of the Sanhedrin in terms of the relation between public and private morality. He examines the passage relating to the founding of the Sanhedrin not from the point of view of historical veracity, but from the point of view of what it is taken to be in the text. The Mishnah describes its composition in the following way:

> The Sanhedrin sat in the form of a semi-circular threshing floor, so that they might see one another, and two judges' clerks stood

before them, one to the right and one to the left, and wrote down
the arguments of those who would acquit and those who would
condemn. R. Judah said [there were] three, one to record the arguments for acquittal, a second those for conviction, and a third to
record the arguments for conviction and acquittal. And three rows
of scholars sat in front of them each knowing his own place. In case
it was necessary to ordain [another judge] he was appointed from
the first [row] in which case one of the second row moved up to
the first, one of the third to the second, and a member of the assembled [audience] was selected and seated in the third [row]. He
did not sit in the place vacated by the first but in the place suitable
for him.[19]

Levinas notes that one never sits with his back toward another.
The face-to-face arrangement is upheld in the architectural arrangement of the court. It is thus symbolically a collective of faces
rather than an anonymous society (QLT 155/NTR 72). It is an
open circle: the court is open to the world. Two clerks record the
proceedings. The act of recording is bearing witness, that is, the
truth of facts reverts to the credibility of the persons who attest it.
In the case of the third clerk the testimony is attested for a second
time. Students of the law are also assembled before the magistrates. Actual jurisprudence and the study of the law are carried
on simultaneously.

Levinas also notes that the number of members of the Sanhedrin that concerns us is twenty-three. This number is extended by
the presence of the students of the law. The Sanhedrin of supreme jurisdiction, which does not concern us here, had seventy-
one members. The reason for the unusual arrangement of the
court is that according to the law a death sentence cannot be
passed by a simple majority. Thus, if it turns out that a decision is
reached that results in condemnation by one vote alone, the
ranks of the court must be increased. It is for this reason that a
procedure is established for moving up in which the order of persons is meticulously maintained. Each one knows his own place.
If one person moves up into the next row, he does not move into
a seat that has been vacated but takes his place at the end of the
row in which he now finds himself. The swelling of the ranks of
the court proceeds until the maximum number of seventy-one is
reached. If the verdict of guilty is handed down by only a single

vote, that is, if thirty-six votes are counted in favor of declaring the defendant guilty, he is automatically acquitted.

The rabbis of the Gemara often seek the scriptural source for the text of the Mishnah. In the case of the structure of the Sanhedrin there may be an additional reason for this procedure, an attempt to establish Jewish roots for an institution borrowed from Hellenism. The text of the Gemara reads as follows:

> *Thy belly is like a heap of wheat* (S. of S. 7:3). Whence is this derived?
> R. Aha b. Haninah said: Scripture states, *Thy navel is like a round goblet wherein no mingled wine is wanting* (ibid.). Thy navel,—that is the Sanhedrin. Why is it called a navel?—Because it sat at the navel of the world. (Why) *aggan?* Because it protects (*meggin*) the whole world. (Why) *ha sahar?*—Because it was moonshaped. (Why) *in which no mingled wine was wanting?* [For] if one of them had to leave, it had to be ascertained if twenty-three, corresponding to the number of the minor Sanhedrin were left,[20] in which case he might go out; if not, he might not depart. (Sanhedrin 37a)

The foundation of justice stems, for Levinas, from the necessity of exerting domination over the sexuality of life, over an equivocacy that must be mastered at every moment. It may not be allowed to overwhelm the right order of the world (QLT 163/NTR 76). What is particularly dangerous in the sexual is that it seems to belong to the private sphere and therefore is of no concern to society. It does not compromise the ethical status of the individual in his public relations.

What is the connection between the Sanhedrin and the "navel" of the Song of Songs text? The Sanhedrin is located at the navel of the universe (QLT 164/NTR 77). It is the center from which absolute justice radiates.[21] Levinas ties the omphalic symbolism of the text to his own thought in the following way: the creature has been severed from the source that nourishes him, but the place where justice is dispensed is the trace of creation (QLT 165ff./NTR 77ff.).

Levinas is drawn to a comparison with another similar tradition. In Greece, Delphi is seen to be the navel of the world and is implicated in the foundation of Athenian justice. This relation is attested in the *Eumenides* of Aeschylus. Athena retains the ancient deities of vengeance and finds a function for them in the city.[22]

Does not every nation conceive itself to be at the center of the world? What is unique in the text in question? The Sanhedrin is seen to be an *aggan*, which is tied to the root of the word *meggin*, which means "to protect." The Sanhedrin protects the universe. Without the justice dispensed there the right order of the universe would disintegrate. The role of Judaism is a unique diaconate.

The passage concerning the conditions under which one might leave the chamber of justice, if twenty-three members were present, testifies to the priority that public service took over any other possible occupation. This service is prior to all individual rights.

The text continues this theme and adds that the men of the Sanhedrin are impervious to temptation:

> *Thy belly is like a heap of wheat.* Just as all benefit from a heap of wheat so all benefit from the deliberations of the Sanhedrin. (Sanhedrin 37a)

The deliberations of the Sanhedrin are nourishing to Israel; they are ingested and feed the life of the spirit:

> Set about with lilies (S. of S. 7:3): Even through a hedge of lilies they would make no breach. In this connection there is the story of a *min* who said to R. Kahana: Ye maintain that a menstruant woman is permitted *yihud* (privacy) with her husband: can fire be near tow without singeing it? He retorted: The Torah testifies this of us. *Set about with lilies*—even through a hedge of lilies they make no breach. (Sanhedrin 37a)

How do the men of the Sanhedrin who have the destiny of the universe in their hands dispose of their private lives? They are total masters of instinct separated from sin by nothing more formidable than a hedge of blossoms. This enclosure is worse than no enclosure at all, or it is itself alluring, more likely to arouse than to withstand instinctual life. The *min* (heretic) knows the weakness of man and assumes that the presence of what is forbidden cannot therefore be shut out by this "enclosure of roses from evil." Rabbi Kahana extends the moral excellence of the Sanhedrin to all Israel. Judaism tries to teach what is possible for man. This is the way in which it differs from the life world of the *Eumenides*. The text in question develops, according to Levinas, a new *typos,* a man who does not need the protection of institutions to keep him from wrongdoing. The internalization of Torah, though merely a border of roses which separates him from sin, is sufficient.

NOTES

1. Levinas, "A Man-God?" EN 70ff./ENT 53ff.

2. In this sense Levinas can be interpreted as a descendant of post-Kantian German Jewish idealism. For thinkers of this tradition, religion becomes the arena for ethical activity and the proper field for its expression. In the work of Moritz Lazarus only an ethical motive is seen in man's relationship to God. Preceptive teaching is emphasized. Hermann Cohen, leader of the Marburg school, integrates Jewish faith in a divinely grounded moral order into a Kantian framework. (Levinas, in his early work, takes exception to Cohen, among others of the Marburg school, whom he sees as identifying philosophy with a theory of consciousness understood as a reflection upon science. See TIPH 17/TIH xxxv). While these thinkers give expression to liberal and progressive tendencies, Levinas rejects an interpretation of prophetic futurism that makes the political arena the sphere of its operation. For the Jewish neo-Kantians see Nathan Rotenstreich, *From Mendelssohn to Rosenzweig: Jewish Philosophy in Modern Times* (New York: Holt, Rinehart & Winston, 1968), and Julius Guttmann, *Philosophies of Judaism* (New York: Holt, Rinehart & Winston, 1964).

3. Levinas also says in E. Amado Lévy-Valensi et Jean Halpérin, eds., *La conscience juive: Données et débats* (Paris: PUF, 1963), 289: "Something very strange is produced in Talmudism, a reason which in the final analysis is revealed as personal. Insofar as there is an impersonal synthesis, the person is lost in reason as in Spinozism. . . . In Talmudic method, the solution is always the person who chooses . . . each time in his own way."

4. In Sean Hand's translation of *Difficile liberté* (Paris: Albin Michel, 1963), "Elijah" is erroneously rendered "Eli."

5. The influence of Rosenzweig is discernible in this regard. In "Franz Rosenzweig: Une pensée juive moderne," *Hors sujet* (Montpellier: Fata Morgana, 1987), 82; translated by Michael B. Smith as "Franz Rosenzweig: A Modern Jewish Thinker," in *Outside the Subject* (Stanford: Stanford University Press, 1993), 56, Levinas writes that for Rosenzweig the relation between God and the world is not a formal link or an ab-

stract synthesis, but is specific and concrete. The link between God and the world is creation; between God and man it is revelation; between man and the world it is redemption. Levinas sustains the concreteness of this viewpoint.

6. While Levinas does not refer to the work of Rudolf Bultmann, it is instructive to compare his view with that of the latter regarding the requirement that all interpretation of sacred texts be related to existential concerns. In *Jesus Christ and Mythology* (New York: Scribner's Sons, 1958), 51, Bultmann writes: "This is then the presupposition for every form of exegesis: that our own relation to the subject matter prompts the question you bring to the text and elicits the answer you obtain from the text."

7. Levinas holds the view that all ideas of consequence have already been formulated in the major classical texts directly preceding and following the common era. In one of his more moderate statements to this effect, he writes (QLT 15–16/NTR 5–6): "Has everything already been thought? The answer must be made with some caution. Everything has been thought, at least around the Mediterranean during the few centuries preceding or following our era." Levinas's claims regarding the classical texts of Athens and Jerusalem may seem exaggerated, but they differ little from the oft-quoted remark of Whitehead that the history of philosophy can be read as a series of footnotes to Plato.

8. While accepting the fruits of historical research, Levinas rejects structuralism as a tool for the analysis of the Talmud on the grounds that critical differences subsist between "primitive" thought (as understood by Lévi-Strauss's anthropology) where such analyses may seem valuable and Talmudic reasoning. See QLT 19/NTR 7.

9. Levinas claims that in this way the possibility of the symbol is respected. Ideas are never divorced from what both suggests and limits them. See QLT 48/NTR 21.

10. Spiegelberg, *The Phenomenological Movement* (The Hague: Martinus Nijhoff, 1960), 2:700.

11. By hermeneutics I mean an attempt to interpret what is not immediately apparent to our modes of apprehension in certain phenomena. Spiegelberg, ibid., 695ff., writes: "Hermeneutics is an attempt to interpret the 'sense' of certain phenomena. . . . Its goal is the discovery of meanings which are not immediately manifest to our intuiting and describing. . . . The interpreter has to go beyond what is directly given. In his attempting this he has to use the given as a clue for meanings which are not given."

12. The Talmudic discussions of pardon and the sections that follow on Jewish messianism and the Talmudic view of "doing and hearing"

take up problems that are generally considered in the context of Judaic studies. I have, however, discussed these questions at some length since Levinas derives his view of eschatology, of pardon, and of nondiscursive thought that play so prominent a role in his philosophical work from these religious texts. Moreover, it is also clear from the methodological presuppositions discussed that sacred texts look forward as well as back in the sense that they incorporate insights which historically speaking have appeared only later. This point of view legitimates for Levinas the use of these texts as a basis for his philosophical insights.

13. The translation I provide differs somewhat from that of Sean Hand. He renders "*Si vous revenez à Moi, Je reviens à vous*" as "*Return unto me, and I will return unto you,*" omitting the conditional "if." See DL 113/DF 77.

14. Hand entirely omits this passage from his translation. Levinas's French texts reads: "*La retour à la bestialité que Rabbi Yochanan redouterait, est-il plus terrible que la politique et l'économie inhumaines du monde où nous vivons?*" (DL 116)

15. Hand renders "*pitié*" as "favour." I prefer the English cognate "pity."

16. Kant, *Religion within the Limits of Reason Alone* (New York: Harper and Row, Publishers, 1960), 148.

17. Levinas does not take note of the Gnostic implications of his interpretation. Hans Jonas, *The Gnostic Religion* (Boston: Beacon Press, 1958), 57, writes in characterizing Gnosticism: "The antithesis of light and darkness . . . meets us everywhere in gnostic literature. . . . In the given state of things, the duality of darkness and light coincides with that of 'this world' and 'the other world' since darkness has embodied its whole power in *this* world, which now there is *the* world of darkness."

18. In this context Levinas's view coincides with that of Martin Buber, *The Eclipse of God* (New York: Harper, 1952), 119, who writes in criticism of Kierkegaard: "Ours is an age in which the suspension of the ethical fills the world in caricaturized form . . . ever and ever again men are commanded to sacrifice their Isaac. . . . Stored away in men's hearts there were . . . images of the Absolute, partly pallid, partly crude, altogether false."

19. Sanhedrin 37a cites Rashi's commentary upon this arrangement: "Also in semi-circular form, but on the floor. Each row numbered twenty-three, making a total of sixty-nine. They were there for completion purposes in case there might be a majority of only one for condemnation. Although forty-eight would have sufficed for that purpose, since the completion goes on till the number of seventy-one is reached, some difficulty would have been experienced in arranging that number into

rows. It would not have been proper to make two rows of twenty-four, since these would have been larger than that of the Sanhedrin, nor three rows of sixteen, which would have seemed too small, nor two rows of twenty-three and a third one only of two. Hence the sixty-nine."

20. We have seen that the number required to try capital cases is twenty-three, one-third of the maximum number seventy-one. Sanhedrin 37a notes that the Aggadists compare the court to mingled wine of which one-third is pure, the other two-thirds water.

21. The symbolism of the center is well known to phenomenologists of religion. Not only are cities, temples, and so on seen to have celestial archetypes, but they are also invested with the prestige of the center. The center is frequently a cosmic mountain at which the three regions of the cosmos, heaven, earth, and hell, are joined. There are numerous texts that bestow such prestige upon, for example, Jerusalem, Eden, and Zion. In the cosmogonic process, the navel is seen as the center so that the world is created from the navel outwards. See Eliade, *Cosmos and History* (New York: Harper, 1959), 12–17.

22. The following lines indicate this change:

> Pass thitherward ye powers of Dread,
> With all your former wrath allayed
> Into the hearts of this loved land;
> With joy unto your temple wend.

See *The Eumenides* of Aeschylus in *Complete Greek Drama,* ed. Whitney Oates and Eugene O'Neill Jr. (New York: Random House, 1938), 1:307.

VIII

Conclusions

THE THESIS that is argued throughout Levinas's work is that the worldviews opened by science and history presume their standpoints to be final. Thus, they fail to take into account their origin in a life world that lies outside the jurisdiction of the methods which they use and from which these methods derive. In this respect Levinas's thought is continuous with that of Husserl. But the failure of science and history, in Levinas's view, lies not only in the objectification of consciousness—in considering consciousness as an object in the world and therefore failing to recognize its absolute uniqueness—but also in the proposed corrective. The critique of science and history requires more than the recovery of the intentional structures of consciousness, for these very structures must themselves be judged by a self anterior to their upsurge. Not only do history and science as worldviews stand under judgment, but a proper critique of these worldviews must rest, not on a recovery of the machinery of consciousness, but upon moral foundations.

What are the consequences of these worldviews in terms of life within the framework of totality? The error of the historical viewpoint is to exonerate all conduct because man is the victim of his era. Plato uncovers the dictum of this position: man is the measure of all things. The error of psychologism that stems from the worldview of science is the fruit of regarding consciousness as another object in a field of objects. It leaves us with a dehumanized anthropology in which man is an alien presence to himself. But the recovery of the structures of consciousness still leaves untouched a fundamental point at issue: how is a moral critique of history, of polity, possible if consciousness itself is under judgment? The account of axiology provided by Husserl and his followers that allows for an understanding of values by consciousness itself cannot found the thoroughgoing critique demanded by Levinas.

We have seen that for Levinas the moral self is anterior to all positing even when such positing is axiological; it is anterior to all decision-making processes. Levinas is forced to put the matter thus not only because the source of values lies outside consciousness itself, but also because consciousness as positional is destructive of the very exteriority from which all values derive. To insist that consciousness is, among other things, axiological is to destroy the foundations of all valuing by uprooting its source, the alterity of the other. Consciousness is active. For Levinas this is Husserl's great discovery. Once valuing is construed as an act, it commandeers the Other for its own purposes, makes him part of the same, destroys his uniqueness. Thus, the moral self must be pure passivity. It cannot become anything else in the way that Aristotelian matter becomes a "this" or a "that" through the imposition of form. The moral self must be passivity without potency. Levinas has thus put forward a radical version of the view that values are objective, founding all objectivity beyond consciousness itself.

It might be argued that there *is* nothing besides what is or becomes a given for consciousness. Levinas would agree. Therefore the objectivity of values lies beyond ontology. This assumption forces Levinas to account for their presence without reintroducing a noumenal realm beyond the world of appearances. To do so would be to overthrow one of the fundamental insights of phenomenology: that there is no "backstage" behind the proscenium, no world behind the world with which we are confronted. If this is so, we see why Levinas is compelled to concede that there are foci within the phenomenological realm, gathering points or knots of value that are known in all of their phenomenality but that in their very upsurge attest the transcendence of ontology. Such a concentration of value is the face of the other person, who appears not as spiritualized but as embodied. Indeed, his carnality becomes the source of his moral appeal, for his appearing as flesh is his vulnerability. It might be conceded that the Other is indeed a given and a veritable presentation of sense, "there" in his *Leibhaftigkeit* through sensory intuition. It might even be conceded that this presence appears at once in its very upsurge as a source of value, as an object of such axiological intuition. But it might reasonably be objected: why does Levinas insist upon the transcendent, that is, upon the supraontological origin of the Other, as a source of value, as the object of such axiological intuition? Is this not to disguise theology in phenomenological garb, to slip a new natural theology into what is presumably a phenomenology of the moral self? The answer to this question can only be affirmative, yet it is a qualified affirmation in a sense that I shall try to show directly.

Levinas has taken pains to establish the notion of "trace," which attests il-leity, the third presence whose past can never be made present. To speak of a trace is to attest what cannot be spoken about, reduced to the same, or unveiled. It can never be brought to full and plenary presence as is the being of objects or made clear and distinct as are concepts and their relationships. To say that the trace can neither be brought into full presence nor made clear and distinct is not to say that we intuit the interstices of phenomena, perceive the coda rather than the theme, for the negative aspect of a phenomenon in Levinas's thought belongs to the phenomenon itself. It is rather to refuse all discourse that attempts to attribute either positive or negative qualities to God. It is to theologize by reinaugurating the *via negativa* of the mystics, which is a refusal to attest the existence of God as a "this" or a "that."

Does the trace lodged in the phenomenal world, which is more than what is presented, whose meaning can only be shown negatively and that enigmatically always remains only what it is, justify designating Levinas a natural theologian? To the extent that the phenomenal realm provides empirical foundation for affirming a realm that transcends it, Levinas can be viewed as belonging to this tradition. But he is far from asserting that there is a design in nature that reflects divine purpose and that can be ascertained by a careful scrutiny of the operations of nature. When we look at the face of the Other we know that we are commanded to honor the alterity of the Other by recognizing an asymmetry between us. We also know that something has "happened" in the intersubjective "space" between us that transcends any knowledge we may have of it. But far from gaining an objective knowledge of God's purpose, we feel a deepened sense of responsibility, the weight of the Other's suffering, an enhanced sense of the Other's creatureliness. We do not interpret what we feel as belonging to a teleological nexus, but as bearing a moral imperative. Moreover it is a moral imperative lodged within the particularity of encounter, one that cannot be made into a universal law. What is absent from the perceptual field of moral encounter in Levinas's thought is beauty, order, and arrangement, which lie at the foundation of classical conceptions of natural theology. It is important to note that Levinas prescinds all aesthetic elements from this broken natural theology, confining himself to attesting transcendence only within the field of human relations.

Once the Other is beyond ontology it could be argued that Levinas's point of view represents a return to Hegelian thought in which objectivity is determined by the reflecting subject, the alterity of an in-itself seen to be merely apparent and reduced by the reflection of the subject to an in-itself for itself. It is true that, for Levinas, Hegel has correctly sketched the programmatics of egoity, that is, of the modes in which the self conducts its totalizing operations. It could be argued, correctly I believe, that the self of totality is the Subject of Hegel's *Phenomenology of Spirit*. But what for Levinas is the actual state of affairs of the totality and thus ought to be brought under judgment is for Hegel the desired state of affairs. For Levinas, as for Heidegger, this de facto state of affairs is the culmination of the decline of Western metaphysics. The *Phenomenology* is a dazzling portrayal of *homo homini lupus* who appropriates his world not only through war and violence, the concrete activities of polity, but also through the very modalities of cognition themselves. The Absolute Subject can bring to light and conserve the spiritual forms of the past as history, but these forms themselves (as well as the intellectual comprehension of the forms) stand under absolute judgment. Such judgment lies entirely outside the province of history. It is in the matter of judgment that strict objectivity prevails. Thus, if we are to elicit the primordial meaning of objectivity in Levinas's thought, we must realize that what is objective to Levinas is not what is known or what is present before historical consciousness; in that sense no theory of history could ground objectivity. The historical is always the reductive work of a historizing subject who cannot incorporate the subjectivity of others into the framework of his project. Thus, the perspective of history is always distorted. What is apprehended with certainty (not subject to doubt because doubt itself is what it is only within a cognitive framework) is the guilt of history. Both the spiritual forms of the past and our knowledge of them stand under moral judgment. All modes of founding and understanding the just social order can only be approximations. Objectivity is not lost to Levinas because of the sublation of alterity by the self-aggrandizing historical subject. It simply lies elsewhere.

If for Levinas objectivity is not grounded in cognitive experience, is it founded in any affective experience that recurs throughout his work as a key motif? Is there at the foundation of his thought an affective intentionality such that something suprahistorical and supraontological is intended? These questions are difficult to answer because by and large Levinas's interpretation of intentionality is tied to the fulfillment of an intuition. Whether what is intended is obscure or distinct, the fruition of intentionality lies in the sense of satiety obtained when what is "found" coincides with what is intended. The salient feature of intentionality is that it yields fulfilled expectation, establishes the presence of what is intended. What is strictly objective is the other person, but the structure that intends the Other is desire, in and of itself incapable of satisfaction. Thus, in the strictest sense desire cannot be considered an intentional structure. Note that even the intentionality of an experience that is strictly sensory results not in *mere* presence, but in *meaningful* presence. What is present before consciousness already in its very upsurge "means." But the difficulty of Levinas's approach lies in the insistence that the Other means precisely because his transcendence lies beyond ontology. It is a transcendence that is *eo ipso* incapable of being brought into correlation with its object. The difficulty is a real one. It raises the specter of abandoning the phenomenological frame of reference altogether or leaving unresolved the dualism that subsists in an acceptance of intentionality of consciousness when dealing with problems of ontology and an abandonment of ontology whenever the strictly unimpeachable (objective) datum of the other person is meant.

It could also be argued against Levinas that being, as present to consciousness, gives itself in all its originality in accordance with its own structures. There is an irreducibility of the presented that wells up before the knowing subject who perceives this manifestation without exerting any constitutive activity. Husserl's development of the material a priori could certainly give rise to such a fundamentally ontologizing phenomenology in which being gives itself to thought. The role of the thinker is minimized. Has Levinas not misunderstood the fundamentally ontologizing thrust of phenomenological thought by claiming that the subject subordinates being to the categories of thought, to the a priori structures of consciousness? The ontological bias of phenomenology has been thought through in a radical way by such thinkers as Mikel Dufrenne, for whom the a priori structures of consciousness are not the work of the subject but come from being itself. They manifest themselves as, for example, value or affective quality. They are no longer the formal subjective basis for objectivity. The object is merely *completed* formally in consciousness. The a priori itself is for the subject rather than a consequence of the subject. This a priori seen in being allows things to make themselves known.[1]

To argue thus is to pretend that Levinas tries to demolish the presented world by asserting it to be fictive, the mere creation of subjectivity. Nothing could be further from his aim. His effort is directed at revealing the presented both as amenable to representation and as absolutely resistant to it. To represent is at once to seek correlation of the intending with what is intended. Whether the a priori belongs to consciousness or somehow wells up from being itself is an indifferent question. The relation of intending to intended is one of correlation in either case. There is, however, a presentation that is not subject to the limiting requirements of correlation. Its form is always inadequate to its content; it is a presentation such that the content is always experienced as breaking through the shell of its form. This presentation is the other person. He transcends ontology not in the sense that he is an extramundane apparition like a docetic Christ whose carnal manifestation belies his underlying spiritual reality. On the contrary: the Other presents himself well within the range of the phenomenal. But the presented now "means" beyond the phenomena and is given as nonrepresentable. Thus, in denying the finality of ontology, Levinas furnishes a critique of representation that underlies all of our cognitive processes and that has been made to serve as the model for all experiencing rather than a critique of ontology from the point of view of idealistic metaphysics. There is no doubt that for Levinas being is present, richly present, as his careful analyses of the elemental and the *il y a* make clear. Nor does he deny the transcendence of the object even in the case of representation. But radical transcendence is possible only at those points in the phenomenal world that are unrepresentable, that require an "intentionality" (if the term "intentionality" in our present context has not been traduced by the contradictory usages to which it is subject, as shown above) that must always remain to some degree empty.

Morality and Metaphysics

The prime objective of Levinas's work has been to develop a metaphysics upon ethical foundations by showing man's being in the world to be moral being. The self that precedes the disjunction of freedom or necessity and precedes such functions of egoity as thinking, beginning, or understanding must be recovered by showing that these mediatory functions of egoity inhibit its spontaneous operation. It might be argued that an ethic that proposes spontaneity without reflective mediation raises the danger of reverting to instinctual conduct based upon hedonic self-interest. Levinas has himself shown that need instigates unmediated activity designed to put an end to an experienced discomfort. The satisfaction of need at the most primitive levels is unreflective; the techniques required for satiety are stimulated in the very upsurge of need itself. Thus, eating, the technique for alleviating hunger, is not a well-designed scheme thought up in advance and then put into operation to appease the emergence of certain types of bodily malaise. It is an operation born in hunger itself. Only when spontaneous satisfaction is, for some reason, impeded and gives rise to anxiety does the self interpose cognitive modes of mediation. It is, as we have seen, the proliferation of these cognitive modes of operation that give rise to economy.

How does the spontaneity of the self that fulfills its needs differ from the spontaneity of the moral self? The answer lies in the principle of strict objectivity that controls the nonmediated oper-

ation of the moral self totally absent in the picture of egoity presented by the self of need satisfaction. This principle is the
presence of the other person; without him there is no moral self.
It is the Other whose face means "thou shalt not kill" that provides the objective criterion for all moral action. I should like to
point out that the principle of objectivity is negative: "thou shalt
not." Were it otherwise, that is, were the underlying principle of
moral action positive, demanding that certain measures however
broad be made the foundation of morals (e.g., "act on behalf of
the greatest good for the greatest number"), the nature of the
moral self as passivity would be undermined. Measures can be
initiated only by egoity. The self of responsibility is infinitely passive. Does this entail a sterile morality, paralyzing all action and
even all reflection? I believe that to interpret Levinas in this way
would be to misread the principle of passivity. For it would be to
understand the passivity of the moral self as enjoining one to refrain from action, a restraint that itself is an activity of a very special type. The passivity of the moral self is thus not a suppression
of activity. In and of itself, it enjoins nothing. It is an experience
of responsibility in the process of expansion with no end in sight.
It functions negatively not as a repression of egoity but as a focus
for the realignment of egotistical forces in a new field. Instead of
gravitating about the self as center, which seeks to bring the intended into correlation with the intending, it now gravitates
around the other, empties itself of itself, distinguishes its asymmetry with regard to the other.

For all of its phenomenological underpinnings, is not Levinas's
self of responsibility a reversion to radical Kantian ethics?

> A good will is good not because of what it performs or effects, not
> by its aptness for the attainment of some proposed end, but simply
> by virtue of the volition, that is, it is good in itself, and considered
> by itself is to be esteemed much higher than all that can be brought
> about by it. . . . Even if it should happen . . . [that] this will should
> wholly lack power to accomplish its purpose, if with its greatest ef-
> forts it should yet achieve nothing, and there should remain only
> the good will . . . then like a jewel it would still shine by its own
> light, as a thing which has its whole value in itself.[2]

There is certainly a good deal to be said for placing Levinas in
the Kantian tradition.[3] When Levinas claims that only the Other

"means" as command, does he not thereby transform the command into universal law? For despite Levinas's insistence that the Other wells up in his particularity, what the Other "means," irrespective of which particular Other he happens to be, is always the same: thou shalt not kill. The upsurge of the face guarantees this meaning.

Has Levinas evaded the major pitfall of Kantian ethics, the separation of the phenomenal realm from the noumenality of practical reason? For Kant, the absolutely good will obedient to the moral law cannot be empirically founded. The problem of the separation of values from the phenomenal world could be overcome through the direct intuiting of values so that values are given in the same way as other essences. Husserlian phenomenology opened the way for this approach, but, while guaranteeing the apodicticity of moral values sought by Kant, it leaves these moral values as instantiations within the ontological sphere. To do so is unacceptable to Levinas. Moral values still arise in the phenomenal realm, but they are now borne by persons and are intuited in the very appearance of their bearers as being of transcendental origin. The problem is further complicated for Levinas by the fact that while responsibility, which alone can attach itself to values, remains inert in the phenomenal sphere, it is even more radically separated from the phenomenal than is demanded by a strictly Kantian framework, since the foundation of its values lies outside its own will. Kantian ethics requires strict autonomy of the will; the will is to itself its own law. Yet Levinas insists upon strictly heteronomous rule. The moral self is to itself its own foundation in the sense that it remains independent of the self of egoity. Yet with regard to other persons, it remains strictly dependent upon others. The Other is one's teacher; his transcendence guarantees the moral self. Levinas remains Kantian in insisting upon the immediate and apodictic upsurge of value and in rejecting an empirical foundation for the moral self. Yet we have seen that the Other appears as phenomenon: he is a unique given who breaks through the form of his appearance to become a transcendent source of value. Thus, while the moral self does not need the presented world insofar as it can be represented, it is subject to the presented when what is presented is the other person who is the source of all moral value.

Still another problem, that of the relationship between duty and inclination (rather simply solved by Kant), poses a number of thorny questions for Levinas. Kant shows that the origin of moral evil lies in the ground of our maxims. If we base our actions upon maxims grounded in inclination rather than in duty we have failed to act in accordance with the moral law. In the simple subordination of inclination to reason the Kantian solution is not altogether un-Platonic. Kant transcends the Platonic framework in that the improper ordering of duty and inclination is seen to arise from an evil will rather than from a simple lack of knowledge as in the case of Plato. Nevertheless, if inclination were properly subordinated to duty, we could not but act in accordance with the moral law, for to act morally is to act precisely in accordance with this correct order. But Levinas has detached reason altogether from the moral self so that what is moral can no longer be sought as it was for Kant, "a priori, simply in the conception of pure reason." Indeed, there is at this juncture a profound break with Kantian principles, for now, as we have seen, morality for Levinas is attached to an affect. Affect is no longer, as it was for Kant, at best an incidental but unwarranted intrusion upon the ground of maxims, sullying the purity of an otherwise moral act and at worst upsetting in its very upsurge the possibility of moral action itself. Affectivity in Levinas's thought becomes the lived mode of morality. This means that for Levinas there is an affect such that it is trustworthy; it procures, not a runaway upsurge of instinctive life as the rebellious steed of the *Phaedrus,* but an immediate and instinctive attachment to the Good. Inclination has been rehabilitated so that motive and duty separable in Kant are united in Levinas's thought as "desire."

The problem of judging a particular action is a relatively simple matter for Kant, since all we need do is to ask whether we are acting such that we might will our action to become a universal law. Hegel has already remarked in this regard that "ethical consciousness . . . is the simple, pure direction of activity towards the essentiality of ethical life, i.e. duty. In it, there is no caprice and equally no struggle. . . . [T]he ethical consciousness . . . knows what it has to do."[4] It is true that another person cannot gauge the sincerity of our motives and the rectitude of our maxims; he can only judge conditionally, that is, *if* our maxim is in conformity to the moral law, and if our action springs from this maxim, then this action is not only in apparent conformity to the moral law, but in actual conformity to it. But it can be objected that since action for Levinas, insofar as it is action, cannot originate in the moral self but only in egoity, all actions stand under judgment. We again are confronted with a Kantian bias radicalized: not only is the value of all action ambiguous as in the case of Kant, for whom the observer can make some judgment regarding its merit but cannot know whether the action proceeded from an absolutely good will, but for Levinas action per se is corrupt because proceeding from egoity. I have already suggested that Levinas does not conclude that the passivity of the moral self need paralyze all action; rather it serves to reorient the self around a new and supraphenomenal source of values. Indeed, as we have seen, the self cannot do other than act, for even restraint from activity is a modality of action; this is not to prescind from the argument that action proceeds from one or another mode of egoity, and therefore all action stands under judgment. While for Kant acts—detached from a final knowledge of the ground of the maxims from which they spring, a knowledge we can never achieve—remain acts of ambiguous moral character, for Levinas there is an inevitability of taint. Once an act falls into the politico-historical order, it is released into a realm of cause and effect and enters into a complex social nexus over which its perpetrator no longer has any control. Thus, even if one's motives are absolutely pure, the act has been alienated and takes on an independent life. Levinas thus interprets every act as Marx interpreted the product of work within an economy: it acquires a strange autonomy, a power quite removed from its origin, and can spring into action against its creator or against others. Thus, Levinas does not merely separate the act from the moral self, so that from the appearance of the one we cannot make any conclusive inferences with regard to the nature of the other, but proclaims the radical independence of the one from the other. It is fair to conclude that "authenticity" for Levinas consists in the recognition of this state of affairs so that the moral self becomes increasingly aware of its burden of guilt.

It could be argued against Levinas that by separating the moral self from rational life he has undercut the very basis upon which all moral disputes can be settled, including those that arise from his own position.[5] To do so would be to misunderstand the crucial role that reason, as evinced in law and institutional life, plays in Levinas's thought. Man lives within totality and must be subject to the prudential rules that govern the political order. These rules are subject to formalization in accordance with the laws of thought. They are vital to the governance of affairs within the totality. The totality is the realm in which the universal is legitimately ensconced, that is, the sphere in which we must think out appropriate measures of conduct for all men. But these rules of conduct must not be mistaken for the moral order anterior to the appearance of any and all rules, an order that in its very nature we have seen to be an-archic. This is not, however, to deny three serious considerations that are entailed by the separation of the moral from the discursive self. First, it makes impossible any but oblique references to the moral self (what I have called a *via negativa* of the moral self), since what is truly moral lies beyond discursive language. Second, it may lead to a conflation of moral issues with legal issues. What can be argued is whether or not our actions conform to a law. What determines whether the law is a moral law cannot be argued since all human laws stand under judgment as products of the politico-historical complex of totality. Third, there is an assimilation of reason to actual violence, which puts reason, the desire to know and experience, under somewhat the same condemnation as outright violence.

In reply to the first objection, Levinas could claim that in accordance with phenomenological principles language arises from the phenomenon. We cannot commandeer language from other realms of being to suit the demand for clarity and precision, but we must be true to the opaqueness of the phenomenon itself, and the phenomenon of the moral self requires this *via negativa*. To the second objection, Levinas could reply that the weight of what lies beyond discursive language is not to be interpreted as an incentive to irrational action. It is to realize that the value of the Other absolutely transcends the possibilities of discursive language and cannot be incorporated into any legal framework. Nevertheless we ought to discuss practical moral questions. There is no logical necessity whatever that should make us conclude that thoughtless and irrational action follows from the assumption that the self of responsibility cannot be described. On the contrary, with the growth of responsibility of the self an ever-increasing caution in the conduct of life affairs is a more likely outcome. The third objection would constitute for Levinas no objection at all, since the point of his work is to elicit the violent substructure of reason itself.

LANGUAGE

We have seen that for Levinas genuine language "expresses"; that is, the bearer of language ultimately both conveys and limits the meaning of language. Beyond the content of discourse, language is in its very foundations ethical. This approach to language raises problems on two levels. First, while placing a high premium upon language not merely as the milieu of the ethical but as the ethical itself, this approach nevertheless regards language as the onset of violence; second, it in effect makes Levinas's own program unsayable. Let us examine these difficulties more closely. For Levinas human communion does not bypass language. Rather, the face of the Other opens up the right to the spoken word because it is the sine qua non and warranty for the authenticity of language. But language is an original phenomenon; Heidegger insists on the simultaneity of thought and language and the impossibility of predicating any sequentiality in their emergence. Thought and language are born together. Language as an original phenomenon means that the possibility of metaphysics is the possibility of the word. Metaphysical responsibility is already a responsibility for language. Levinas goes so far as to exempt art from the domain of language since it fails precisely on these grounds; that is, it fails to take responsibility for itself as language. What is critical is that there is not first the face and then language, but a simultaneous upsurge of face, language, and responsibility. Language wells up with the face. Yet, in its very appearing, the face undergoes a primordial act of violence. We have seen that for Levinas the Other, starting from his appearing for us as Other, is a drawing of his alterity into the light. But no discourse can evade the necessity of the Other's appearing to us, a drawing forth through violence into discursive possibility. War is inherent in phenomenality as such.[6] When Levinas attempts to found metaphysics in ethics, the ethical foundation itself is shaken by the necessity of language to become phenomenal, that is, by the necessity of the face to appear. The emergence of true peace can only appear as an end to language, as deferred to the "not yet" of an indefinite future. Such a peace must be silence. Thus, the *telos* of language would not lie in its very upsurge, which is an act of violence, but in something other than itself, in silence.

The second problem relates to the difficulty of philosophizing itself. We have seen that for Levinas there is an inherent incompatibility between the Greek *logos* and the prophetic word. For this very reason he seeks to uncover nondiscursive phenomena, phenomena of appearing that found language so that the worn-out metaphors of philosophical discourse can be avoided. Heidegger has achieved this by seeking to recover the original meanings of a philosophical language traduced by its history without discarding the language itself. Levinas's rejection of ontology closes this possibility, for the language of being that such an enterprise recovers is for him not a genuine rebirth of language, but an efflorescence of the same. He therefore works through metaphors that essentially convey a sense of the infinite through descriptions of epiphany. This is the very meaning of the face, the trace, and enigma. The divine appearing, elusive and enigmatic, is recovered by bringing to discursive clarity this very obscurity and vagueness, by opening to interpretation what the phenomenon itself guides but does not legislate. In this task Levinas has no alternative but to use the outworn language, which for him is the language of totality. It is a language of spatiality, of inside and outside, which is irreducible. It might be argued that such language served negative theology well, but it must be recalled that negative theologians did not ground the possibility of ethics in the upsurge of language and did not consider the word spoken between men the foundation of ethical life. Thus, language itself is undermined by the requirements of what Levinas calls "formal logic," that is, the structure of language that brings into correlation the intending with what is intended.

THE IDEA OF THE INFINITE

There is one idea such that the intending and the intended can never be brought into correlation, which transcends the self who thinks it. As we have seen, this is the idea of the infinite. It is important to note that Levinas's reflection on the idea of the infinite derives from Descartes's Third Meditation, where, for the first time in the *Meditations,* the idea of the infinite appears. Yet the idea of the infinite is introduced by Descartes after the notion of methodical doubt has been thought through and accepted, and after the establishment of the *cogito* in the first two meditations.[7] In our present context, the existence of the infinite is discovered in the idea that Descartes has of it as the cause of his idea. Descartes leaves little doubt that the idea of the infinite in the new context of the Third Meditation appears as positive and prior to the recognition of the finite:

> And I must not think that, just as my conceptions of rest and darkness are arrived at by negating movement and light, so my perception of the infinite is arrived at not by means of a true idea but merely by negating the finite. On the contrary, I clearly understand that there is more reality in an infinite substance than in a finite one, and hence that my perception of the infinite, that is God, is in some way prior to my perception of the finite, that is myself. For how could I understand that I doubted or desired—that is, lacked something—and that I was not wholly perfect, unless there were in me some idea of a more perfect being which enabled me to recognize my own deficiencies by comparison?[8]

If the infinite is prior to the finite, how can the existence of the infinite itself be reached without the starting point of the *cogito* and the certainty of its intuition so carefully established in the first two meditations? There is a reciprocity, a mutual dependence that is at the origin of what has been designated as the "Cartesian circle."[9]

I believe that this puzzle in Descartes's work is of critical importance in the development of Levinas's thought, for the relation of the idea of the infinite to the *cogito* is carefully worked through phenomenologically as a central concern of *Totality and Infinity.* We have already established that for Levinas the idea of the infinite is the foundation for all objective reality. Is this idea anterior to the separated self? How is the question of the "Cartesian circle" resolved? For Levinas the *discovery* of the relation to the infinite is possible only by a separated self; discovery follows rather than precedes the self-certainty of the *cogito:* "The present of the *cogito,* despite the support it discovers for itself *after the fact* in the absolute that transcends it, maintains itself all by itself—be it only for an instant, the space of a *cogito*" (TeI 25/TI 54). The position of the *cogito,* to which Levinas refers as "atheism," is, as we have seen, not the rejection of the proposition "God exists" but a stance anterior to all negation, the moment at which participation in being is severed and the self emerges as separated from the matrix of being.

In his work after 1968, separated self is not described as prior to the ownmost self, that is, to the self of responsibility that carries the weight of the other person. Levinas writes: "Ipseity is not an abstract point, a center of rotation, identifiable by way of the trajectory traced by a movement of consciousness. It is here and now identified without having to identify itself in the present, nor having to 'decline' its identity, already *older than the time of consciousness*" (S 494/BPW 85/AE 135/OBBE 107; my emphasis). This seemingly paradoxical view can now be seen as developing from the Cartesian problem, for insofar as the infinite is placed in us, it is from the logical point of view anterior to our own discovery of it, an anteriority that does not therefore prejudice the case for its posteriority in terms of our discovery of it.

I would argue that a theology grounded in ethics is also made possible by the view that the separated self is at least historically prior to the discovery of the infinite: "The atheism of the metaphysician means, positively, that our relation with the Metaphysical is an ethical behavior and not theology, not a thematization, be it a knowledge by analogy of God's attributes. God rises to his supreme and ultimate presence as correlative to the justice rendered to men" (TeI 50/TI 78). The relation to the infinite succeeds separated self because the infinite is ethically rather than theologically founded. Our theological suppositions are only possible after the ethical has been firmly established.[10]

This opens to question a second point raised by Descartes: that there is an infinite that cannot be clearly comprehended, that remains inaccessible to thought because of the finite nature that thinks it. Levinas insists that the relation to the infinite arises in the domain of intersubjective relations. The idea of this infinite arises in the presence of the face of the Other. But is this infinite consistent with the Cartesian intention? The infinite that emerges from the upsurge of the Other is inherently mortal. Indeed, the ethical imperative "thou shalt not kill," which the face expresses, relates the infinity of the Other as face precisely to his mortality by locating the meaning of the Other in the interdiction of murder. The exclusion of phenomenality and death from the Cartesian infinite separates it decisively from Levinas's "other person."

What is even more fundamental is the link that Levinas establishes between language and the face. First, Levinas insists, as we have seen, that language belongs to thought indissolubly, that is, there is no thought which precedes language. He writes: "Modern investigations in the philosophy of language have made familiar the idea of an underlying solidarity between thought and speech. Merleau-Ponty, among others . . . showed that disincarnate thought thinking the speech before speaking it, thought constituting the world of the speech, adding a world of speech to the world antecedently constituted out of significations in an always transcendental operation, was a myth" (TeI 180/TI 205–6).[11] Levinas contends that "meaning surprises the very thought which thinks it." This view establishes the simultaneity of the thought and its language, the absence of a gap between the thought and its meaning, which is language. For Descartes, therefore, it is perfectly consistent and appropriate to speak of a thought that cannot be contained by its idea, of a discrepancy between contained and containing, but Levinas (if he is consistent in his approach to language) cannot imagine a thought for which language is inadequate, an idea that is not, in its very upsurge, language. Levinas could certainly object that the face is not intended by an objectifying act, that it is rather intended by an affective intentionality, by desire, so that plenary presence of the intended is out of the question. But in that case he would be compelled to jettison the Cartesian scheme based on the model of cognition, of clear and distinct ideas.

Levinas also contends with a second notion of the infinite that is an underlying motif rather than an explicit problem in his work. This is the idea of the infinite as it appears in Hegel's *Ency-*

clopedia Logic. Hegel declares that wrong or negative infinity is the endless passage of something into its opposite. We start out with a something (determinate being), which then passes into another, which itself only becomes a something and which as a something again changes into another ad infinitum. The difficulty for Hegel is that the something that has changed into another has not, in becoming other, forced the other to become other to itself: that is, no higher level of rationality has been achieved. The change involved in this case subsists always at the same level. In genuine infinity, that which passes into the other shares with the other into which it passes the same attribute: that each is other to the other. What is altered is the alterity of the original other. What was previously the other has become other than the other. Alterity is no longer what it was. For Levinas the true infinite is the other that is other than the same. It functions *always* and forever, as the other of the same never incorporating into itself what is other to it, namely the same. Thus, it remains simple alterity, never raising itself to the level of the "other than the other" required by Hegelian dialectic for the true infinite. Levinas remains within the dualistic framework that Hegel describes: "Dualism, which makes the opposition of finite and infinite insuperable, fails to make the simple observation that in this way the infinite itself is also just *one of the two,* [and] that it is therefore reduced to one *particular,* in addition to which the finite is the other one. Such an infinite, which is just one particular, *beside* the finite, so that it has precisely its restriction, its limit, in the latter, is *not* what it ought to be. It is not the Infinite, but is only *finite.*"[12]

It may thus be argued that Levinas's infinite is Hegel's bad infinite.[13] Levinas maintains that while Hegel reverts to the Cartesian position by sustaining the positivity of the infinite, Hegel excludes anything (determinate being) that sustains a relation with the infinite, that would thereby limit the infinite. Hegel's infinite thus can only overwhelm all other relations. For Levinas one can enter into Hegel's infinite only by suppressing one's proper finitude, so that we recognize in Hegel's infinite the finitude of man before the elemental, where the elemental which is other than man overwhelms him (TeI 170–71/TI 196–97). Hegel's infinite thus haunts all of Levinas's work as the possibility of return into undifferentiated being.

NOTES

1. See DEHH 179–86. Levinas sees the ontological thrust of Dufrenne as avoiding a Hegelian account of the subject as submerging an in-itself in a for-itself (183).

2. Kant, *Fundamental Principles of the Metaphysics of Morals* (New York: Library of Liberal Arts, 1949), 12ff.

3. Jean Lacroix, "L'infini et le prochain selon Emmanuel Levinas," *Panorama de la philosophie française contemporaine* (Paris: PUF, 1966), 116–23, writes that the very root of Levinas's thought is Kantian because there is only true consciousness of the other as ethics.

4. Hegel, *Phenomenology of Spirit,* trans. A. V. Miller (Oxford: Oxford University Press, 1977), 279–380.

5. Derrida, "Violence et métaphysique: Essai sur la pensée d'Emmanuel Levinas," in *L'écriture et la différence* (Paris: Seuil, 1967), 164 (translated by Alan Bass as "Violence and Metaphysics: An Essay on the Thought of Emmanuel Levinas," in *Writing and Difference* [Chicago: University of Chicago Press, 1978], 111), argues that Levinas gives us neither ethical precepts nor a theory of ethics but an "ethic of ethics." He writes: "let us not forget that Levinas does not seek to propose laws or moral rules, does not seek to determine *a* morality but rather the essence of the ethical relation in general. But as this determination does not offer itself as a *theory* of ethics, in question then, is an ethics of ethics. . . . Is this ethics of ethics beyond all laws?"

6. Derrida, "Violence et métaphysique," 171, 188–90 ("Violence and Metaphysics," 116, 128–30). Also see Maurice Blanchot, "Knowledge of the Unknown," translated by Susan Hanson in *The Infinite Conversation* (Minneapolis: University of Minnesota Press, 1993), 49–58.

7. In the discussion following "Transcendence and Height," Levinas confirms the importance of Descartes's Third Meditation for his own thought (BPW 25): "And yet, if Descartes begins with the *cogito,* he says a little later that in fact it is the idea of God that is primary, that is, the idea of the infinite. The idea of God was prior to the *cogito,* and the *cogito* would never have been possible if there had not been already been the idea of God."

8. René Descartes, *Meditations on First Philosophy,* ed. John Cottingham (Cambridge: Cambridge University Press, 1996), 31.

9. S. Decloux, "Existence de Dieu et rencontre d'autrui," *Nouvelle Revue Théologique* (1964), 709.

10. See also Plat, "De mens en de oneindige ander bij Emmanuel Levinas," *Tijdschrift voor Filosolophie* 26 (1964), 457–99: "Man is sustained all alone in existence without participating in the being from which he

is separated; it is only from this condition that he can exist as atheistic, as free being" (499).

11. See Merleau-Ponty, *Phenomenology of Perception,* trans. Colin Smith (London: Routledge and Kegan Paul, 1962), 177ff.

12. Hegel, *The Encyclopedia Logic,* trans. T. F. Geraets, W. A. Suchting, and H. S. Harris (Indianapolis: Hackett, 1991), 151.

13. Plat, "De mens en de oneindige ander," 500, writes that Levinas "introduces the paradoxical notion of an infinite limited in some way, which allows room for beings separated from it."

KEY TO SPECIAL
TERMINOLOGY

Being (*être*). Roughly comparable to Heidegger's *Sein*. It is contrasted with the existent, *Seiendes*. To be understood as the light in which existents become intelligible.

Desire (*le désir*). Used, except in very early works, to designate an affect that intends the other person and is therefore inadequate to its object. It is a want that remains insatiable.

Dwelling (*la demeure*). Compared with Heidegger's *Wohnen*, which is a fundamental being-structure of Dasein, the way in which Dasein abides or sojourns. Its fundamental characteristic is tending. In dwelling human activity begins. For Levinas, man is in the world as coming from a private domain. It is an indispensable condition for representation and contemplation. Recollection is concretized as existence in a dwelling.

Eschatology (*l'eschatologie*). Institutes a relation with being beyond the totality and beyond history. It relates to a surplus outside the totality, to the infinite that transcends totality.

Existent (*l'étant*). Comparable to Heidegger's *Seiendes* but used by Levinas to designate the other person to whom one relates prior to an understanding of being, the other who is one's interlocutor.

Expression (*l'expression*).

Manifestation of the presence of being but not as a mere uncovering of a phenomenon. In the face, an appeal, teaching, or entry into relation, what is immediately presented is the one signifying rather than a sign or what the sign signifies.

Face (*le visage*).

Disincarnate presence of the Other. It prevents totalization and the triumph of totality. It is the source of revelation of the other who cannot be encompassed in cognition. It calls separated being, egoity, the self into question.

Hypostasis (*l'hypostase*).

The appearance of something that arises from anonymous being and that now carries being as its attribute. The term is largely confined to early works.

Il y a. Related to Heidegger's *es gibt.*

Il y a as a translation of *es gibt* in Sartre's work is called into question by Heidegger. *Il y a* does not convey the sense of the *es* in *es gibt* since *es* refers to being and not to beings. Levinas uses *il y a* to designate the being that persists in the face of the destruction of the world, a presence despite the absence of individual things, the sheer fact of being when there is nothing at all.

Intentionality (*l'intentionalité*).

Understood by Levinas in Husserl's sense: a fundamental characteristic of consciousness, an animating act that bestows upon elements not yet animated by intention their transcendent meaning. For Levinas it is consciousness's way of being in the world, the subjectivity of the subject.

Living-on (*vivre de*).

A relation to the content of life that

	goes beyond the mere assurance of the continuation of life to include the love of life, the value of life. It is the enjoyment of the I, its happiness and independence.
Metaphysics (*la métaphysique*).	Metaphysics is a going-forth from the familiar world to what is outside of oneself. It describes a desire for what is absolutely other than the self, for the infinite, a desire that remains insatiable.
Need (*le besoin*).	A want capable of satisfaction that implies a dependence on the world.
Ontology (*l'ontologie*).	The comprehension, the embracing of being. It fails to call into question the reduction of the Other by the self to the same. It therefore leads to philosophies of power and injustice.
Optics (*l'optique*).	Unmediated relation with the Other. Describes the spiritual condition of ethical life.
Other (*l'autrui*).	Reserved for the special alterity belonging to other persons who resist reduction to the same. The Other stands in an asymmetrical relation with oneself. The Other is always higher, commands, is the teacher of the self.
Same (*le même*).	The possibility of suspending the otherness of the world by sojourning in it, by being at home with oneself in it. What is other is so only relative to the self. The reduction of the Other to the same occurs in a concrete relationship to the world and is not merely formal.
Totality (*la totalité*).	That view of the whole that destroys the alterity of the Other and is therefore a primal act of violence.

WORKS CITED

The list below does not include those works of Levinas already included in the list of abbreviations. For a complete English-language bibliography of works by and about Emmanuel Levinas, the reader is referred to Henrik Petersen, "Bibliography," *Philosophy and Social Criticism* 23, no. 6 (1997): 109–38.

WORKS OF EMMANUEL LEVINAS

L'au-delà du verset: Lectures et discours talmudiques. Paris: Minuit, 1982.

Beyond the Verse: Talmudic Readings and Lectures. Translated by Gary D. Mole. Bloomington: Indiana University Press, 1994.

Difficile liberté. Paris: Albin Michel, 1963.

Hors sujet. Montpellier: Fata Morgana, 1987.

"Liberté et commandement." *Revue de Métaphysique et de Morale* 3 (1953): 264–72.

Noms propres. Montpellier: Fata Morgana, 1976.

Of God Who Comes to Mind. Translated by Bettina Bergo. Stanford: Stanford University Press, 1998.

Outside the Subject. Translated by Michael B. Smith. Stanford: Stanford University Press, 1993.

"Pluralisme et transcendence." In *Actes du Xeme Congrès Internationale de Philosophie*, edited by F. W. Beth, H. J. Pos, and J. H. Hollak, 1:381–83. Amsterdam: North American Publishing, 1949.

Proper Names. Translated by Michael B. Smith. Stanford: Stanford University Press, 1996.

Review of Leon Chestov, *Kierkegaard et la philosophie existentielle.* *Revue des Etudes juives* 1, nos. 1–2 (1937): 139–41.

"Transcendance et hauteur." *Bulletin de la Société Française de Philosophie* 56 (1962): 89–113.

"Envers Autrui: Texte du traité 'Yoma' (851–85b)." In *La Conscience juive, donnés et débats,* edited by E. Amado Levy-Valensi and Jean Halpérin, 289–304. Translated by Annette Aronowicz as "Toward the Other," in *Nine Talmudic Readings,* 9–29. Bloomington: Indiana University Press.

WORKS ABOUT EMMANUEL LEVINAS

Bataille, Georges. "De l'existentialisme au primat de l'économie." *Critique* 4 (1948): 127–41. Translated by Jill Robbins and Marcus Coelen as "From Existentialism to the Primacy of Economy," in Jill Robbins, *Altered Reading: Levinas and Literature,* 155–80. Chicago: University of Chicago Press, 1999.

Bernasconi, Robert, and Critchley, Simon, eds. *Re-reading Levinas.* Bloomington: Indiana University Press, 1991.

Boehm, Rudolf. "De Kritiek van Levinas op Heidegger." *Tijdschrift voor Filosophie* 25, no. 3 (1963): 585–603.

Catesson, Jean. "Un penseur enraciné." *Critique* 9 (1953): 961–72.

———. "Une philosophie de l'inégal." *Critique* 21 (1965): 629–57.

Chalier, Catherine. *Figures du féminin: Lecture d'Emmanuel Levinas.* Paris: La nuit surveillée, 1982.

Cohen, Richard A., ed. *Face to Face with Emmanuel Levinas.* Albany: State University of New York Press, 1986.

Derrida, Jacques. "Violence et métaphysique: Essai sur la pensée d'Emmanuel Levinas." In *L'écriture et la différence,* 117–228. Paris: Seuil, 1967. Translated by Alan Bass as "Violence and Metaphysics: An Essay on the Thought of Emmanuel Levinas," in *Writing and Difference,* 79–153. Chicago: University of Chicago Press, 1978.

Dondeyne, A. "Inleiding tot het denken van Emmanuel Levinas." *Tijdschrift voor Filosophie* 25 (1963): 555–81.

Gerber, Rudolf J. "Totality and Infinity: Hebraism and Hellenism—The Experimental Ontology of Emmanuel Levinas." *Review of Existential Psychology and Psychiatry* 7 (1967): 177–88.

Kwant, R. C. "De verhouding van mens tot mens volgens Emmanuel Levinas." *Streuven* 19 (1965–66): 609–21.

Lacroix, Jean. "L'infini et le prochain selon Emmanuel Levinas."

In *Panorama de la philosophie française contemporaine,* 116–23. Paris: PUF, 1966.

Llewelyn, John. "Levinas' Critical and Hypocritical Diction." *Philosophy Today* 41, supplement (1997): 28–40.

Martin, Jean. "Une philosophie nouvelle devant l'athéisme contemporaine." *Revue Diocésaine de Tournai* 19 (1964): 226–41.

Peperzak, Adriaan. "From Intentionality to Responsibility: On Levinas' Philosophy of Language." In *The Question of the Other,* edited by Arleen B. Dallery and Charles E. Scott, 3–22. Albany: State University of New York Press, 1989.

van Peursen, C. A. "Philosophen der Kontingenz." *Philosophische Rundschau* 12 (1964–65): 1–12.

Plat, J. "De mens en de oneindige ander bij Emmanuel Levinas." *Tijdschrift voor Filosolophie* 26 (1964): 457–99.

OTHER WORKS CITED

Aeschylus. *The Eumenides.* In *Complete Greek Drama,* edited by Whitney Oates and Eugene O'Neill, Jr. Volume 1. New York: Random House, 1938.

Aquinas, Saint Thomas. *Basic Writings of St. Thomas Aquinas.* Edited by Anton Pegis. New York: Random House, 1945.

Barth, Karl. *Church Dogmatics,* vol. 3, part 2. Translated by G. W. Bromiley. Edinburgh: T. & T. Clark, 1960.

Benjamin, Walter. *Illuminations: Essays and Reflections.* Translated by Harry Zohn. New York: Schocken, 1968.

Blanchot, Maurice. "Knowledge of the Unknown." In *The Infinite Conversation,* translated by Susan Hanson, 49–58. Minneapolis: University of Minnesota Press, 1993.

Brown, N. O. *Life against Death.* New York: Random House, 1959.

Buber, Martin. *The Eclipse of God.* New York: Harper and Row, 1952.

———. *I and Thou.* Translated by Ronald Gregor Smith. 2d ed. New York: Scribner's Sons, 1958.

Bultmann, Rudolf. *Jesus Christ and Mythology.* New York: Scribner's Sons, 1958.

Decloux, S. "Existence de Dieu et rencontre d'autrui." *Nouvelle Revue Théologique* (1964): 706–24.

Descartes, René. *Meditations on First Philosophy*. Edited by John Cottingham. Cambridge: Cambridge University Press, 1996.

Dufrenne, Mikel. *The Notion of the A Priori*. Translated by Edward S. Casey. Evanston, Ill.: Northwestern University Press, 1966.

Eliade, Mircea. *Cosmos and History*. Translated by Willard R. Trask. New York: Harper, 1959.

Eliot, T. S. *Collected Poems, 1909–1935*. New York: Harcourt, Brace, 1936.

———. *Four Quartets*. New York: Harcourt, Brace, 1943.

Guttmann, Julius. *Philosophies of Judaism*. Translated by D. W. Silverman. New York: Holt, Rinehart & Winston, 1968.

Hegel, G. W. F. *The Encyclopedia Logic*. Translated by T. F. Geraets, W. A. Suchting, and H. S. Harris. Indianapolis: Hackett, 1991.

———. *The Phenomenology of Spirit*. Translated by A. V. Miller. Oxford: Oxford University Press, 1977.

Heidegger, Martin. *Being and Time*. Translated by John Macquarrie and Edward Robinson. New York: Harper and Row, 1962.

———. *Holzwege*. Frankfurt am Main: Vittorio Klostermann, 1957.

Husserl, Edmund. *Cartesian Meditations*. Translated by Dorion Cairns. The Hague: Martinus Nijhoff, 1960. French translation by Emmanuel Levinas and J. Pfeiffer. Paris: Colin, 1930. 2d. ed. Paris: Vrin, 1947.

———. *Ideas Pertaining to a Pure Phenomenology and to a Phenomenological Philosophy, First Book*. Translated by F. Kersten. The Hague: Martinus Nijhoff, 1982.

———. *Logical Investigations*. Translated by J. N. Findlay. New York: Humanities Press, 1970.

James, William. *The Varieties of Religious Experience*. New York: Mentor, 1958.

Jaspers, Karl. *Spinoza*. Volume 2 of *The Great Philosophers*. Translated by Ralph Mannheim. New York: Harcourt Brace Jovanovich, 1964.

Jonas, Hans. "Heidegger and Theology." In *The Phenomenon of Life*, 235–61. New York: Harper and Row, 1966.

Kant, Immanuel. *Fundamental Principles of the Metaphysics of Morals*. New York: Library of Liberal Arts, 1949.

————. *Religion within the Limits of Reason Alone.* New York: Harper and Row, 1960.

Kierkegaard, Søren. *Philosophical Fragments.* Translated by David Swenson and Howard V. Hong. Princeton: Princeton University Press, 1962.

Kwant, Remy C. "Merleau-Ponty's Criticism of Husserl's Eidetic Reduction." In *Phenomenology,* edited by Joseph C. Kocklemans, 375–93. New York: Doubleday, 1967.

Marion, Jean-Luc. *God without Being: Hors-texte.* Translated by Thomas A. Carlson. Chicago: University of Chicago Press, 1991.

Marx, Karl. *German Ideology.* Moscow: Progress Publishers, 1964.

Merleau-Ponty, Maurice. *The Phenomenology of Perception.* Translated by Colin Smith. London: Routledge and Kegan Paul, 1962.

Nietzsche, Friedrich. *The Birth of Tragedy.* New York: Doubleday, 1956.

Plato. *Complete Works.* Edited by John M. Cooper. Indianapolis: Hackett, 1997.

Richardson, William J. *Heidegger: Through Phenomenology to Thought.* The Hague: Martinus Nijhoff, 1963.

Ricoeur, Paul. *Husserl: An Analysis of His Phenomenology.* Evanston, Ill.: Northwestern University Press, 1967.

Rieff, Philip. *Freud: The Mind of the Moralist.* New York: Viking Press, 1959.

Rosenstock-Huessy, Eugene, ed. *Judaism Despite Christianity: The "Letters on Christianity and Judaism" between Eugene Rosenstock-Huessy and Franz Rosenzweig.* Translated by Dorothy Emmet. Birmingham: University of Alabama Press, 1969.

Rotenstreich, Nathan. *From Mendelssohn to Rosenzweig: Jewish Philosophy in Modern Times.* New York: Holt, Rinehart & Winston, 1968.

Russell, D. S. *The Method and Message of Jewish Apocalyptic.* London: SCM Press, 1964.

Sartre, Jean-Paul. *Being and Nothingness.* Translated by Hazel E. Barnes. New York: Philosophical Library, 1956.

Spiegelberg, Herbert. *The Phenomenological Movement.* 2 vols. The Hague: Martinus Nijhoff, 1960.

The Babylonian Talmud. Translated under the editorship of I. Epstein. London: Soncino Press, 1935–48.

Thévanez, Pierre. *What Is Phenomenology?* Translated by James M. Edie. Chicago: Quadrangle, 1962.

Weil, Simone. *Waiting for God.* Translated by Emma Cranford. New York: G. P. Putnam's Sons, 1951.

Wisdom, John. "Gods." *Proceedings of the Aristotelian Society* 1944–45.

Wyschogrod, Edith. *Saints and Postmodernism: Revisioning Moral Philosophy.* Chicago: University of Chicago Press, 1990.

INDEX